Chris Klicka's message on education and parenting is sobering, practical, biblical, and to the point. He teaches that home schooling is not merely an alternative to public school but rather our best choice in raising godly children, God's way! Thanks, Chris (once again), for waking us Christian parents from our worldly slumber.

Dean and Karen Andreola
Book reviewers for CBD books,
Speakers, Authors, *Charlotte Mason Companion*

A passionate commitment to Christ and His kingdom purposes is reflected in each page of this book. It mirrors Chris's heart to encourage parents in their great calling to build a godly heritage for eternity by home schooling their children. Very practical insight and biblical instruction will give each family a clarity of purpose and encouragement to keep going in their journey toward God's design for families.

Sally Clarkson
Author, *The Whole Hearted Child* and *Lessons from a Mother's Heart*
Producer, Whole Hearted Mother conferences

Many of you know what Chris Klicka does, now you will know why. This book is the bottom line for all that he is and does. Out of the "abundance of the heart," he has shared what is nearest and dearest to him. I heartily recommend *The Heart of Home Schooling* to those of you who share this "like precious faith." I have known the Klicka family for several years and can attest that by God's grace what they say, they do. In addition to the heart, Chris and his wife Tracy devote several chapters to practical advice and ideas that have passed the test in their family. This book will help all of us to remember why we do what we do.

Steven P. Demme
President, Math-U-See (math curriculum company)
Author, Speaker

Any writer who regards the topic of home schooling as a "spiritual revival" has to bring to the work a sense of dedication and obligation. Christopher Klicka goes far beyond that as he provides the experience and the training of many years in this important field. With public schools failing to transmit the minimum principles of basic learning, cultural adjustment, patriotism fed by a genuine knowledge of American history, and sound moral instruction, home schooling is a secure haven for concerned parents who do not have the availability of a good Christian school. This book is timely, practical, readable, and extremely helpful for such a time as this because of its Christian testimony.

D. James Kennedy
Senior Minister, Coral Ridge Presbyterian Church

At a time when it is estimated that Christian families are losing between 50 to 70 percent of their children to the world by the time they graduate from high school, it is imperative that we take a new look at home schooling as the alternative to public education. In his book *The Heart of Home Schooling*, Chris Klicka, a home school father and attorney, speaks from personal experience when he challenges both fathers and mothers to rethink their responsibility to safeguard the hearts and minds of their children from the secular seduction of public education.

Chris Klicka speaks especially to home school fathers and mothers and urges them to teach their children what really matters. He reminds the fathers of their heavy responsibilities to train their children in the Lord and to love their wives unconditionally. Chris Klicka calls all home schoolers to draw closer to the Lord and seek Him with their whole heart.

In our pastoral ministry of more than thirty-seven years, we have never once met home school parents who regretted home schooling their children. On the other hand, however, we have met scores of parents who have deeply regretted sending them to the public school system.

Read this book; your child's future depends on it!

Beverly LaHaye
Founder, Concerned Women of America
Tim LaHaye
Best-selling author, Left Behind series, Pastor, Speaker

The Heart of Home Schooling is truly "for such a time as this," even as Mordecai challenged Esther in the Old Testament account. With the modern home schooling movement growing by leaps and bounds, we need to return to the foundational principles of the 1970s and 1980s. I remember those days very well. The battle was raging, and our families were under attack. We spent weeks as expert witnesses in the courtrooms of America, defending the liberties of home schoolers. Chris has been there since 1985, arguing cases and handling legal conflicts on behalf of home schoolers. Without question the key to success, which made possible the millions now engaged in the education of their children at home, was that the early pioneers put Jesus Christ at the center of their schooling activities. The sovereign God was honored, and He abundantly blessed the fledgling movement with His good pleasure. "Only take heed to yourself, and diligently keep yourself, lest you forget the things your eyes have seen, and lest they depart from your heart all the days of your life. And teach them to your children and your grandchildren" (Deut. 4:9). If we as parents fail to do this, the next generation of home educators will be overrun by humanistic ideologies. Home schooling may well become just another pawn of big government, and, most serious of all, we will lose the precious ones God has given us to train in the light of His eternal truth.

Paul Lindstrom
President, Christian Liberty Academy Satellite Schools (CLASS)
Publisher, Christian Liberty Press

The goal of home schooling is not home schooling for its own sake. It is the rearing of children who will walk with God and will be fully equipped to serve Him and their fellow man. Speaking from his heart, Chris Klicka shows that he understands.

The Heart of Home Schooling is so chock-full of practical admonitions to parents, especially fathers, and words of encouragement to those committed to this multiyear endeavor, that I recommend it wholeheartedly. This book contains a much needed perspective to help us all concentrate on what really matters.

John Morris
Scientist, Author, Home schooling father
President, Institute for Creation Research

Chris Klicka has it exactly right. Home schooling is not just an educational alternative; for Christian home schoolers, it can be the first step on the road to spiritual revival. But *The Heart of Home Schooling* is not a fluffy devotional book; it's more of a how-to manual for Christian warriors and those who want to raise Christian warriors! From his years battling for home schoolers in the legal trenches and battling serious illnesses and the day-to-day challenges of the home school life, Klicka provides down-to-earth help for the spiritual side of Christian home schooling. Highly recommended.

Mary Pride
Publisher, *Practical Home Schooling*
Author, *The Big Book of Home Learning* and *The Way Home*

In *The Heart of Home Schooling* Chris Klicka focuses on the core of home education, providing a fresh perspective on the most common as well as the most serious challenges facing home schooling today. While this book contains sound, practical how-to principles, you will also be challenged to evaluate why home schooling is effective.

Chris invites parents to instill more than just academic excellence in their children. Anyone who is considering home education for their children will find inspiration and instruction within each chapter of this book. Those currently home schooling will find *The Heart of Home Schooling* packed with new ideas to energize their daily pursuit of raising a godly generation.

Jim Ryun
Congressman from Kansas
Olympic Silver Medalist in 1500-meter race, Home schooling father

What a wonderful book! As I read it, I found myself encouraged, challenged, inspired, and, at times, completely overwhelmed. I only wish I had this book when my wife and I began teaching our children at home seventeen years ago. *The Heart of Home Schooling* is filled with insight, wisdom, and practical suggestions that will be a tremendous help not only to new home schoolers but to seasoned ones as well.

As Chris Klicka explains, the home schooling movement is really a movement to restore families. This is critical in our day. Christian families today are not alert to the destructive forces in our society that are stealing the hearts of their children away from them and from the Lord. This book is needed today. I highly recommend it.

George W. Sarris
Actor/Narrator/Spokesman, *The World's Greatest Stories*

As a veteran home schooling father, Chris Klicka knows home schooling. As a veteran of the school wars, he knows the costs. *The Heart of Home Schooling*, I pray, will fill thousands of hearts with the courage to discover the joy that is at the heart of home schooling.

R. C. Sproul Jr.
Editor, *Tabletalk*

The Heart of Home Schooling is really the heart of Chris Klicka. I have had the privilege of knowing Chris for eighteen years and can say without hesitation, Chris is the genuine article. When he tells us how to nourish our own souls, we can be confident in knowing that he practices what he teaches.

Chris's first book, *The Right Choice*, convicted us as Christians of our obligation before God to take responsibility for the education and spiritual training of our children. This book tells us how we can be successful in doing both.

As Chris has shaped the home school movement with his legal skills, dogged determination, authorship of legislation, public speaking, and personal counseling, he will positively influence our relationship with our spouses and our children with his invaluable information in this book. Additionally, the book gives clear application on how each of our families can advance the kingdom of God.

For fathers who have wanted to be able to follow through on our commitment to a daily quiet time with the Lord and family devotions, this book will lead us step-by-step through the process.

There are a lot of books that give us guidance and direction to better live out the Christian life. This book does that, but it is unique in that through the sharing of Chris's personal and family tribulations, it motivates us to see why it is all worth it.

When the history of Christian home schooling is written many years from now, *The Heart of Home Schooling* will be referenced as one of the foundational books behind the Christian renewal known as the modern home school movement."

J. Michael Smith
President, Home School Legal Defense Association

The Heart of Home Schooling is a wonderful book because its focus is right. Chris Klicka aims at the heart, providing excellent encouragement and direction for home schooling families. You will find practical how-to and what-to advice, but even more, you will appreciate Klicka's superb focus on motivation and empowerment flowing from the grace of Jesus Christ. This book will be an impetus not only to tell the gospel to our children but also to live the gospel for them. *The Heart of Home Schooling* is the book I'll be telling home schooling dads (and moms) to read.

Tedd Tripp
Pastor, Speaker, Author, *Shepherding a Child's Heart*

The Heart of Home Schooling is more than just another book on how to teach our children at home, although it is certainly that. It is an instruction manual that shows us how to live as Christians in light of eternity. It teaches us how to interpret and handle suffering, how to love our spouses, and how to evangelize the world as we keep the home fires burning brightly. In a book on home schooling, Chris Klicka succeeds in teaching us to aim higher, work harder, love unconditionally, and embrace Christ tightly. Every mother and father need to read this book and be reminded of the really important things in life.

Zan Tyler
Senior Education Editor, Crosswalk.com
Coauthor, *Anyone Can Homeschool*
Home schooling mother since 1984, three children

THE HEART
of HOME
SCHOOLING

THE HEART
of HOME
SCHOOLING

TEACHING & LIVING WHAT REALLY MATTERS

CHRISTOPHER KLICKA
Author of Home Schooling: The Right Choice!

Nashville, Tennessee

978-0-8054-2597-0

Published by B&H Publishing Group, Nashville, Tennessee

SUBJECT HEADING: HOME SCHOOL

5 6 7 8 9 10   10 09 08 07

Contents

To all parents
who are diligently training
the never-dying souls entrusted into their care
by our loving Lord
and to all husbands and wives
who are running the race to win.

Foreword

Christopher Klicka answers the important question, "What really matters in the training of children?" His practical tips and spiritual insights on how to teach our children what really matters mirror my own experience.

My parents had never heard of home schooling, but every morning after breakfast (We had to be at the table at seven o'clock sharp! No dawdling!), we went to the living room where either our father or mother sat down to the piano and we six children joined in singing whichever hymn our parents had chosen. We memorized dozens, perhaps hundreds, of the great hymns of the faith. They have stayed with us. Our father then read a passage from the Bible (explaining its meaning for the younger ones), whereupon we all knelt as Daddy prayed for each child by name and then all joined in the Lord's Prayer before going off to school. Every evening we were not excused from the dinner table until we had listened to the evening portion of *Daily Light*, and then our father prayed again. In my day, public schools were required to read the Bible to the class every day. Of course a great deal of it went "out the window," as it were, yet it is surprising how much the school children learned.

Because few schools nowadays are permitted to read the Bible in class, I agree with Mr. Klicka that it is essential that many families home school their children. I am strongly in favor of this practice, and I thank God for home schoolers. It is not always easy for the mother or father to find the time needed for teaching, but surely the Lord will help, no matter how difficult it may seem.

I have watched my own daughter as she home schooled all eight of her children, and I marvel at the happy results. Of course there have been times when she has felt her own inadequacy and wondered whether she was doing a good job, but her perseverance is evident whenever I have the privilege of visiting them.

For those who wonder if they could possibly teach their children at home, I want to say, "The Lord GOD will help me; therefore shall I not be confounded: therefore have I set my face like a flint, and I know that I shall not be ashamed" (Isa. 50:7 KJV). *The Heart of Home Schooling* is overflowing with encouragement to home school mothers and fathers to keep on keeping on.

I commend parents who have made the decision to home school. The Klicka family made the decision to sacrifice a large amount of their personal time, well aware that their children were precious gifts from the Lord and therefore "worth every moment of investment." Christopher and Tracy Klicka certainly live what they share in this book. They relate the constant struggle of how to balance time—Chris spends forty or fifty hours a week at work; and Tracy performs countless tasks, including balancing the budget, cleaning, cooking, washing, child training, and shopping. I have seen this struggle in the life of my daughter, Valerie. She prayed for a large family, having observed the dynamics between her aunts and uncles and me. The Lord gave her eight children in whom she finds great delight.

Mr. Klicka helps us find the solution to this balancing problem. It is necessary to set priorities, the first being the condition of one's soul. He explains, "Our soul is the most important thing on earth because we will leave everything else behind us when we die." That is a sobering thought. Mr. Klicka explores the feelings parents face when they have work deadlines, when a child needs to learn to read, when dishes pile up, when the grass needs to be cut, and when the car needs repairs. He explains that everything is yelling for our attention, "but our soul is quiet." At these times God is squeezed out.

So is a daily meeting with God impossible in a busy family? Martin Luther said, "If I am going to have a busy day, I spend one hour with the Lord. If I am going to have a very busy day, I spend two hours with the Lord." Mr. Klicka shares that it takes effort to schedule a regular time with Him, but by His grace it can surely be done.

And the result of spending time with the Lord is wonderful peace. It is supernatural. It is a gift from God. The writer of this very helpful book is thirty miles away from work and travels at least twelve times a year to speak at home school conferences. He emphasizes that the Bible teaches fathers to nurture their children spiritually, to "bring them up in the nurture and admonition of the Lord" (Eph. 6:4 KJV). But how can he spiritually nurture his children when he is away from home?

Mr. Klicka shares many practical tips on how home school fathers can and must make time to shepherd the hearts of their children in the Lord. I especially like his one very creative way of maximizing time with his children by using a tape recorder, on which he tells many stories.

Who does not love stories? The Shepard children in Greer, South Carolina, beg for stories every time I, the grandmother, come to visit. There is nothing I love more than to sit between two or three eager children and read them stories. To sit in a rocking chair in the sunny window upstairs when my mother offered to read when I was a child was the loveliest treat for me.

Through stories, your children can learn many spiritual lessons and much knowledge about God's world. In fact, your children may have read a book called *My Savage, My Kinsman,* which tells the story of how and why Valerie and I were living with the Auca Indians in the jungle of Ecuador when she was three years old. She loved living with the Auca Indians, the very tribe who had killed her Daddy and four other missionaries. (To this day, she loves showing her own children the blowgun, the spear, the quiver, and the darts that the Indians gave us to take back to the States.) We lived in a house made of six poles and a thatched roof: no walls, no floors, and no furniture. Valerie slept in a little sleeping bag beneath my hammock. She learned how to take care of fires as all the other little children learned. True stories like this can inspire children to fervently serve the Lord. Reading to our children and training them in the Lord is such a blessing. Ask the Lord to give you wisdom regarding the books and videos you want your children to use.

My description gives only a fraction of the content and the value of this book to help home schooling parents, or any parents, teach what really matters to their children. Mr. Klicka gives many heartfelt and practical tips for mothers, fathers, husbands, and teenagers on how to serve the Lord with their whole heart and to let their light shine in this dark world.

It is my privilege to have been asked to look over Mr. Klicka's excellent book, *The Heart of Home Schooling*. I have never seen a better one for parents who are seeking to bring up their children in the nurture and admonition of the Lord.

Elisabeth Elliot

Author and speaker

My Heart to Your Heart

This book is from a father's, a husband's, and a parent's heart. God has taught me through many hard times to make every day count for Him in these areas.

The subjects covered in this book, I believe, represent *the heart of home schooling.* I pray the principles and practical tips in this book will help you to both *teach and live what really matters.*

This book is directed first and foremost to home school parents. But the spiritual principles and practical tips extend far beyond home schooling and *apply to all parents* who are serious about serving the Lord and faithfully training their children.

My purpose in writing this book is to encourage parents along the way. Raising children is hard work. Raising children *and home schooling* is really hard work! From my own experience, I know it is easy from day to day to lose sight of the goal. Many times we will be tempted to cut corners or even give up.

I hope these chapters will bless you and refresh you. I hope you will be renewed in your vision as to why you are home schooling, and I hope you will commit to "run the race to win" in your relationship with your spouse, your children, and those around you. I hope this will encourage you to not grow weary in well doing but to *make every day count* in raising your children and home schooling for His glory.

The principles on which each chapter is based come from the Word of God.

The ways to apply these principles come primarily from my wife Tracy's and my own experience training seven very strong-willed children. We also have learned from other Christian brothers and sisters who are treading or have trod the same path. God has been merciful to us to show us these ways before it was too late.

This book is meant to *focus on what really matters*. I try to explain the primary importance of being faithful in the spiritual aspects of our home schooling—not just the academics. In the busyness of home schooling, we can sometimes forget.

Therefore, these chapters are intensely practical. I want to share specific steps to take and goals to pursue that will fulfill what God requires of us.

Chapter 1 gives the big picture of how God is using the home school movement "TO TURN THE HEARTS OF THE FATHERS BACK TO THE CHILDREN" (Luke 1:17). Home schooling is rebuilding families and raising a godly generation. It is in many ways a "spiritual revival."

Chapter 2 gives the foundations of why we are home schooling. I review dozens of Scripture passages that demonstrate how serious God is about the education of our children.

Chapter 3 focuses on the most important thing: the nurturing of our own souls. If we do not get this priority right, our home schools, children, family, relationships, and work will suffer.

Chapters 4 through 6 are for fathers. We fathers carry the heaviest responsibility before God in the training of our children. Moms, make sure dads read these chapters. My prayer is that we fathers will be more faithful in being godly leaders in our homes. Chapter 5 especially is filled with practical tips for fathers to help them shepherd the hearts of their children. Chapter 6 shows dad how he can train his children through storytelling. This can be fun!

Chapter 7 is another must for dads in their all-important role as husbands to love their wives as Christ loved the church and gave Himself for her. One of the best ways for us as fathers to ensure the success of our home school is to faithfully and unconditionally love our wives. Loving our wives can often be ignored as we spend so much time with our children in home schooling. We must provide consistent support for our wives, who end up doing, by far, the lion's share of the work.

Chapter 8 is specifically for mothers. My wife Tracy, a faithful mother of seven, who is fighting an incurable illness herself, shares how she has peace in the midst of the commotion and pressure of day-to-day home schooling. God is definitely her strength.

Chapter 9 gives parents tools and reasons to teach their children a biblical worldview.

We must teach our children not only to believe as Christians but also to think as Christians. Therefore, we must make a conscientious effort to apply biblical principles to each and every subject. God has something to say about subjects like government, law, math, literature, and history, and we must take the time to search His Word.

Chapter 10 is specifically for home school teenagers, to warn them of the culture's attempt to mold them and shape them into its image. It is a sobering and encouraging challenge to teenagers to keep their eyes fixed on Jesus and have the teachings of their parents ever before them.

God has personally spent a great deal of time with me in writing chapter 11, "Understanding Suffering in the Midst of Home Schooling." God has shown me that hard times and suffering are blessings from Him. He uses these times to conform us more to the image of His Son. I tell the true story of the near death of our twins Amy and Charity, my wife's battle with ulcerative colitis, and my struggle with the debilitating disease of multiple sclerosis. Yet God is faithful, and He is with us every step of the way, enabling us to keep on home schooling. The Scriptures in this chapter will minister to all who have suffered in some way.

What better way to let our light shine than to evangelize those around us? I have found home schooling parents are often asked, "Why are you home schooling?" This is God's cue to you to share the gospel. In chapter 12, I point out many ways you and your family can share the gospel. Chapter 13 tells how home schooling is spreading around the world. As we work to help legalize home schooling and establish national home school associations in dozens of countries, we are also spreading the gospel. Learn practical ways you can support the home school missionary effort around the world.

I am thankful to God for leading my family to home schooling. As long as we remember what really is the *heart of home schooling* and consistently teach and live what really matters, we will be found faithful before God.

Christopher Klicka

June 2, 2002

Acknowledgments

My deepest thanks is to my Savior and Lord, Jesus Christ. Oh what unconditional love He has shown to this miserable sinner! He has willingly purchased my soul by His precious blood that He shed on the cross. By no merit of my own, Jesus has given me eternal life and everlasting mercy. What sweet assurance He has given me that He has prepared a place for me in His heavenly kingdom, where there will be no more tears or sorrow. Jesus has spent so much time with me in the midst of suffering, tenderly holding me up so that I have come to see that "though our outer man is decaying, yet our inner man is being renewed day by day" (1 Cor. 4:16). I finally realize, by His lovingkindness, that "this momentary, light affliction is producing for us an eternal weight of glory far beyond all comparison" (1 Cor. 4:17).

God alone has graciously taught me the principles I share in this book to help me become a better father, husband, and disciple. He has opened the eyes of my heart. He alone is my strength, because I have none.

I give heartfelt thanks to my wife Tracy who loves me unconditionally. Her love helps keep me from giving up. Through her contentment and peace in many hardships, I see the light of Christ shine brightly. Her constant witness and example to those around us, our children, and me is an endless blessing. I thank Tracy for the support, loyalty, patience, and wisdom that she has given me to complete this project. She truly is a Proverbs 31 woman in every way. Our love only grows deeper each year as we become more and more one. She is truly a gift from the Lord.

I give thanks to each of my seven children: Bethany, Megan, Jesse, Susanna, Charity, Amy, and John. I am thankful that they are a mirror to my soul—training them helps me to see my sin and to grow closer to God. They bring me so much joy. They are the most important reason for this book! Training, raising, and loving them are among the greatest privileges God has given me. They have taught me never to grow weary in well doing. They have helped teach me how I must walk by faith.

I want to give gratitude and honor to my pastor, Jack Lash. Through his faithful preaching and teaching from the Word and his godly example, I have learned how to be a better father and husband.

Finally, I thank my good friend Matt Jacobson for encouraging me to keep writing and making this book possible by offering me the original contract. I also thank David Shepherd of Broadman & Holman Publishers for believing in me and making this book a reality.

Home Schooling:
A Spiritual Revival

H ome schooling is back. More and more parents are beginning to teach their children at home. God is beginning to "restore the hearts of the fathers to their children and the hearts of the children to their fathers" (Mal. 4:6). During the first hundred years of this nation, home schooling was one of the leading forms of education. Then it died out for a period of nearly seventy-five years. The 1970s ushered in a resurgence of home schooling and a trend away from institutionalized schooling and standardized educational methods. It brought a return to the traditional tutorial process involving individualized instruction and apprenticeships. The home school movement also brought a healthy understanding of the role of parents and the role of government in education.

Most important, the home school movement developed because parents wanted to teach their own children at home in order to implant traditional Christian values in their children's hearts and to unite their families.

There never was nor is there yet a single organization that has spurred the rebirth of the home school movement. It seems apparent that the change in parents' hearts toward their children is supernatural; the Holy Spirit has moved on hundreds of thousands of families in the United States and around the world to understand the need for training their children in His ways. They are realizing that the Bible is filled with commands to parents as to how they are to train their children. These conditions must be met in order to obey God, the great Lawgiver and our Redeemer.

CHAPTER ONE

Surveys conducted within the home school community reveal that 85 to 90 percent of home school parents consider themselves born-again Christians. These parents are committed to training their children in the way they should go so when they're old they won't depart from it (Prov. 22:6).

In other words, the home school community at large desires to home school—not for home schooling's sake—but for the glory and honor of God. Home schooling is a means to an end, not an end in itself. The end is that their children will come to know Jesus Christ as their personal Savior and live with Him as Lord of their lives. Although these home school parents would love to see their children become geniuses here on earth, their higher goal is that one day their children will be standing together with them in heaven. *Home schooling teaches what really matters.* Home schooling enables parents to teach the Word of God to their children. Paul reminded Timothy to "continue in the things you have learned and become convinced of, knowing from whom you have learned them; and that from childhood you have known the sacred writings which are able to give you the wisdom that leads to salvation through faith which is in Christ Jesus. All Scripture is inspired by God and profitable for teaching, for reproof, for correction, for training in righteousness; so that the man of God may be adequate, equipped for every good work" (2 Tim. 3:14–17).

Home schoolers take seriously the truth that their children need to be diligently taught the Word of God when they rise up, when they lie down, and when they walk by the way. It needs to be tied to their doorposts, put on their walls, and hung on their wrists (Deut. 6:6–8). This command requires parents to teach their children God's principles in a comprehensive way—something the public schools cannot do.

Home school parents do not want their children to learn the way of heathen nations, which God commands them not to learn (Jer. 10:2).

Human life is short, and none of us know how long our children will be with us. We need to make every minute count. In home schooling, we can best fulfill the commands that God has given to parents in His Word. We can make sure that we "provoke not your children to wrath; but bring them up in the nurture and admonition of the Lord" (Eph. 6:4 KJV). We can focus on "godliness [which] is profitable for all things, since it holds promise for the present life and also for the life to come" (1 Tim. 4:8).

In many ways, home schooling is a moral and spiritual revival in which children are being seriously trained in God's Word, not only to believe as Christians but also to think and live as Christians. Today even Christians are thinking like non-Christians because they have been taught in a secular school system in which knowledge is learned apart from an understanding of God's absolute truths. But home schooling parents are dying to themselves and putting their children before themselves in order to fulfill God's commands.

Home schooling is a spiritual revival, a revival that brings many blessings but demands great sacrifice. The greatest rewards are in heaven, and one day we will be able to go before God's judgment throne, where we will give an account of faithfully and diligently training our children in His Word so that He will be able to say, "Well done, good and faithful servant."

What Does the Bible Say about Home Schooling?

W hen we make a decision, we should always make certain our decision pleases God and is in accordance with His Word. The type of training we want our children to have is one of the more important decisions we must make as parents.

No doubt many readers of this book are presently home schooling. You started out strong, diligently teaching your children. Sometimes, however, you can lose sight of your goal as you become bogged down in the day-to-day drudgery, repetition, and hard work of home schooling. If you lose the vision for home schooling (or do not have one), your home school will fail. It will not last.

The temptations of satisfying self are all around us. Our culture tells us to be fulfilled and to seek our own pleasure. Home schooling is hard. We yearn for time for ourselves. Often we have doubts about the quality of education our children are receiving. We occasionally find ourselves wondering if our children will ever graduate or go to college. Will they possess enough skills to find a job and succeed? Will they really have what it takes to be leaders in our needy world?

We remember the public school around the corner and reason that the public schools are not so bad. They are convenient, and they are free. We begin to believe that sending our children to a good church on Sunday will be enough to keep them on the straight and narrow path.

This is why it is important to return to the foundational principles found in the Word of God. We need to be thoroughly familiar with God's Word so

CHAPTER TWO

that we can know His will for the training of our children. If we know His commands concerning how our children must be trained, we will be careful to obey them and not surrender to temptations.

The Word of God is the source of all truth. It is the standard by which all things are measured. We want our children not only to believe as Christians but also to think as Christians. Therefore, we must make sure that they become biblically literate. This requires a consistent and methodical training of our children in God's principles as found in the pages of the Bible. They must be taught to apply these principles to every area of life.

When the United States was formed, the framers of the Constitution and many of the citizens had a biblical mind-set. Some of them may not have had a personal relationship with Jesus, but they respected the Bible as defining right and wrong and providing a foundation on which to build the country. For this reason, the country prospered. Today, the biblical mind-set has been replaced by a secular mind-set. Public schools are abandoning children to biblical *illiteracy* and ignoring God's absolute moral values. The negative effects are being felt throughout the country. In many ways we "sow the wind and reap the whirlwind" (Hos. 8:7 NIV) as we allow children's minds to be wasted in the public schools, void of godly values and truth. As home schooling parents, we are working to restore that biblical mind-set in our children as we work to fulfill the commands of God through their education.

If we are honest with ourselves, we cannot escape the fact that public schools are no longer a safe place for children academically, physically, or most important of all, spiritually.

If you want a thoroughly researched and current analysis of the public schools, steeped with footnotes and quotes from the founders of public schools, I urge you to read my book *Home Schooling: The Right Choice* (Nashville: Broadman & Holman Publishers, 2000).

Let us waste no more time and look to God's Word for a summary of the biblical principles of education that support Christian home schooling. You will find that God delegated to parents the authority and responsibility to teach and raise children. You can delegate the *authority* to train your children to someone else, but you never delegate the *responsibility*.

A close and prayerful Bible study will demonstrate that sending your children to public school is *no longer an option*. But do not rely on my opinion. Examine the following verses yourself, and let God speak to your heart.

The Scripture states that "From everyone who has been given much, much will be required" (Luke 12:48). Because we are free to choose in this country, we will be even more at fault if we send our children to a clearly secularized public school.

Whenever you begin to lose sight of the goal, meditate once again on these passages from the Word of God. He will speak to you and replant your feet on solid ground. I am convinced that *home schooling is the best way* to fulfill these commands.

God Delegates the Raising of Children to Parents

According to the Bible, children belong to God, but God has delegated the responsibility and authority to raise and educate them to their parents. The psalmist says that children are a gift from the Lord to the parents:

> Behold, children are a gift of the LORD;
> The fruit of the womb is a reward.
> Like arrows in the hand of a warrior,
> So are the children of one's youth.
> How blessed is the man whose quiver is full of them;
> They will not be ashamed
> When they speak with their enemies in the gate.
> —Psalm 127:3–5

Our children are a reward! They are a blessing from God. What wonderful gifts they are to us! Abortion, however, not only murders the babies but also denies the parents a blessing from the Lord.

Also, God describes our children as arrows in the hands of a warrior! Consider that for a moment. What kind of arrows are we making as we educate and train our children? Are we following the heavenly blueprint for designing "arrows" (child training), the perfect plans given by the Maker Himself? Are we following the blueprint closely so our *arrows* will be straight and not slightly bent? Or have we delegated the authority to *craftsmen* (teachers) who are not allowed to or who do not want to follow the heavenly blueprint? As a result, our arrows are incomplete, flimsy, and not properly balanced.

Have we *diligently* crafted our arrows according to the biblical blueprint so they can be trusted to hit their target as we launch them into the world? Or have we simply worked on our arrows in a haphazard manner whenever we can fit time into our busy schedules? Have we personally guaranteed that our arrows (whom God entrusted to us) are carefully crafted according to the biblical blueprint and have a razor-sharp point, or did we hire a stranger who is ignorant of the Creator's design? Are we *truly* training our children to be well-prepared warriors for God? What kinds of flawed arrows are the public schools crafting?

We must ask ourselves these serious questions as we raise our children. *Our children are never-dying souls whom God has entrusted to us.*

Jacob introduced his children to his brother Esau as "the children whom God has graciously given your servant" (Gen. 33:5), and similarly the prophet Isaiah says, "I and the children whom the LORD has given me" (8:18; see also Heb. 2:13 and Gen. 48:8–9). Nowhere in Scripture can a reference be found in which God delegates the authority to raise and educate children to government officials.

The only times the government educated God's people were in instances of coercion. Most often this happened when the children of Israel were dominated by a heathen nation that allowed them no options. Some of the more famous persons educated this way were Moses, Joseph, Shadrach, Meshach, Abednego, and Daniel. God truly preserves His people when they endure severe circumstances, but this does not apply to us in America. Here we have the freedom to train our children thoroughly in the Lord.

God has clearly delegated the primary responsibility and authority to teach and raise children to the parents. Parents can delegate their *authority* to raise and teach their children to someone else (such as a tutor or church school, or to a private or public school), but they can never delegate their *responsibility* to teach their children to anyone else. God will always hold parents responsible for the education their children receive. For this reason parents need to be aware of who is teaching their child, what is being taught in class by both the teacher and the peers, and what is being taught in all their textbooks, supplemental books, and projects. Many of us take this responsibility so seriously that we believe we must retain the authority by home schooling our children and being their primary teachers.

Children Still Belong to God

Although God has *given* children to parents, children are a *gift of steward-ship*. This means that parents do not really *own* their children. Therefore, we are not free to raise our children any way we want, because God gives us certain conditions that must be met. God considers our children to be His children. God refers to Jacob's children as "the work of My hands" (Isa. 29:23). David gave thanks to God for being "fearfully and wonderfully made" while in his mother's womb (Ps. 139:13–14. See also God's claim to unborn children whom He has made and called while they were in their mother's womb in Jer. 1:5; Ps. 139:13–16; Job 10:8–12; Isa. 49:1–5; and Luke 1:41–44).

In Ezekiel 16:20–21, the Lord emphasizes again that the children are His: "Moreover, you took your sons and daughters whom you had borne to Me and you sacrificed them to idols to be devoured. Were your harlotries so small a matter? You slaughtered *My children* and offered them up to idols by causing them to pass through the fire."

God judged these parents severely because they did not meet God's conditions for raising His children. They gave up their children to an idolatrous system that hated God. We, as home schooling parents aware of the anti-God curriculum and lack of absolute values in the public schools, must not allow ourselves to be tempted to sacrifice our children to such a system.

The Bible states further that parents must "render to Caesar [the state] the things that are Caesar's; and to God the things that are God's" (Matt. 22:21). In some of the legal cases that I have handled, the prosecutor has asked the home school parent on the stand why he is not obeying the law, since he says that he believes the Bible and the Bible commands: "Render to Caesar the things that are Caesar's." Of course the prosecutor never finishes the verse. Since the children are not Caesar's in the first place, but rather God's, parents do not have any obligation to render their children to the state by enrolling them in public school or by complying with excessively restrictive state controls of their children's education and training.

God's Conditions for Educating Children

As part of parents' stewardship responsibility in raising children, parents must follow certain commands and conditions in raising and educating His children. For example, concerning children's education: "And, ye fathers, provoke not your children to wrath: but bring them up in the nurture and admonition of the Lord" (Eph. 6:4 KJV). This is a heavy command to fathers! In verses 1 and 2 of the same chapter, God gives commands concerning both mothers and fathers. However, in Ephesians 6:4, the command is to fathers only. We, as fathers, therefore, definitely carry the heaviest responsibility in training our children. The word *nurture* involves loving, providing for, and carefully instructing them. Of course, the instruction must be "in the Lord."

The word *admonition* is the same word as *discipline,* and it involves using the biblical methods of spanking and other admonitions in order to ensure our child's obedience and ability to stay the course. We must not provoke our children by acting hypocritically, ignoring them, or being preoccupied with our work. I believe we are provoking our children when we send them to public schools to learn the ways of the world, outside of godly training and nurture. Let us train our children diligently in order to sear the truth of God into their very souls.

The all-important role of dads in personally training their children is discussed in detail in chapters 4 and 5. Many practical tips are shared on how home school fathers can fulfill God's commands in Ephesians 6 and the following passages.

In Deuteronomy 6:6–9, the Lord, after restating His moral law, declares: "These words, which I am commanding you today, shall be on your heart. You shall teach them *diligently* to your sons and shall talk of them when you sit in your house and when you walk by the way and when you lie down and when you rise up. You shall bind them as a sign on your hand and they shall be as frontals on your forehead. You shall write them on the doorposts of your house and on your gates." (Also see parallel passages in Deut. 4:9, 11:18–21, and Ps. 78:1–11.) In other words, parents must teach God's commands and truth to their children, and they must teach them *diligently.* Children are to be brought up in the instruction of the Lord. How can this be achieved if a child spends six to seven hours daily receiving a public education that teaches him to think as a non-Christian?

It is clearly the parents' primary responsibility to teach their children "so that your days and the days of your sons may be multiplied" (Deut. 11:21).

These commands to educate our children, of course, cannot be accomplished once a week at Sunday school. They require a comprehensive approach to education on a daily basis. The commands of God should be taught to our children when we sit in our homes, when we rise up, when we lie down, and when we travel. In other words, all the time.

This comprehensive educational program is to be based on God's commands. Two of the goals of godly education, therefore, are that children will put their confidence in the Lord and that they will keep His commandments.

> For He established a testimony in Jacob
> And appointed a law in Israel,
> Which He commanded our fathers
> That they should teach them to their children
> That the generation to come might know, even the children yet to
> > be born,
> That they may arise and tell them to their children,
> *That they should put their confidence in God*
> *And not forget the works of God,*
> *But keep His commandments.*
> —Psalm 78:5–7

Many other verses emphasize that parents have the weighty responsibility of teaching their children what God has done so that the children will not forget (see Exod. 13:8 and 14 and Josh. 4:20–22, 24).

In Proverbs 22:6, God commands, "Train up a child in the way he should go, / Even when he is old, he will not depart from it." We need to train our children now so they will follow the path of righteousness as adults. If they do stray from the path, they will be more likely to return to God if we instruct them thoroughly in the Word of God while they are children.

Of course children also have some responsibility. They must obey the commandments of their parents who, in turn, are obeying God:

> My son, observe the commandment of your father
> And do not forsake the teaching of your mother;
> Bind them continually on your heart;
> Tie them around your neck.
> When you walk about, they will guide you;

When you sleep, they will watch over you;
And when you awake, they will talk to you.
For the commandment is a lamp and the teaching is light;
And reproofs for discipline are the way of life.
—Proverbs 6:20–23

The thorough teaching of God's commands is light to our children and leads them to the way of life. A side effect of a comprehensive, daily, biblical education, then, can be the salvation of our children's souls for all eternity. Learning God's law and His principles will "become our tutor to lead us to Christ" (Gal. 3:24).

If the very souls of our children are at stake, should we risk having them taught thousands of hours of information that is contrary to God's truths and in an atmosphere that denies God's existence?

The prophet Isaiah wrote about a tremendous blessing our children will receive from godly instruction. "All your sons [children] will be taught by the LORD, / and great will be your children's peace" (54:13 NIV). In the New American Standard version the word *peace* is translated as *well-being*. "All your sons will be taught of the LORD, / And the well-being of your sons will be great." As our children are consistently taught of the Lord and trained in His ways, God promises to bring our children peace. It seems apparent that the children's peace will affect the parents by contributing to a peaceful home and minimal rebellion. As I travel around the country and observe thousands of home school children, I see the fruit of this godly training. The orderly and disciplined behavior of the children speaks for itself.

My family and I traveled to Virginia Beach to visit the Marine Science Museum. As our seven children, aged two through twelve, viewed the exhibits and asked questions about marine life, one museum employee who supervised the starfish and sea urchin exhibit watched us intently. Then she asked me if we home schooled our children. When I responded in the affirmative, she quipped, "I knew it!" She continued by explaining she had worked at the museum for several years and could always recognize a home schooler by various common traits. "Your children, like other home schoolers, are articulate and ask good questions. They are well behaved, cheerful, and focused. They are helpful to their siblings, and they are content. You can see it in their eyes." She added, "All of the children on field trips from the public schools seem to care more about each other than about the exhibits. They goof around and do not focus on the wonderful opportunity to learn what is all around them."

What a wonderful testimony of God's work in the lives of home schooled students. Sometimes we as parents do not see the fruit as clearly because we are with our children day in and day out, month after month. We find ourselves needing to discipline our children time and time again and constantly repeating instructions. We wonder if they will ever learn how to behave, be wise, and accept responsibility.

Many times it takes an outsider looking in to help us see the progress our children are making. God's promises hold true. He will bring our children peace and well-being as long as we do not give up. "Let us not lose heart in doing good, for in due time we will reap if we do not grow weary" (Gal. 6:10).

Many parents who send their children to public school for six or more hours a day of ungodly instruction and peer influences wonder why they have chaotic homes in which the children regularly challenge the parents' authority and mistreat siblings. The reason is simple: their children are not being taught of the Lord in a comprehensive manner.

Commands to Train Our Children's Minds

None of us want to waste the minds of our children. Unfortunately, Christians often do this when they send their children to the modern public school. It is estimated that approximately 80 percent of Christian parents send their children to public schools. Yet God commands His people in Jeremiah 10:2: *"Thus saith the LORD, Learn not the way of the heathen"* (KJV). The public schools are teaching children the "way of the heathen," while ignoring God's ways. Are we not disobeying God's clear command by allowing our children to be taught knowledge from a comprehensive and consistent humanistic perspective?

Furthermore, David explains that we need to "meditate" on God's law day and night (Ps. 1:2). Home schooling helps parents create an atmosphere conducive for our children to truly meditate on the Lord. How can our children meditate on God's law when they are never even taught God's law in the public schools? We as Christians "are taking every thought captive to the obedience of Christ" (2 Cor. 10:5). Home schooling gives us the opportunity to train our children in how to do this.

This responsibility is immense. Parents must train their children to think God's thoughts. A godly education, therefore, is learning not only to believe as a Christian (for salvation) but also to *think* as a Christian. Christian home schooling teaches children to think as Christians. In contrast, public schools and some private schools are teaching children who believe as Christians to think as non-Christians. These children are suffering from a type of *spiritual schizophrenia.*

Since Christian parents in the past have neglected their *duty* to follow this comprehensive approach to education, generations of adult Christians now apply ungodly principles in their lives and workplaces while simultaneously believing as Christians. For example, I have met U.S. senators and congressmen who faithfully attend virtually every prayer breakfast but consistently vote for abortion.

In essence, many Christian parents today are raising humanistic Christian children who are *lukewarm* and who do not think God's thoughts after Him. We know too well the results of being lukewarm to our Lord. God says, "So because you are lukewarm, and neither hot nor cold, I will spit you out of My mouth" (Rev. 3:16). What a huge risk parents are taking by sending their children to be trained in a comprehensively secular atmosphere!

Proverbs 23:7 states, "For as he thinks within himself, so he is." If a child is trained to think as a humanist, he will tend to act and live as a humanist. Moreover, Scripture states, "Everyone, after he has been fully trained, will be like his teacher" (Luke 6:40). This passage continues by describing the blind who lead the blind into the pit. This is why it is so important that parents teach their children to *think* as Christians and that children be taught by godly teachers. Parents must not let their children be conformed to the pattern of this world, but they must be transformed by the *renewing of their minds,* that they may prove what is the good, acceptable, and perfect will of God (see Rom. 12:2). Much of television and public education is working hand in hand to conform our children's minds to the pattern of this world.

Peter, thinking like a humanist, told Jesus that He would not have to die. Jesus' response to him was harsh: "Get behind Me, Satan! You are a stumbling block to Me; for you are not setting your *mind* on God's interests, but man's" (Matt. 16:23). Some Christian parents are casting a stumbling block before their children by having them trained to think man's thoughts, instead of God's thoughts, for more than thirty hours a week in public schools.

Rather, God commands us to "Keep seeking the things *above*, where Christ is. . . . Set your *mind* on things above, not on the things that are on earth" (Col. 3:1–2). The Bible and its principles are things from above—the blueprint that God has given to show us how we are to live. Jesus commanded, "'YOU SHALL LOVE THE LORD YOUR GOD WITH ALL YOUR HEART, AND WITH ALL YOUR SOUL, AND WITH ALL YOUR *MIND*.' This is the great and foremost commandment" (Matt. 22:37–38). How can children love God with their minds when the public school and some private schools train their minds to ignore God's principles and to think as humanists?

Home schooling enables families properly and comprehensively to train the mind of each child to think God's thoughts and to develop a biblical mind-set rather than a secular mind-set. However, it is important to make sure you are using a good curriculum and books that are grounded in God's Word. Even a home-schooled child's mind can be wasted if the parents, for instance, just "baptize" humanist textbooks. By this I mean that sometimes parents use humanistic textbooks and merely pray over those books or try to do "damage control." With all the excellent Christian textbooks available and countless Christian books covering every subject, we are without excuse to give our children the most truth we can while they are being educated under our roofs. They will only be stronger and more grounded in God's principles, until truth becomes second nature to them. In chapter 8 I give many practical tips and resources for teaching a biblical worldview to your children.

Negative Socialization in School

Even though parents are commanded to give their children a biblical education, they must also protect them from negative socialization. The Scripture warns, "Do not be deceived: 'Bad company corrupts good morals'" (1 Cor. 15:33). Proverbs 13:20 states, "He who walks with wise men will be wise, / But the companion of fools will suffer harm."

The public schools fail miserably in the area of socialization, with the abundance of crime, drugs, immorality, and gang warfare rampant in the school system. Home schooling helps parents fulfill this responsibility by fostering positive socialization. Nonetheless, home school parents must remain vigilant in this area and closely monitor their children's contact with children in the neighborhood and even their church youth group.

Content of True Education

It is clear from the passages above that God delegates to parents the authority and responsibility for teaching children. God requires us to make certain that His Word and principles are applied in a daily, comprehensive manner to the education and upbringing of our children. Furthermore, He will hold us responsible for how we direct the education of our children. We must be careful not to subject them to an ungodly education. Christ explains, "But whoever causes one of these little ones who believe in Me to stumble, it would be better for him to have a heavy millstone hung around his neck, and to be drowned in the depth of the sea" (Matt. 18:6; also see the consequences of disobedience in Col. 3:25).

Parents must therefore be careful to provide their children with an education in which the *content* is based on His Word. "*From childhood you have known the sacred writings* which are able to give you the wisdom that leads to salvation through faith which is in Christ Jesus. *All Scripture* is inspired by God and profitable for teaching, for reproof, for correction, for training in righteousness; so that the man of God may be adequate, equipped for every good work" (2 Tim. 3:15–17).

"The fear of the LORD is the beginning of knowledge" (Prov. 1:7; also see Ps. 111:10). "The LORD gives wisdom; / From His mouth come knowledge and understanding" (Prov. 2:6; also see 9:10). In fact, James 1:5 affirms that we find all the treasures of wisdom in Christ. Further, James 3:13–17 says that wisdom not from above is earthly, natural, and demonic; but wisdom from above (found in the heavenly blueprint, the Bible) is "pure, then peaceable, gentle, reasonable, full of mercy and good fruits, unwavering, without hypocrisy." Which form of wisdom is being taught to your children? Does your home school curriculum reflect the "wisdom from above" or are you using humanistic textbooks? The public schools and some private schools certainly are not teaching wisdom from above.

We must regularly remind ourselves of God's goals for education. Psalm 119:97–101 presents some of these goals: to train children in God's laws so they can govern themselves, be wiser than their enemies, have more insight than their teachers, and understand more than the aged. If we train our children this way, God will no doubt find us faithful stewards of the children He has placed in our care.

Scripture speaks to every area of life. Education is inescapably religious. Every subject, as a result, needs to be studied through the lens of God's Word. If parents do this, their children will be equipped for *every* good work and be able to apply God's principles to every area of life. Their beliefs will not be separate from their thoughts and actions, as is so often the case with nominal Christians today.

Does Sending Our Children to Public School as Missionaries Make It Right?

Many Christian parents rationalize that they send their children to public school in order for them to be *missionaries* to unsaved children. However, there are no biblical examples of children being used as missionaries. The missionaries are always adults. This means it is important for adult Christians to become public school teachers and administrators, school board members, truant officers, and social workers. Adult Christians must work to take dominion of every institution under Christ's lordship.

As far as our own children are concerned, the command is different. God commands us to provide our children with a comprehensive education based on His principles. Sending our children to public school to "save souls" while they receive six or more hours of secular brainwashing does not relieve us of our responsibility before God. Disobeying God by doing something in the name of God does not justify our sin.

For instance, in 1 Samuel 15:1, 23, King Saul directly disobeyed God's command to destroy all of the Amalekite animals by sparing the animals and then offering them as sacrifices to the Lord. God rebuked Saul through Samuel, saying,

Has the LORD as much delight in burnt offerings and sacrifices
As in obeying the voice of the LORD?
Behold, to obey is better than sacrifice,
And to heed than the fat of rams.
For rebellion is as the sin of divination,
And insubordination is as iniquity and idolatry.
—1 Samuel 15:22–23

Are we trying to make a sacrifice to God by sending our children to public school to save souls while disobeying God's commands to us concerning raising our children? When we are burned out with home schooling and become tempted to take the easy way out by sending our children to public schools, we must remember the Word of God: "to obey is better than sacrifice."

These Biblical Principles Also Apply to Children in High School

Sometimes families are tempted to educate their children only *until* high school. At that point, they rationalize that the child is ready to be trained in a secular setting or elsewhere. The biblical principles discussed above, however, still apply to high school-aged children. In fact, the high school years are generally the most difficult and formative years for a child. Therefore, consistent biblical training is more important than ever.

Also, the high school years are crucial for the training of the child's mind in God's principles and teaching him how to apply those principles in his life and in the world around him. A high school-aged child is more mature and often ready for learning the weightier matters of God's laws and principles. The four high school years should be the final phase of training the child for adulthood so that he can thoroughly think as a Christian and apply biblical solutions to his future work, family, or college. These years are too valuable to waste and much too risky, considering the peer pressures and subtle humanistic training. God calls our children "arrows," and we need to be sure they are finished arrows that are straight, sharp, and sure of their mark. We do not want to shoot partially finished arrows that are not fully sharpened into the secular world. Such arrows will often miss their mark and make no impact.

Home Schooling Is a Biblical Form of Education

It is beyond dispute that we find support for home schooling in the Word of God. I am convinced it is the best way that we as parents can fulfill God's command to provide our children with a comprehensive biblical education while restoring and preserving our families. The key goal of home schooling must be to raise our children so that each of them will "be diligent to present [himself] approved to God as a workman who does not need to be ashamed, accurately handling the word of truth" (2 Tim. 2:15).

From the verses above, we know that God's truth and His principles are the foundation of all knowledge. Our children must be taught not only to *believe* as Christians but also to *think* as Christians. We must teach God's principles to our children in a comprehensive manner on a daily basis. God's truth speaks to every academic discipline.

Never become tempted to send your children to public school. That would be similar to the Israelites wanting to return to Egypt. To do so violates almost every biblical principle described above. It is tantamount to sending your children to be trained by the enemy. If Satan could choose which school system he wanted you to send your children to, he would choose the public school system. Sending them to public school, knowing what the public schools have become, is like playing Russian roulette with their souls! Christians play a dangerous and deadly game when they send their children to public schools.

We need to encourage our pastors to start preaching these truths from the pulpit. Until pastors take the lead in urging an exodus from the public school system, the minds of many children from Christian families will be wasted and, in some instances, their hearts will be lost. You may want to give a copy of this book, or at least this chapter, to your pastor and encourage him to take a stand on this issue for the sake of your children. Let the Word of God do its work. It will not return void.

As parents, we cannot escape our responsibility for training and educating our children. God will hold us responsible for the choices we make in regard to our children and to whom we delegate the authority to teach our children.

Home schooling is truly a biblical form of education. It is clear that God is raising up the home school movement from which properly trained children will one day assume leadership. God is blessing the home schooling movement, not because families are home schooling for home schooling's sake but because families are faithfully teaching their children to obey and glorify God! God will bless you as you "seek first His kingdom and His righteousness" in educating and training your children, and "all these things shall be added to you" (Matt. 6:33).

It may not be easy for you to start home schooling. Once you start, the road will not always be smooth. But remember that God will honor those who honor Him! When you make your children and their training a priority, God will bring you many invaluable blessings.

The most important thing to me is the salvation of my children. I would much rather have Bethany, Megan, Jesse, Susanna, Charity, Amy, and John standing with me in heaven than have them live as geniuses in terms of their secular education on this earth and lost forever in hell.

The apostle John said it all when he said: "I have no greater joy than this, to hear of my children walking in the truth" (3 John 4). This is why I home school. This is my hope. I trust it is yours as well.

Help! How Do I Balance Home Schooling and My Life Responsibilities?

H ome schooling takes time. When we decided to home school, we simultaneously made the decision to sacrifice a large amount of our personal time. We willingly chose to die to ourselves and faithfully and diligently train our children in the nurture and admonition of the Lord. Our children are precious gifts that God gave us, and they are worth every moment of our investment in them.

We thought we were busy before we started to home school! Now time is even scarcer. Therefore, we must engage in a battle over how we will spend our time each day.

The Battle for Our Time

This battle for our time involves many different battlefronts. One of those battlefronts is the father's work, which may include forty to fifty hours a week in addition to commuting time. A father must work because the Scripture says, "If any provide not for his own, and specially for those of his own house, he hath denied the faith, and is worse than an infidel" (1 Tim. 5:8 KJV). Determining how the father will use each available hour of the week requires constant prioritization.

Another battlefront takes place in the home where the mother is engaged in home schooling one or more children. The larger the family, the

CHAPTER THREE

greater the demand on the mother's and father's time. At home the mother must run the household. She performs countless tasks that include balancing the budget, cleaning, cooking, washing, ironing, providing for the needs of small children, child training, and shopping. A growing number of mothers must balance their time with operating their own home businesses or sharing the work with their husbands.

A battlefront common to all families is the repair and maintenance of household equipment and property. The law of entropy always prevails! Everything deteriorates: the van breaks down, the stove-top burner burns out, the vacuum makes a grinding noise, the drain is plugged, the lawn tractor engine blows up, the garden needs weeding, the bushes need to be trimmed, toys break, the ax is dull, the house paint is chipping off, the bathroom door lock is broken, the heating element in the clothes dryer burns out, the towel rack is pulled down, more book shelves must be built, home improvements are in process, and the list continues. These are just some of the recent experiences we have had in our family. (I do not know about you, but this makes it clear to me that the theory of evolution's claim that everything is getting better and improving is certainly false!)

Another battlefront is the time spent in Christian ministry. Church and your local home school support group activities can absorb large segments of your time. For example, maybe you heard that workers are needed for Vacation Bible School, you teach a Sunday school class, and you host a Bible study at your house. It takes time to minister to your neighbors and share the gospel, but you do it to fulfill God's command in the Great Commission. If you are a support group leader, you receive calls from distraught parents who want to remove their children from school . . . right now! They need advice immediately. Talking with them takes time away from your family. You have just one more activity to organize for your support group. Maybe you agreed to write an article for your local home school newsletter, and the deadline is coming up fast.

What about the battle for freedom that is being waged around us? We need to make time to be involved in local political races and crisis pregnancy centers. We need to try to educate others. We must make calls to our legislators to defeat bad bills and pass good ones. The price of freedom is eternal vigilance. This takes time.

We have so much to do, but where do we stop? How do we balance our time?

My wife and I can relate to this battlefield. My wife has an incredible responsibility with teaching seven children, caring for them, running the household, keeping up with the special diet for my multiple sclerosis, ministering, singing at church, providing music lessons, gardening, and much, much more.

I have an intense job at the Home School Legal Defense Association, where I have served as senior counsel since 1985. I typically spend about forty-five hours each week in my job. I make at least ten trips each year to speak at state home school conferences. I handle all the legal work for seven states, supervise the contract lawyers in our legal department, direct the lobbying for home school freedoms in the fifty states, network and communicate with state home school leaders throughout the country, and write articles. I lobby on home school issues in Richmond while the legislature is in session. I handle most of our foreign home school legal work and serve on the boards of the home school legal defense organizations in South Africa, Germany, and Canada. At home, I try to keep up with home repairs and tending our garden. I am involved in our church and local politics. My struggle with multiple sclerosis takes time because I cannot move fast physically and I read regularly on the subject and plan for my diet. I write books, too.

Oh, yes. How can I forget. I am also a husband, a father of seven children, and a disciple of Jesus Christ! Whew!

The Balancing Act

There is a constant tension among all these responsibilities. Everything pulls at us. It demands a balancing act. It is hard, but I believe God meant it to be hard. God does not promise that the road to heaven will be easy. We should, therefore, accept the privilege of laboring in God's service. First Corinthians 15:58 tells us, "Be steadfast, immovable, always abounding in the work of the Lord, knowing that your toil is not in vain in the Lord." This tension is healthy, but we cannot afford to become slack. We need to take *dominion* of our time as part of the command God gave us in Genesis 1:28. This requires work. This requires discipline.

So, what can we do? We must start with the Word of God. We must observe the priorities in the Word of God.

We Must Set Priorities!

My pastor, Jack Lash of Gainesville Presbyterian Church, is a man after God's own heart. He balances his innumerable church responsibilities with raising and home schooling his ten children. The success he has had with his children is incredible. Through his sermons I learned several of the biblical principles I have written about in this chapter.

The Word of God is filled with priorities. We need only look. For example, the Bible tells us to "*first* take the log out of your own eye, and then you will see clearly to take the speck out of your brother's eye" (Matt. 7:5). In another passage, "*first* be reconciled to your brother, and then come and present your offering" (Matt. 5:24). "*First* clean the inside of the cup and of the dish, so that the outside also will be clean" (Matt. 23:26 NIV). The Pharisees were preoccupied with the tiny matters of the law while neglecting the weightier matters.

Even more important, the Bible says, "Seek *first* the kingdom of God and His righteousness, and *all* these things shall be added to you" (Matt. 6:33 NKJV). Also, "'LOVE THE LORD YOUR GOD WITH ALL YOUR HEART, AND WITH ALL YOUR SOUL, AND WITH ALL YOUR MIND.' This is the *great and foremost* commandment" (Matt. 22:37–38).

John wrote to the church at Ephesus: "I know your deeds and your toil and perseverance, and that you cannot endure evil men, and you put to the test those who call themselves apostles, and they are not, and you found them to be false; and you have perseverance and have endured for My name's sake, and have not grown weary. But I have this against you, that you have left your *first love*" (Rev. 2:2–4). Jesus said, "For what shall it profit a man, if he shall gain the whole world, and lose his own soul?" (Mark 8:36 KJV).

From these commands of God, it becomes apparent what is the most important priority for each of us.

Our #1 Priority Is the Condition of Our Souls

We can forget about balancing our home schooling, work, and family responsibilities if we do not nurture our own souls.

Our souls are the most important thing on earth because we will leave everything else behind us when we die. Everything else is screaming for our attention, so we make time.

- Our boss wants the project done now.
- Our child needs to be taught how to read.
- The field trip we are leading must happen on schedule.
- The dishes are piling up, and the grass is getting longer.
- Our car must be fixed.
- Friends are arriving in the evening, and the house needs to be cleaned.
- The dentist appointment must be kept.
- We must check our children's math and science assignments.
- We believe we have to read the newspaper or see a certain movie.
- Our children are yelling, "Feed me, feed me!" or "Change me!"

These responsibilities are real and urgent. But our souls are quiet. The soul does not scream out for our attention. We leave our relationship with Jesus Christ behind in the commotion. Our daily appointment with God is squeezed out. We know we should nourish our souls with daily time in communication with Him, but we keep putting it off until tomorrow.

Our love for Christ wanes, and we lose our first love. We distance ourselves from sweet communion with God, our Abba Father. Our prayers become impotent. Our faith weakens, and we give in to circumstance, worries, and anger. We forget that "the anger of man does not achieve the righteousness of God." We abandon following the law of kindness referred to in Proverbs 31. We develop a critical spirit. Bitterness sets in. We whine back at our children in frustration. We snap at our wife or husband. We do not live by the fruits of the Spirit: love, joy, peace, patience, kindness, goodness, faithfulness, gentleness, and self-control (Gal. 5:22–23).

When the afflictions come—and God promises they will come: "Many are the afflictions of the righteous" (Ps. 34:19)—we fall apart.

We finally realize at those times of hardship, that Jesus is all we have. Our relationship with Him is the only thing that will get us through. But have we been regularly nurturing our relationship? Are we ready?

If we do not nurture our souls, our trust in God diminishes and our souls slowly grow weak from starvation. When we neglect our souls, it affects and infects every area of our lives, including our marriages, work, home schooling, ministry, witness, and relationships. We can become a "whited sepulcher" as God stops filling us up with comfort, peace that passes all understanding, security, wisdom, love, and the power of the Spirit. We forget that God is in control. He alone is sovereign. We forget "that God causes *all things* to work together for good to those who love God, to those who are called according to His purpose" (Rom. 8:28). *All things* include suffering and hard times.

The problem is not so much busyness—ultimately it is pride. We actually think we can make it without Him every day. As John wrote to the Laodicians, "You say, 'I am rich, and have become wealthy, and have need of nothing,' and you do not know that you are wretched and miserable and poor and blind and naked" (Rev. 3:17).

Who Is This God We Are Neglecting?

Because we do not take time to know God and meditate on His Word, we have forgotten who He is. We forget whom we are messing with! The prophet Isaiah wrote several passages that remind us of how big God is and how small we are:

> All flesh is grass, and all its loveliness is like the flower of the field.
> The grass withers, the flower fades,
> When the breath of the LORD blows upon it;
> Surely the people are grass.
> The grass withers, the flower fades,
> But the word of our God stands forever.
> —Isaiah 40:6–8

> Who has measured the waters in the hollow of His hand,
> And marked off the heavens by the span,
> And calculated the dust of the earth by the measure,
> And weighed the mountains in a balance
> And the hills in a pair of scales?
> Who has directed the Spirit of the LORD,
> Or as His counselor has informed Him?
> With whom did He consult and who gave Him understanding?
> And who taught Him in the path of justice and taught Him
>   knowledge

And informed Him of the way of understanding?
—Isaiah 40:12–14

"Surely the nations are like a *drop in a bucket;* / they are regarded *as dust* on the scales . . . All the nations are as nothing; / they are regarded by him as worthless / and less than nothing" (Isa. 40:15, 17 NIV).

Do you get the picture? God is infinite—far beyond our understanding. He does not need us. We are insignificant. We are like grass before God, a mere drop in the bucket. In fact, the nations are as nothing before Him. We cannot get much lower than nothing . . . can we? Read the words from Isaiah again, "All the nations are as nothing; / they are regarded by him as worthless / and *less than nothing*" (Isaiah 40:17 NIV). We are so low, that before God we are less than nothing:

It is He who sits above the circle of the earth,
And its inhabitants are like *grasshoppers.*
Who stretches out the heavens like a curtain
And spreads them out like a tent to dwell in.
He it is who reduces rulers to nothing
Who makes the judges of the earth *meaningless.*
Scarcely have they been planted.
Scarcely have they been sown . . .
But He merely blows on them, and they wither,
And the storm carries them away like stubble.
"To whom then will you liken Me
That I should be His equal?" says the Holy One.
Lift up your eyes on high
And see who has created these stars,
The One who leads forth their host by number,
He calls them all by name;
Because of the greatness of His might and the strength of His power
Not one of them is missing.
—Isaiah 40:22–26

There is simply none like Him! There is none to compare. We cannot understand His infinite power and wisdom. Yet we think we can skip our daily time with Him because we are too busy. We think He won't notice or care. We neglect the nurturing of our souls day after day.

Isaiah asks why the people say,

"My way is hidden from the LORD,
And the justice due me escapes the notice of my God"?
Do you not know? Have you not heard?
The Everlasting God, the LORD, the Creator of the ends of the earth
Does not become weary or tired.
His understanding is inscrutable.
—Isaiah 40:27–28

God does care. God does notice. "For God will bring every act to judgment, everything which is hidden, whether it is good or evil" (Eccles. 12:14). We cannot escape His watchful eyes.

We are foolish to neglect nurturing our relationship with Him—every day. Especially since this awesome God—the one, true God, and our Creator—sent His Son to die on the cross for us. He willingly suffered for us and rose again. While we were yet enemies, God stooped way, way down to love us. He chose to love us even though we are like grasshoppers, mere drops in a bucket, and less than nothing. He wants to be close to us, as a father wants to be close to his child. What an incredible picture of God's amazing love! What a privilege it is to know Him and spend time with Him. He created us for the purpose of bringing Him glory. Feeding our souls must be our number one priority. God wants it that way. We should too.

So How Do We Feed Our Souls?

We need to learn to *walk with God and wait upon Him.* Then we will begin to be conformed more to the image of His Son and think His thoughts after Him. We will begin to know His will.

In Genesis 2, the Bible explains that Adam walked with God—as close as anyone could walk—but Adam let pride get in the way, and he destroyed that close relationship with God. Enoch walked so close with God that suddenly "he was not, for God took him" (Gen. 5:24).

In Genesis 6:9, we are told Noah "walked with God" and was a righteous man. Instead of relying on his own strength and good works, he made the necessary time to walk with God. As a result of his close relationship with God, Noah *"did everything just as God commanded him"* (6:22 NIV).

So how can we walk with God? We need to "walk by faith, not by sight" (2 Cor. 5:7). It is a spiritual walk with God by faith, always trusting in His sovereignty. What is faith? "Faith is the substance of things hoped for, the evidence of things not seen" (Heb. 11:1 KJV). Not seeing God or the future but still trusting our Heavenly Father and knowing He loves us is what God has called us to do. Jesus explained, "Blessed are they who did not see, and yet believed" (John 20:29). "The things which are seen are temporal, but the things which are not seen are eternal" (2 Cor. 4:18). God is spirit and wants us to worship Him in spirit and in truth. This walk with God is a spiritual walk, a walk accomplished by following His Word closely. We must trust Him even though we do not know the outcome. Even though we do not see, "we know that God causes all things to work together for good to those who love God, to those who are called according to His purpose" (Rom. 8:28).

As human beings, we see with our eyes. Walking by faith is a different experience. Many churches cater to human nature by making images for people to pray to or with. These icons distract from the worship of the true God, who is spirit. This is why the second commandment is so clear: "Thou shalt not make unto thee any graven image, or any likeness of any thing" (Exod. 20:4 KJV). God, at this time, does not want us to see but rather to believe and trust in Him without seeing.

This walking with God involves trusting Him and waiting on Him in faith. Jesus commands us, "Abide in Me, and I in you. As the branch cannot bear fruit of itself unless it abides in the vine, so neither can you unless you abide in Me. I am the vine, you are the branches; he who abides in Me and I in him, he bears much fruit, for apart from Me you can do nothing" (John 15:4–5). We cannot live a righteous, godly life without an intimate and personal relationship with Jesus. And we need to wait on Him.

We need to apply these truths to home schooling. We will not always have the answer to our child's questions. At times we do not see immediate results, and we find ourselves repeating instructions over and over again. Our teaching may only take root years later. We do not know if our children will succeed in life. We are never certain our children are receiving a sufficient education in everything they need to know. But this is exactly where God wants us to be—depending on Him and trusting Him completely. He wants us to wait on Him while we trust and obey.

We need to follow the examples set by Zacharias and Elizabeth, who waited on the Lord for a baby. We can also imitate the trust and patience of Simeon and Anna, who waited so long for the coming of the Messiah. In the Old Testament we read about Joseph. He was torn from his family and homeland, sold into slavery, immersed in a pagan culture, tempted and falsely accused by Potiphar's wife, and imprisoned for two years. Yet he kept his faith in God. Understanding God's sovereignty, he boldly declared to his brothers, "As for you, you meant evil against me, but God meant it for good" (Gen. 50:20). Joseph walked with God and trusted Him, no matter how bad his circumstances were.

On the other hand, the Bible is filled with people who did not wait on the Lord. Remember how the Israelites turned from God time and time again? They pursued false idols simply because they would not wait on God. They wanted to enter the promised land now. They wanted meat now. They wanted to see God now.

Don't we feel like that with our home schooling? Aren't we often frustrated when we do not see results? I know I begin to trust in my training of the children to change their hearts rather than trusting God and begging for His mercy on their souls. I have to remind myself that those who honor Him, He will honor—but it will be in His timing and in His way. I need to remember that all of my good work and busyness can get in the way of my deep communion with my Lord and Savior.

The prophet Isaiah promises,

> He gives strength to the weary,
> And to him who lacks might He increases power.
> Though youths grow weary and tired,
> And vigorous young men stumble badly,
> Yet those who *wait for the* LORD
> Will gain new strength;
> They will mount up with wings like eagles,
> They will run and not get tired,
> They will walk and not become weary.
> —Isaiah 40:29–31

In Hebrew, the term *wait* means "to bind or twist together"—like with ropes. We need to bind ourselves to Jesus so that our relationship will be as close as strands of rope twisted together!

So What Can We Do?

Even if we know the answer, we still don't act. It is not necessarily premeditated disobedience, but rather the result of hundreds of decisions over time. We simply allow other things to squeeze God out. We are behind in doing our lesson plans. We get up late because we stayed up too late. Maybe our three-year-old gets up too early. We take too long getting ready in the morning. Soon we are off working, and our busy day overtakes us. Intimate, quiet time with God is lost.

We need to repent.

Jesus has an incredible feast for us, but we are too busy to come. He has an important word for us, but we are too preoccupied to listen. Jesus is the manna from heaven, the living water, and the bread of life. God is speaking, feeding, comforting, leading, and warning us, but we are too busy to listen. The Bible is God's love letter to us. It is so precious that people in communist and Islamic countries are willing to die to obtain a copy. Yet we find ourselves too busy to read and meditate on it.

Only One Thing Is Needed:
A Close Relationship with Jesus

Remember Mary and Martha? Martha worked hard doing good works, and she was very busy. Martha became very frustrated with Mary because Mary sat at Jesus' feet, talking and listening to Him. Jesus gently rebuked her saying: "Martha, Martha . . . you are worried and upset about many things, but only one thing is needed. Mary has chosen what is better, and it will not be taken away from her" (Luke 10:41–42 NIV). Only one thing is needed, and that is our relationship with Jesus. We must never put activity at the center of our lives, even if it is good activity.

Trusting Jesus must be at the center. "Trust in the LORD with all your heart, / And lean not to your own understanding; / In all your ways acknowledge Him, / And He shall direct your paths" (Prov. 3:5–6 NKJV). The most important aspect of this relationship is to trust God with our souls. We must know Him as our personal Savior. We must believe that He lived a sinless life on this earth and willingly died for our sins. If He had not paid the penalty for our sins, we would go straight to hell. But God, in His mercy, gave us His Son to be a substitute for us. Paul instructed the believers in Rome: "If you confess with your mouth Jesus as Lord, and believe in your heart that God raised Him from the dead, you will be saved" (Rom. 10:9). We must realize that we cannot save ourselves. We cannot earn our salvation through good works and staying busy for God. We are saved by God's grace alone. It is nothing that we do, but it is everything that God does.

Our relationship, then, must constantly grow closer to Jesus. Relationships take time. If we want to have a relationship with our son, daughter, wife, or friend, we need to talk with them on a regular basis and listen. That is what Jesus requires of us if we are to have a real relationship with Him. We must seek His face on a daily basis. We need to talk to Him through prayer and to hear Him speak to us through Bible reading. We must make time to talk with Him and thank Him. Scripture says, "In everything give thanks; for this is God's will for you in Christ Jesus" (1 Thess. 5:18). David instructs us to meditate on His Word day and night. The closer we walk and the more time we spend with Him, the better we will know His will for our lives. We must not be afraid to share our feelings with Him either, and this includes our hurts and our fears. We need to cast all our burdens on Him, then He will sustain us (1 Pet. 5:7).

One aspect of building our relationship with Jesus is to take time to nurture strong relationships with God's people. I never fully understood what the body of Christ is until I had a powerful experience at my church, Gainesville Presbyterian Church. I had just announced my diagnosis with multiple sclerosis at our church's Thanksgiving service. After the service, the church body surrounded my wife and me. As various members laid hands on us, the tears began to flow. For the first time, I realized that Jesus has chosen to manifest Himself through His people whom He calls His body. That night, it was as though God gave us a gigantic hug through His people. I will never forget the love of God that was poured out on us at that time and how we felt His overwhelming presence. The Scriptures tell us to meet together to encourage one another (Heb. 10:25). I believe this is an important aspect of developing a close relationship with God.

What Does Your Soul Look Like?

If we could take away your body for a minute and expose your soul for all to see, would it be underfed? Would it look malnourished? Would it be parched and dehydrated? Or would it be a soul that was vibrant, well-nourished, and strong? Would everyone see that your soul was eating regularly of the bread of life and of the manna from heaven? Would your soul look like it had been drinking deeply and consistently from the living water?

Unfortunately, we often spend more time each morning preparing our outward appearance than we do our souls. To keep our souls healthy, we need to meditate on God's Word and pray to Him. We must recommit to "seek first the kingdom of God and His righteousness, and all these things shall be added to you" (Matt. 6:33 NKJV). We need to return to our first love.

God wants us to be faithful in the little things. It is a little thing to read our Bibles to hear what God has to say to us and to pray to Him. Below are a few practical steps we can take to develop a habit of spending daily time with the Lord.

Practical Tips on Having a Daily Meeting with God

The first question that comes to many people's minds is, "How much time do I need to spend with the Lord each day?" Well, that is between you and God. Martin Luther jealously protected his time with the Lord. He said, "If I am going to have a busy day, I spend one hour with the Lord. If I am going to have a very busy day, I spend two hours with the Lord." Martin Luther is a good model. He made the effort to plan a regular time with the Lord each day. It takes action on our part. David wrote, "Seek peace and pursue it" (Ps. 34:14). That requires action. Peace is not passive. Peter said, "Whoever would love life and see good days. . . . he must seek peace and pursue it" (1 Pet. 3:10–11 NIV). Paul instructs the church at Philippi: "Be anxious for nothing, but in everything by prayer and supplication with thanksgiving let your requests be made known to God. And the peace of God, which surpasses all comprehension, will guard your hearts and your minds in Christ Jesus" (Phil. 4:6–7).

When we spend time with the Lord each day, we receive a rich, wonderful peace that we can enjoy no matter what the circumstances. This peace is supernatural. It is a gift of God. Our circumstances may not change, but our hearts are at peace with God.

However, this peace is not automatic. God assigns certain conditions by which we can receive this gift.

- We must not be anxious. This means that we must trust that God has ordained all circumstances and that they are for our good.
- We must sincerely bring our burdens and requests before the holy and living God.
- There must be a heartfelt expression of thanks, which involves a recognition of God's goodness and a recognition of His faithfulness to us in the past.
- We must realize that He is in control. Everything that He allows in our lives is for our good.
- We need to learn to completely trust Him and surrender all.

If these conditions are met, God promises that He will send His peace.

When Should We Meet with God to Nurture Our Souls?

When is the best time to have this special time with the Lord? Jesus left us an example, "In the *early morning*, while it was still dark, Jesus got up, left the house, and went away to a secluded place, and was praying there" (Mark 1:35). The psalmist seems to reinforce the importance of coming to the Lord at the beginning of each day: "*In the morning*, O LORD, You will hear my voice; / *In the morning* I will order my prayer to You and eagerly watch" (Ps. 5:3). "It is good to give thanks to the LORD / And to sing praises to Your name, O Most High; / To declare Your lovingkindness *in the morning* / And Your faithfulness by night" (Ps. 92:1–2). "But I, O LORD, have cried out to You for help, / And *in the morning* my prayer comes before You" (Ps. 88:13). "I rise *before dawn* and cry for help; / I wait for Your words" (Ps. 119:147). "As for me, I shall behold Your face in righteousness; / I will be satisfied with Your likeness *when I awake*" (Ps. 17:15). We have other examples in the Word of God, including Daniel who prayed regularly three times every day. Certainly, the first time was in the morning.

An Old Testament prophecy about Jesus stresses the importance of starting the day in communion with the Lord.

> The Sovereign LORD has given me an instructed tongue,
> to know the word that sustains the weary.
> He awakens me morning by morning,
> wakens my ear to listen like one being taught.
> The Sovereign LORD has opened my ears,
> and I have not been rebellious;
> I have not drawn back.
> I offered my back to those who beat me,
> my cheeks to those who pulled out my beard;
> I did not hide my face
> from mocking and spitting.
> —Isaiah 50:4–6 NIV

The right way to begin each day is in the joy of the Lord. As the Scriptures state, "This is the day which the LORD has made; / Let us rejoice and be glad in it" (Ps. 118:24). We can remember another promise, "The LORD's . . . compassions never fail. They are new every morning" (Lam. 3:22–23).

Skipping daily time with the Lord is easy to do because nobody is watching. Of course, if we are honest with ourselves, we know that God is watching. Paul wrote, "I discipline my body and make it my slave" (1 Cor. 9:27). The Bible teaches us to be diligent and faithful in developing this relationship and walk with the Lord.

Home schoolers have busy days. Training our children is a huge responsibility. We need to set aside time with the Lord, because it won't happen automatically. We might go to bed earlier so that we can rise earlier. The psalmist warns us, "It is vain for you rise up early, / To retire late, / To eat the bread of painful labors" (Ps. 127:2). God doesn't want us to burn the candle at both ends. He wants us to lead sane lives. Home schooling, in the midst of all our other ministries and work, can make our lives insane if we allow it. God admonishes, "Make it your ambition to lead a quiet life, to mind your own business and to work with your hands . . . so that your daily life may win the respect of outsiders" (1 Thess. 4:11–12 NIV). God wants us to pursue peace, but we can only find that peace in Him, not in our circumstances. As we dedicate a daily time to Him each morning to worship, praise, and search out His will, this peace will come. Our outward circumstances may not change, but we will enjoy incredible inner peace.

But I Can't Find a Quiet Time with the Lord

You might be thinking, *I've tried, but I cannot find a consistent time for devotions*. I have felt that way many times over the years. After reading a book by Ron Hutchcraft, I adopted some practical steps that have helped considerably (*Living Peacefully in a Stressful World* [Grand Rapids, Mich.: Discovery House Publishers, 2000], 43–45). He gives five action steps that help establish uncompromised time with God each day.

- Find a place. Set aside a corner of the house that you can walk to when your alarm goes off. Your Bible, notebook, and prayer list should be waiting for you.
- Clear your mind. Pray that God will help you focus on Him. "Be still, and know that I am God" (Ps. 46:10 NIV). As Ron Hutchcraft says, "The rest of the day can't be allowed to fill up our Jesus time. Instead, let His time fill up the rest of the day."

  This is my biggest obstacle to time with the Lord. My mind usually runs one hundred miles per hour, and when I wake up, I begin to plan out the day and organize all the things that need to be done. Often when I pray, I find these many, many tasks drive away my concentrated worship of God. My prayers become nothing more than my thoughts about what I have to do during the day. One helpful technique is to pray out loud, even if it is barely audible. This helps me discipline my mind, and it focuses my prayers to God.
- Let go and cast your burdens on the Lord. Let go of the frustrations from the day before and give your burdens to the Lord in prayer along with your thankfulness.
- Get an assignment. You are not meeting with a book, but with a person. Ron Hutchcraft says, "We are looking for something to do today, not just something to know." Pray diligently through the Scripture passage that you are reading. Ask God to help you apply

the principle and the truth to your life. Let the Word of God change your heart, your attitudes, and your actions for this day and every day thereafter.

I tell my children not simply to read and hear the Word, but to do it. If we don't act on the teachings, then our reading is in vain, and we are hypocrites.

- Set your course. Pray about your work, the people with whom you will interact, and aspects of your day that you know about. We can ask for God's blessings on our plans and wisdom for our responsibilities. It is prideful to think that we can complete any aspect of our day without Him.

I have found that a helpful way to ensure that the content of my prayer each day is complete is to pray through the elements of the Lord's Prayer. Obviously, this is the way that God wants us to pray, because Jesus specifically instructed us.

- Praise God and recognize His awesome and incredible majesty.
- Pray that His will be done and His Law and Word be established.
- Ask God for our daily sustenance and present our requests and burdens to Him.
- Ask Him to protect us from temptations, because they abound in our culture today. We must always keep our guard up.
- Ask the Lord for forgiveness of our sins. Confess them honestly, and be prepared to forgive others.
- Give God all the glory.

Don't Compromise Your Time with the Lord

We all need to purpose in our hearts to guard our time with the Lord. God must be first in our lives. Let us show how serious we are about our love for Him by making Him a priority. If we have to lose sleep at first, God will provide. If we have to write down a specific time in our organizer or calendar to meet with Him, we must do it. If an unforeseen event throws off our morning devotions, we must reschedule devotions for later in the day.

Of course, none of this discipline of meeting with God in the morning replaces a prayerful attitude throughout the day. The Bible tells us that we are to "pray without ceasing" (1 Thess. 5:17). Thus, we always want to have regular communion with God. As I struggle with multiple sclerosis and have difficulty climbing stairs, getting in and out of cars, and putting my socks on in the morning, I'm learning to be in a much more regular attitude of prayer. I'm calling out for Him and His strength. We're all in the same boat because we depend completely on His strength, and He's helping me appreciate the importance of my devotional time. When I am struggling, I pray for the persecuted church and for other brothers and sisters who are struggling. I want my time of hardship to be productive for God's service.

The Condition of Your Soul Will Directly Affect Your Success in Every Other Area of Life

What your family needs most is the godliness of your own soul. What your work needs most is the godliness of your own soul. What your ministry needs most is the godliness of your own soul. Remember, we are home schooling, not for home schooling's sake, but for the glory of God. Home schooling is a means to an end. It is not an end in and of itself. Home schooling is a means to train our children's hearts and souls for God's work on earth and for eternity.

My number one priority is walking close with the Lord and reading His Word so that it is truly "a lamp unto my feet, and a light unto my path" (Ps. 119:105 KJV). We all need to work out our salvation with fear and trembling; this requires us to have a daily time of communion with our Lord. Once we firmly establish this time with God each day, I believe the rest of our work and priorities will fall into place.

Sin Is the Greatest Time Waster of All!

If we are not continually hiding the Word of God in our hearts that we might not sin against God (Ps. 119:11), we will fall into various temptations and sins. If you are honest with yourself, you know that the biggest time waster for you each day is your own sin. It may be the sin of rebellion, laziness, or impatience. It may be the sin of selfishness, pride, or lack of faith. Whatever sin we are engaged in makes us less efficient and sends us off the

37

path. Let us commit to spending time with the Lord so that we can hide His Word in our heart each day. This is how we put on the full armor of God to stand against the wiles of the devil and the temptations of this world (Eph. 6:10–18).

The Second Priority Is Our Family

After we have our own souls in order and have committed to spending regular time with the Lord, the second priority is our families. I will simply touch on this topic because chapters 4 and 5 explore this issue. God gives the never-dying souls of our children into our care. God calls husbands and wives to love each other. In fact, husbands are to love their wives as Christ loved the church and gave Himself for her (Eph. 5:25). Paul admonishes fathers to "provoke not your children to wrath; but bring them up in the nurture and admonition of the Lord" (Eph. 6:4 KJV).

Paul wrote that each father "manages his own household well, keeping his children under control with all dignity (but if a man does not know how to manage his own household, how will he take care of the church of God?)" (1 Tim. 3:4–5). The instruction to train our children is a priority to God. More than our ministries!

Remember, our children may not always be with us. We do not know what tomorrow will bring. Therefore, we must make every day count with our wives and children. These are necessities. If the rest of our activity and good works begin to squeeze out our ability to faithfully and unconditionally love our wives or our husbands or they make it impossible to bring up our children in the admonition of the Lord, we have to make a change.

Every time we say *yes* to another activity we are saying *no* to our family and our spouses. When we say *no* to an activity, we are saying *yes* to our family and spouses. Let us make sure that our second priority is our family.

The Time to Adjust Our Priorities Is Now

If your priorities are off, do not delay another day to make them right. Do not wait for a disease or tragedy to shake you and wake you up. Take action now to put your relationship with Jesus *first* in your life and your family second. Your soul may depend on it.

How utterly horrible, if on the last day, you explain to Jesus, "Lord, Lord, did we not prophesy in Your name, and in Your name cast out demons, and in Your name perform many miracles?" (Matt. 7:22). Or you say, "Did we not home school in your name, give to the poor and missionaries in your name, and go to church in your name?" Then He turns to you and says, "I never knew you; DEPART FROM ME" (Matt 7:23). How terrible that would be. We would be without hope and without a second chance.

We need to make certain we have a close relationship with the Lord. We need to take the time to truly and intimately know Him. The Lord wants our hearts, not just our works.

As you shift and make adjustments to fulfill these priorities, you will find God's blessing and feel His peace. May God bless you as you faithfully teach your children at home for His glory and as you love Him with your whole heart, soul, and mind. Remember to "seek first the kingdom of God and His righteousness, and all these things shall be added to you" (Matt. 6:33 NKJV).

A Challenge to
Home School Fathers:
The Biblical Foundation

What a wonderful privilege it is to be a father! As a father of seven children, I can honestly say that few gifts in this life compare to the privilege of raising children. Being a father, however, also requires hard work and an enormous amount of time. Often it is time that we as fathers do not have, or at least, we do not *think* we have. At the writing of this book, Bethany, our oldest, is thirteen years old. She is followed by Megan, ten; Jesse, eight; Susanna, seven; the six-year-old twins, Charity and Amy; and three-year-old John.

Whew!

My wife and I gladly sacrifice to home school our children because we believe that God has delegated to us both the authority and the responsibility to train our children in accordance with His principles. We can delegate that authority to someone else, but we can never delegate the responsibility. God will always hold us responsible for the training these children receive. In order to best fulfill this responsibility, we are committed to home school them.

The psalmist tells us,

> Behold, children are a gift of the LORD;
> The fruit of the womb is a reward.
> Like arrows in the hand of a warrior,

CHAPTER FOUR

So are the children of one's youth.

How blessed is the man whose quiver is full of them.

—Psalm 127:3–5

Although our children are a gift, it is clear from the Word of God that this is a gift of stewardship. We, as parents, do not own our children; God owns them. Our God-given stewardship responsibility carries with it clear commands from the Word of God as to how our children must be raised.

Yet fathers are abandoning their God-given responsibilities at an alarming rate.

Fatherhood Is in Danger

The National Center for Health Statistics released its report on the 1999 birth data. It found that a record 1.3 million babies were born out of wedlock in 1999. This was the first time that one-third of all U.S. births were to unwed mothers. This survey found that the increases are the result of "an increasing tolerance for couples to have children without marrying" (Cheryl Wetzstein, "Unwed Mothers Set a Record for Births," *Washington Times*, 18 April 2001, A1).

Many industrialized nations around the world are suffering from the same symptoms.

A recent report from the U. S. Census Bureau showed that traditional families lost ground in America during the 1990s. Significant increases occurred in cohabitating couples, single parent households, and non-family groups. Married couple households dropped from 55.1 percent of all households in 1990 to 51.7 percent in 2000. Households in which married couples actually lived with their own children also fell from 25.6 percent to 23.5 percent. Meanwhile, the number of single mother households grew 25 percent during the 1990s, from 6 million to 7.5 million. There was a 72 percent increase in cohabiting couples, from 3.1 million in 1990 to 5.4 million in 2000 (Cheryl Wetzstein, "Traditional Families Harder to Find," *Washington Times*, 15 May 2001, A3). Something is wrong for sure.

Wanted: Committed Fathers

The home school movement is a beacon of hope as fathers' hearts are being turned back to their children. Many fathers in the home school movement are getting involved with their children. The purpose of this chapter and the next is to encourage fathers to be more than simply involved. Fathers need to be committed. This way, their marriages and families will not become a statistic of failure, and their children will have the strong guidance of a godly father.

The Bible states clearly what the father's responsibility must be. Ephesians 6:4 KJV is one of the most important passages on child training. It is directed not to fathers *and* mothers but to fathers only. It says, "Fathers, provoke not your children to wrath: but bring them up in the nurture and admonition of the Lord." In the previous verses, God refers to both fathers *and* mothers: "Children, obey your parents in the Lord, for this is right. HONOR YOUR FATHER AND MOTHER (which is the first commandment with a promise) SO THAT IT MAY BE WELL WITH YOU, AND THAT YOU MAY LIVE LONG ON THE EARTH" (Eph. 6:1–3). Fathers and mothers are one, and the father is the head of the marriage and the family relationship. The ultimate responsibility of training children, then, falls on fathers, not mothers—although mothers do bear a significant responsibility. God could have easily said father and mothers in Ephesians 6:4, but He chose to limit the command to fathers.

Fathers, therefore, have the greatest responsibility in training their children in the Lord and in disciplining them. As fathers, we must lead in the area of child training and particularly in our home school.

We must be more than simply involved—we must be *committed*. We must be committed before God to stick with home schooling, which is intricately connected with the spiritual and physical nurturing of our children. A farmer once helped me understand the difference between being involved and being committed by illustrating with a plate of bacon and eggs. He said, "Now you see, the hen was involved, but the pig was committed!" To put it bluntly, we fathers need to be more like that pig.

So, the challenge for us as home school fathers is to be Ephesians 6:4 fathers. Here are a few tips you can follow in order to fulfill this command.

Provoke Not Your Children to Wrath

First of all, fathers, God makes it clear to us in Ephesians 6:4 that we are not to provoke our children to wrath. This is also affirmed in Colossians 3:21, "Fathers, do not exasperate your children, so that they will not lose heart."

Why should we not provoke our children? So they will not lose heart; so they do not give up on life; so they do not give up on God. Today, children are turning from the faith of their fathers, and suicide is an epidemic.

In order to obey this command, we need to know what in our life provokes our children to wrath. Below are some possible inconsistencies that can provoke our children.

We Can Provoke Our Children by Losing Our Tempers

It is clear from James 1:20 that "the anger of man does not achieve the righteousness of God." Yet we go into a rage over trivial things. We give the excuse, "I am under a lot of pressure."

Proverbs 22:24–25 says, "Do not associate with a man given to anger; / Or go with a hot-tempered man, / Or you will learn his ways / And find a snare for yourself." What are your children supposed to do? Where can they go? They have to associate with you even though you give in to anger. The consequences are far-reaching as you begin to see your children learn your ways of anger.

Proverbs also says, "A fool always loses his temper, / But a wise man holds it back" (29:11). We can turn our children away from God if we habitually give in to anger, and we will soon find our children imitating our ways. We may very well drive our children from God. We are supposed to represent God the Father. Our children will not want any part of an angry God who always loses control. Fathers, let us stop playing the fool and get control of ourselves.

I know how children can annoy their parents. They can make us madder than anyone else. We tell them many times to do right, but they purposely disobey. We fathers tend to take misbehavior personally, so we lash out at our children in anger, yelling at them or spouting out harsh words. We feel justified because they are disobedient or foolish.

But before God, we are sinning. We need to walk by the Spirit and diligently live by all of the fruits of the Spirit. We must, therefore, treat our children with gentleness, kindness, love, and self-control. I recommend that you take a few minutes periodically and meditate on 1 Corinthians 13 to help you overcome your anger. A practical suggestion I often follow is simply to pray a prayer out loud asking God to help me control my anger when I am ready to let loose on my children. I pause a minute and ask the offending child to go to another room to wait for me. Then I can deal with the problem with calm, reasoned discipline instead of sinful, out-of-control anger.

Not Admitting You Are Wrong Can Provoke Your Children

Fathers need to confess their sins before God and their children. We as fathers must ask forgiveness on our knees and pray with our children.

When I yell at my wife or commit a sin before my children, I always try to repent within a few minutes. I pray to God first, humbling myself, repenting, and asking for His forgiveness. I then gather the children and my wife, and I publicly confess my sin. I tell them I was wrong. I sinned against my God and all of them. I explain I already prayed to God and asked His forgiveness. I tell them I am going to try hard to not do it anymore. I do not give any excuses. I then ask them to forgive me.

There are not many things more wonderful than having your children run to you, throw their arms around your neck with tears in their eyes, and unhesitantly forgive you. Sincere forgiveness and love fill the room. The restoration is complete. You honor God, set an example for your children, and you avoid provoking them to wrath.

Do not be too proud to admit you are wrong. Cast off your pride and humble yourself.

Allowing Double Standards

Many times fathers can intentionally or unintentionally hold up double standards for their children. For instance, fathers can condemn television and prohibit their children from watching it. Then after the children go to bed, they turn on the boob tube and let their minds vegetate on various useless and maybe harmful shows. Another way fathers can hold a double standard is when they discipline their children for bickering and arguing with one another, while in front of their children they argue and bicker with their wives. We need to remember that our children's eyes are watching us, and we are their most powerful and influential example.

This concept is captured in a poem by Herbert Parker called "A Boy and His Dad."

> To get his goodnight kiss he stood beside my chair one night,
> And raised an eager face to me, a face with love alight;
> As I gathered in my arms the son God gave to me,
> I thanked the lad for being good and hoped he'd always be;
> His little arms crept round my neck and then I heard him say,
> Four simple words I can't forget,
> Four words that made me pray;
> They turned a mirror on my soul, on secrets no one knew,
> They startled me, I hear them yet, he said,
> "I'll be like you."

We need to constantly guard our hearts and our mouths and our actions in the presence of our children because we will be held responsible for the influence we have on their lives. Let us not be guilty of provoking our children by practicing double standards.

Neglecting to Give Them Verbal and Physical Love

I have talked with several fathers who lost their children to the world. A common statement they heard from their children is, "You never loved me. All you cared about was that I followed your rules." What a sharp stab in a father's heart when he hears those words! Of course, he loves his child. In fact, that is why he made those rules.

But his child wanted more. He or she wanted obvious, unmistaken signs of affection. No misinterpretations could happen. No hidden feelings of love. The child wanted an open, loving relationship.

How can we make certain we do this? What can we do? We need to apply layer and layer of love in blatant ways upon our children—so they are without excuse. So they can never honestly say, "You do not love me." We need to tell them verbally how much we love them—especially after we have disciplined them. We must regularly give our children hugs, verbal encouragement, and praise. Have the little ones sit on your lap, put your arm around your older children at church, or simply put your hand in their hand.

This outward showing of affection is especially crucial for our daughters. Many surveys of teenage girls testify to the lack of appropriate physical love by the father as the major reason they enter immoral relationships. There will be many boys who will be glad to give our daughters physical affection. We need to be certain our daughters have a secure and safe refuge—the arms of their fathers.

We cannot just think and feel love toward our children and assume they know we love them. We need to tell them to their faces and in front of others. I have found my love is warmly received when I take time to write notes. My daughters keep those notes and reread them. It is proof of my deep love for them. Remember, the entire Bible is God's permanent love letter to us.

We need to keep our relationship close with our children by cultivating it and watering it, just like we would a garden. This takes time, planning, discipline, and commitment. A successful garden does not merely involve planting seeds in good soil and leaving it alone. Rather, it involves regular weeding, watering, sweat, and attention. Children, too, must be diligently and lovingly nurtured.

Love is the key ingredient. If it is missing or if it is not easily seen, our children might think it is missing. This may provoke your children to anger.

Failing to Give Our Children Both Quality and Quantity Time Can Provoke Our Children to Wrath

Our children need to be with us as their fathers. We must have both quantity and quality time with them. We need to develop a strong, unbreakable bond that involves experiencing life together. This takes quantity time. To achieve this, for example, we can have them travel with us when we go on errands or business trips, allow the little ones to carry something as soon as they can walk, and regularly include our children in accomplishing projects around the house.

I take turns taking my children with me when I go to lobbying meetings on Capitol Hill or in Richmond and when I go to work. They bring their home schoolwork to do while I work. We have lunch together and talk during the commute. I also take my children with me on business trips, as I save up frequent flyer miles or find a good fare. These are also great ways to bless my wife by relieving her of a child for a day or a couple days!

Of course, quantity time is not enough. If you have a home business, for example, you can end up zoning out your children. They see you, but do not really talk with you face to face in any deep way. We have to make time for heart-to-heart conversation. We need to shepherd the hearts of our children. We need to know and listen to their feelings and concerns. We need to come alongside them. In my next chapter, I will spend more time on this subject and suggest practical ways to do it.

Sending Our Children to Public School Can Provoke Our Children

God clearly commands us to "learn not the way of the heathen" (Jer. 10:2 KJV). But is that not exactly what our children are learning in public school today? Sending this mixed message to our children certainly can provoke them to wrath as they try to balance the competing instruction they are receiving at home and at school. Public schools create intellectual schizophrenics while they play Russian roulette with our children's souls. Review chapter 2 of this book for a thorough discussion of this topic. I also recommend you read my book *Home Schooling: The Right Choice* to understand the modern dangers, both blatant and subtle, of the modern public school system.

We Can Provoke Our Children by Inconsistent Discipline

We, as fathers, need to be constantly on guard against the many ways we provoke our children to wrath. One of the most common ways is through inconsistent discipline. Our culture demands that children be allowed to have their own way so as not to interfere with their individual rights and their spontaneity. Many fathers have been raised with the thought that it is wrong to discipline a child. We only need to look to the Word of God to see the consequence of inconsistent discipline.

David was a great king and a man of God; in fact, the Scriptures say he was a man after God's own heart. However, David was busy. He had important things to do, and he did not make time for leading and disciplining his children. We read that David did not confront his son Adonijah with his sins. The Scriptures say, "And his father had never crossed him at any time by asking, 'Why have you done so?'" (1 Kings 1:6). David didn't even bother to verbally challenge him.

In another biblical account, we can read about Eli the priest and his two sons, Hophni and Phineas. Eli went a little further than David did. He actually confronted his sons. Eli "heard all that his sons were doing to all Israel, and how they lay with the women who served at the doorway of the tent of meeting. He said to them, 'Why do you do such things, the evil things that I hear from all these people? No, my sons; for the report is not good which I hear the LORD's people circulating'" (1 Sam. 2:22–24).

But Eli had a problem. Although he confronted his sons, he did not do anything about it. See how God interprets his inconsistent discipline. God said to Eli, "Why do you kick at My sacrifice and My offering which I have commanded in My dwelling, and honor your sons above Me?" (1 Sam. 2:29). By refusing to discipline his sons, he was actually honoring them above God—he was disobeying God's clear commands on training his children.

1 Samuel 3:13 declares God's judgment on Eli: "For I have told him that I am about to judge his house forever for the iniquity which he knew, because his sons brought a curse on themselves and he did not rebuke them." By not restraining his sons, Eli brought not only judgment upon his house, but he provoked his children, contributing to their continuing in sin, which led ultimately to their violent deaths.

Of course, Samuel was raised in Eli's household and saw firsthand Eli's lack of discipline and its consequences. You would think that Samuel would have made sure he spent the necessary time to bring his children up in the nurture and admonition of the Lord. But according to 1 Samuel 8:3–5 this apparently was not so: "His sons, however, did not walk in his ways, but turned aside after dishonest gain and took bribes and perverted justice. Then all the elders of Israel gathered together and came to Samuel at Ramah; and they said to him, 'Behold, you have grown old, and your sons do not walk in your ways. Now appoint a king for us to judge us like all the other nations.'" Samuel's lack of consistent discipline in bringing his children up in the nurture and admonition of the Lord not only had consequences for his own sons and their eternal lives but also for the whole course of the nation of Israel. The elders of Israel wanted a king, not to be like the other nations, but because they wanted to avoid having Samuel's sons, who were very wicked, rule over them. Yes, let us be consistent in following God's biblical instruction on diligently disciplining our children while there is hope.

Having a Bad Attitude

Our children often frustrate us by their whining, screaming, and yelling. They keep surprising us with their disobedience, laziness, and bad attitudes. We begin to take it personally. I often think, *How can that child not get it? I have been teaching her not to scream at and pinch her brother for six years!* Or when one of my older children makes a scene, I will be sadly disappointed and frustrated with another repeat performance.

Sometimes I am tempted to imitate their negative or whining tones when I instruct or correct my children. I start responding in kind with a bad attitude, and my tongue lashes out in anger. Then I remember, "If anyone thinks himself to be religious, and yet does not bridle his tongue . . . this man's religion is worthless" (James 1:26). What am I? My sin is obvious and I repent. We need to pray for God's strength to enable us to control ourselves and always exhibit a godly attitude.

Being Selfish

We fathers need to die to ourselves. "Do *nothing* out of selfish ambition or vain conceit, but in humility consider others better than yourselves" (Phil. 2:3 NIV). Do we regard our children, both in words and deeds, as more important than ourselves? Christ set the example of ultimate sacrifice.

We need to be certain our children can see Christ living in us. There are endless ways we can be selfish.

- We yell at our children when they interrupt our reading of the newspaper.
- We spend too much time out with the guys.

- We put work above our children.
- We fail to share our plate of food or treats with them.
- We watch too much television or sports.

We need to balance our time and focus on God's priorities, or we risk provoking our children.

Idolizing our Children

As home schoolers, it is easy to be tempted to provoke our children by holding on too tight. We know what the world is like, and we are afraid to let them go. This can be making an idol out of our children. We are putting them above God and not trusting Him like we should. If we have home schooled them well and grounded them in the Word of God, we need to willingly *send them out* to do the Lord's work. God Himself set the ultimate example by sending out His only begotten Son to do His work and save us through dying on the cross and rising again (John 3:16).

Not Loving Our Wives

Your children notice the lack of love, or the deep love, between you and your wife. Your hypocrisy in this area can easily provoke your children. This will impact their lives and future marriages in a significant way. In chapter 7, I deal extensively with how God wants you to love your wife, and I give practical steps you can follow.

Not Leading Our Children Spiritually

Although there are many ways we can provoke our children, this last one is especially important. We, as fathers, must lead our children spiritually. If we do not, we risk provoking them to wrath. Remember, this is not simply an option—this is a command. In the next chapter I will deal extensively with ways to be the spiritual head of the family.

The Command to Bring Them Up

In Ephesians 6:4 we are commanded to bring up our children. This command requires action. We fathers do not have the option to simply *let* our children grow up, nor can we throw up our hands when they disobey and say, "They will grow out of it." We need to be in charge of bringing them up in the Lord. We must not abdicate this responsibility.

Fathers Must Nurture Their Children

Fathers, we need to lead in bringing up our children "in the nurture and admonition of the Lord" (Eph. 6:4 KJV). The word *nurture* involves intimacy and loving, something a teacher cannot do for a child. The word *nurture* in Greek means "nurture, instruction, and chastening." Nurture involves knowing your child's heart and caring deeply about him. A teacher cannot nurture children as a father can.

Fathers must instruct their children in the Lord. God said of Abraham, "I have chosen him, in order that he may command his children . . . to keep the way of the LORD by doing righteousness and justice" (Gen. 18:19). This means we must teach our children a biblical worldview so that they understand that the Bible speaks to every academic discipline and His wisdom is the foundation of all knowledge. We must diligently and comprehensively instruct our children in these biblical principles. We must sear them into their consciences so that when they are old, they will not depart from them (Prov. 22:6). Children must not only be taught to *believe* as Christians but also to *think* as Christians.

Nurturing also involves *chastening*. "For whom the LORD loves He reproves, / Even as a father corrects the son in whom he delights" (Prov. 3:12). We love our children, so we need to discipline them. Be certain to discipline for attitude, not just overt disobedience. When you tell your child to sit down, you don't want him standing up in the inside although he sits down on the outside. There is a connection from the bottom to the brain. Spanking will teach them the difference between right and wrong.

Proper discipline means you must take the time, when you spank your child, to help him identify his sin, express sorrow for his sin, and pray with you to ask forgiveness before God. A physical hug and expressing your forgiveness to him is also necessary. Sometimes you feel like skipping this process, but you cannot for your child's sake.

Proverbs 23:13–14 says,

> Do not hold back discipline from the child,
> Although you beat him with the rod, he will not die.
> You shall beat him with the rod,
> And deliver his soul from Sheol.

We find there is a spiritual connection between the physical chastisement and the child's soul! (Spanking is really a taste of hell.)

Other scriptural examples include: "He who withholds his rod hates his son, / But he who loves him disciplines him diligently" (Prov. 13:24); "Foolishness is bound up in the heart of a child; / The rod of discipline will remove it far from him" (Prov. 22:15); "The rod and reproof give wisdom, / But a child who gets his own way brings shame to his mother" (Prov. 29:15); "Correct your son, and he will give you comfort; / He will also delight your soul" (Prov. 29:17); "God deals with you as with sons; for what son is there whom his father does not discipline? But if you are without discipline . . . then you are illegitimate children" (Heb. 12:7–8); and "Discipline your son while there is hope, / And do not desire his death" (Prov. 19:18).

Wow! I think God really means it. He is serious about discipline, especially spanking. He could not have been clearer on this subject.

Fathers Are Commanded to Admonish Their Children

The word *admonition* in the Greek means "a putting into the mind." It also means "to say again and again." How well we know, as fathers, the importance of repetition! We might ask, "How many times should we repeat our instruction?" Our responsibility before God is to repeat it until our children get it! This includes shepherding our child's heart, not just controlling his actions. Admonishment is more than making and enforcing rules. It includes coming alongside our children.

Fathers Must Bring Their Children Up in the Lord

Let us not forget, fathers, that we must train our children in God's way, not our way. The training must be of the Lord, not from modern humanistic psychologists. We must know and follow the Word of God.

Overwhelmed?

Being the father is tough. God has laid the responsibility of bringing up our children His way squarely on our shoulders. We cannot escape this responsibility. God will always hold us accountable. Therefore, let us rise to the occasion and play the man—the godly man. Let us recommit ourselves to running the race of child training to win.

The next chapter is filled with practical tips on how we can be better and more Christlike fathers. Let's never grow weary in well doing, for in due season, we will reap *if* we do not faint.

A Challenge to
Home School Fathers:
Practical Tips

F athers, the responsibility is great. Home schooling happens to be the best way to fulfill the responsibility and commands that God has given us. Remember, home schooling is not the end in itself—it is the means to the end. The end we are aiming for is that our children will be arrows that carry God's truth to this world and that one day they will live with us in heaven.

As we read in the last chapter, the responsibility of nurturing these never-dying souls is great. As you read in this chapter about the time and tasks required to fulfill this responsibility, you will feel overwhelmed! It seems impossible that we can ever be adequate fathers who please the Lord.

But remember, when you feel weak, then you are strong. Paul wrote to the Philippian church, "I can do all things through Him who strengthens me" (Phil. 4: 13). God wants us to realize that we cannot accomplish these things by our own strength but by His. May God richly bless you and your family as you strive to be Ephesians 6:4 fathers.

Practical Tips on How to Be Ephesians 6 Fathers

We all have much to learn as we grow to be consistent, godly fathers. When I started down the path of fatherhood, I knew very little. Through trial and error and much grace from God, He has shown me ways I can be more faithful in training my children according to His will.

CHAPTER FIVE

Here are a number of practical tips that I try to use consistently in my own family to help me be a faithful father who is actively bringing his children up in the nurture and the admonition of the Lord. I keep asking for the Lord's strength to fulfill these principles in the training of my children, so that I will be found a good and faithful servant. I hope these tips will help you as you strive to be the most godly father you can be.

Nurture Your Own Soul

The most important thing you can do for your children is to nurture your own soul. Jesus tells us: "Seek first the kingdom of God and His righteousness, and all these things shall be added to you" (Matt. 6:33 NKJV). The condition of our own souls and how closely we walk with the Lord will directly influence our ability to train our children. I don't believe we can lead our children to a closer relationship with God than we ourselves have. So we need to walk closely with our Lord, surrender ourselves daily to His will, and beg for His mercy. Matthew 22:37–38 commands: "LOVE THE LORD YOUR GOD WITH ALL YOUR HEART, AND WITH ALL YOUR SOUL, AND WITH ALL YOUR MIND." This is the greatest commandment.

Loving God with all of our being is more important than anything else. We cannot let the business of our lives squeeze out our daily communion with the Lord. We must read the Bible, which is His word to us, and pray, which is our words back to Him. Jesus wants a personal relationship.

I also urge you to be members of a Bible-believing church, where you will find fellowship, mentoring, and accountability. Chapter 3 discusses this point in greater detail.

Shepherd Your Children's Hearts

It is important that we shepherd our children's hearts and not just control their actions. We need to come alongside our children, take time to understand them, and know their hearts. It is important to have a regular time scheduled with each of our children.

My schedule is as follows: Each night I read Bible stories or read directly from the Bible to my children between the ages of three and seven. I'll often read the Bible by flashlight with all the lights turned out. I've found that children, especially my twins, will completely quiet down and listen to the Word of God this way. I'll ask them questions and we'll interact. They actually beg me to read the Bible or some Bible story to them each night.

I spend a few minutes with my other children, reading the Bible in their rooms before they go to bed. When my son Jesse was six, he said: "My favorite thing I like to do with my dad is read the Bible with him." That's how I want my children to be—now and throughout their lives—lovers of the Word of God.

In addition, I schedule times early in the morning four days a week with my older children. On Tuesday morning, I meet with my eight-year-old son, Jesse. On Wednesday morning, I meet with my ten-year-old daughter, Megan. On Thursday morning, I meet with thirteen-year-old Bethany. And on either Monday or Friday morning, I meet with seven-year-old Susanna. For each of them I go through a book that directs them on how to develop godly character.

For instance, I have gone through the book *Beautiful Girlhood,* edited by Karen Andreola, with each of the girls. This wonderful book deals with many character traits and issues that girls face as they transition from girlhood into womanhood. It is especially helpful for a dad to use this book because it introduces many topics that, as a man, he would not otherwise have thought about or discussed with his daughter. For my son who has had trouble with conflicts with his sisters, I've been going through the Peacemakers series for children. This is an easy-to-read series of booklets with many illustrations that summarize the biblical principles of dealing with conflict and applying them to siblings and friends. I have several other books that I have gone through with my children, which I list as resources in Appendix III.

Love Your Wife Unconditionally

One very important way to avoid provoking your children to wrath and to present them a biblical model of marriage is to love your wife in a visible way before your children. You need to support her 100 percent and *never* argue with her in front of the children. We need to die to ourselves when we come home from work.

Multiple sclerosis puts me in a much weaker condition physically than the normal father. After putting in a full day of work under highly stressful situations and driving my car in a long commute, I am tired. But I've committed myself to coming home and taking over the care of the children each night. My body is longing for rest and relaxation, but I discipline myself and cry out to God for strength to supervise the cleanup after dinner, inspect bedrooms, pick up the stuff throughout the house, and administer all discipline.

I also make certain that I have family devotions with everyone. If I come home late and miss dinner, I go right to family devotions and eat my dinner later at night when the children are in bed.

Another way to love our wives is to honor her before our children. Particularly honor her as a fellow heir of salvation—we are equals before God. Our children need to understand that although our wives are under our authority, we treat them with the love of a fellow heir of salvation.

We also need to have regular times to communicate so that we don't assume anything about each other. This communication must be expressed verbally so as to avoid conflict.

We read in 1 Peter 3: 7 that we need to love our wives so that our prayers will not be hindered. We want our children to be godly, and we pray to God that He will transform their hearts. We don't want these prayers to be hindered because we don't love our wives. Ephesians 5:25 sums it up: "Husbands, love your wives, just as Christ also loved the church and gave Himself up for her." There can't be a higher love than that, and God's Word demands it of us.

In chapter 7, I discuss many ways that we as husbands can better love our wives according to God's teachings.

Be the Principal in Your Home School

Your wife is sacrificing a great deal to teach your children at home. She is giving up much of her own time and possibly a career. You need to generally lead in your home school and also come alongside your wife in the area of academics. You may not have time to teach many classes, but as you are able, make the time. Be available to grade papers and answer questions. Talk to your wife about the academics and discuss the educational plan and schedule for each of your children. Most important, make certain all topics are taught from a biblical perspective. There are many good books and materials that offer solid, biblical instruction.

Administer Discipline When You Are at Home

I make it a practice that, when I am at home, I am in charge of all discipline. This way I am demonstrating support for my wife. I don't want my children to think of me as a dad who is all fun and games and think of my wife as the bad guy because she has to do the disciplining. I want my children to respect my wife and to realize that we enforce the same rules. The message is clear: my wife and I are one.

Many times my wife is very busy during the day teaching all of the children and keeping up with all the household tasks. At times it is difficult for her to administer discipline when a child is acting up. I put a chart on the refrigerator door and created a system whereby she puts a *mark* by the name of the misbehaving child with a note of what he or she did wrong. When I come home, I look on the refrigerator to see if there are any marks, and I dispense the spanks accordingly. My children begin to understand that they will not get away with disobedience or bad attitudes.

Take Care of All Your Legal Troubles

This next point I do not take lightly. I urge you to make sure your family belongs to the Home School Legal Defense Association. As senior counsel of the Home School Legal Defense Association since 1985, I have seen how God has used HSLDA to literally change the legal landscape across this country. In 1985, when I started working at the Home School Legal Defense Association, it was only clearly legal to home school in about five states. After many years of work before the courts and legislatures of this land, God has blessed our efforts with many victories. We can now state with great thankfulness to God that it is legal in all fifty states. This was not always so, and there is no guarantee that it will always be.

The price of freedom is eternal vigilance. Your investment in the Home School Legal Defense Association not only will enable you to protect your family if you ever get an unwanted knock at your door by a truant officer or a social worker, but more important, your investment will help the many thousands of families who are members of HSLDA that we help each year who do have legal troubles and conflicts. It also will support our work on your behalf before the U.S. Congress and the federal government. We have a full-time lobby team that works on drafting laws and amendments and lobbying and building relationships with many congressional offices.

Your investment in joining the Home School Legal Defense Association will also go to help legal cases throughout the fifty states. Furthermore, your membership fee will help us promote the benefits and the cause of home schooling through commissioning research and dealing with the press. In addition, we have now expanded to assist home schoolers throughout the world as they contact us to find out how to legalize home schooling in their countries. We have an E-mail alert system, and we give our members weekly updates on what is happening across the country and other pertinent information regarding home schooling. We also send out state-by-state alerts as bills are introduced that will affect our liberties. We do the same thing on issues before the federal government.

Believe me, the $100 membership fee is worth it. Your right to home school is much too precious to lose. You can join the Home School Legal Defense Association by calling us at 540/338–5600 to ask for an application or join on-line at www.hslda.org. Our legal cases, legislative work, research, and much more are on our Web page.

Provide for Your Family Financially

This point is very obvious in the Scriptures. God says that the man who does not provide for his family is worse than an infidel (1 Tim. 5:8 KJV). Part of this process is to instill in your children a sense of productivity. Apprentice your children as much as possible. Take them to work with you so they can see what the work world is like.

Control the Television Set and Sports

In my experience working with many fathers across the country, I've found two weaknesses in this area. Fathers tend to like watching sports, and others like to watch the television set in general, especially the news. Now, nothing in and of itself is wrong with this. However, since I developed multiple sclerosis and have seen how it is changing my life to the extent that I cannot engage in athletics or go hiking with my children anymore, I realize how important it is for us to redeem the time we have with our children (Eph. 5:16). I've also received many letters from parents whose husband, wife, or child has died suddenly and tragically in one way or another.

My point is simply this: Our time is too precious to waste in watching television and most sporting events. Life is too short. We need to make every day count with our children; there is so much training to do—so much molding and shaping of their characters. Let us make certain our priorities are in order. One day we will be standing before our Creator and Judge to answer for how we spent our time with our children.

Our culture is obsessed with sports and TV. Let us not open the door of our children's hearts to these idols.

Be the Spiritual Head in Your Family

As fathers, we symbolize God the Father. Ephesians 6:4 says we're supposed to bring our children up in the nurture and admonition of the Lord. This is our most important role as a home school father as well. As you approach this responsibility, you need to be organized, just like you would make a plan for some project at work. Don't approach this area with a lackadaisical attitude or in any haphazard way. If you need to, write out a plan in your organizer and a schedule—and stick to it. Here are twelve ideas that I believe God wants us to practice.

1. Lead in family worship. The most important aspect of being the spiritual head in your family is to lead your family every day in family worship. *I do not believe this is a preference, but a command.* A survey was done in New York a few years ago of home school mothers, asking them what was the most important thing a father could do to support them in home schooling. The near-unanimous response of these women was that their husband should lead in family devotions. This was more important to the wives than date nights or time to themselves. The wives know what is important! Therefore, fathers, let us honor our wives by leading in this most important area.

I have to admit that my wife had to push me into leading in this area of family worship. I thought I had it covered in other ways. But once I disciplined myself to lead after dinner each night, the blessings began to flow. To observe my children growing spiritually is a privilege that I would not trade for anything. Making family devotions a priority demonstrates, by action, your commitment to the Lord. This is true especially when visitors come and, instead of canceling family devotions, you include the visitors. Not only is this a witness for the Lord, but a permanent example that you are etching into the minds and hearts of your children.

We have family devotions on the average of five nights each week. If I am traveling or working late, my wife will lead that night. I think it is important that we fathers make the devotions interactive so that the children participate to some degree. In this way we will know if they are actually listening and learning.

We always begin with prayer to ask the Lord's blessing on our time as we come before Him. Next, I read a passage from the Bible. I devote time to reading books of the Bible that are stories or narratives such as Esther, Daniel, the Kings, Chronicles, Samuel, the Acts, and the Gospels. I alternate reading passages in Proverbs. I apply each verse to our own family and discuss examples to which our children can relate. When we read the Scriptures, I always stop and ask questions to make sure each age level understands. I will sometimes substitute a newsletter from the *Voice of the Martyrs* to recount miracles taking place in persecuted countries and to teach examples of the suffering our Christian brothers and sisters endure in China, Sudan, and other countries.

From Proverbs, I help my children understand that if one of their friends should tempt them to do something wrong, they must be wise and resist the foolishness of that friend. I also explain the importance of learning never to repeat the same sin after they are disciplined. Otherwise they will be like a dog that returns to its vomit. I want to ground my children in God's perfect wisdom. I have also read aloud *Courageous Christians, The Child's Story Bible,* and *Training Hearts Training Minds* (See Appendix III for descriptions of these wonderful resources).

We then sing at least four praise songs and/or hymns. There is nothing sweeter than hearing the voices of your own children joined together in praise of their Heavenly Father. We close with a time of prayer. Usually we pray from the youngest to oldest. With seven children and often guests, prayer takes time! But it is truly a blessing to hear and see your children's faith grow as they pray for their neighbors and friends to come to know the Lord, pray for the persecuted church, and pray for those who are suffering various trials. It is an encouragement to hear them pray that they will be obedient and to thank God for all they have.

2. Set spiritual goals for your family. It is important to be the spiritual head of your wife, which includes planning spiritual goals for you, your wife, and your children. Ask your wife how your children are doing in various areas. Then, when you keep your appointed time with each child, you are aware of the particular problem or any hang-up they may have. As you interact with your children, be sure to encourage them as you see their faith grow.

Don't let little sins grow into big sins. It takes effort and discipline to deal with an argumentative child when he or she is young, but you know it is necessary to prevent rebellion as the child gets older. It is important that we nip problems in the bud.

3. Be the spiritual protector of your family and your children. We as home school fathers need to practice intense prayer. We need to lead our family to battle when we pray. If we don't pray for our children, who will? This is one of our greatest responsibilities: to be a prayer warrior. As Steve Camp says in one of his songs from his album *Fire and Ice*: "Do the demons beware when you get down to pray?" We need to pray fervently.

Recently I came to the obvious realization that all the good training in the world will not save my children. If I keep every command in the Word of God and follow all the principles discussed in this chapter, I still cannot save my children. God and God alone saves.

Therefore, I have learned to let go of the results and turn those over to God. Scripture tells us that God gives the increase (1 Cor. 3:6-7 KJV). Of course, I must still be diligent in training my children repeatedly and consistently until they learn each lesson. However, I have learned that it's even more important that we realize we're engaged in a spiritual battle for the souls of our children. Therefore, practicing intense prayer is crucial. We must pray that God will change their hearts. We must beg for His mercy on behalf of our children.

4. Do not delegate older children the responsibility to train the younger children in spiritual matters. Spiritual training should be our responsibility as fathers and mothers. We need to have our older children focus more on practical tasks like changing diapers, getting children dressed, and cleaning the house.

5. Teach your children to develop the habit of personal devotions. As home school fathers who are true spiritual heads, we must teach our children how to have their own private devotions with the Lord God Almighty. It is important that we make them accountable to us as their father and as the spiritual head of the home. I've learned a method that helps my children form a lasting habit of having regular, daily, personal devotions in communion with God. I want my children to learn to nurture their own souls and develop a close, personal walk with the Lord.

I teach accountability by having each child who can read and write keep a journal. Each day they read a prearranged passage of Scripture and write in their notebooks. They are to write out a verse and a sentence or two describing what this verse means to them. At the scheduled time each week that I meet with them, I review the Bible verses they wrote from their personal devotions and their comments from the past week. What a joy it is to peddle through the Scriptures and review what they have been reading for the week. When the child has diligently completed his or her personal devotions every day for a month, he or she gets a special treat from Dad or has a breakfast date with him. These incentives particularly help the smaller children as they begin developing their habits. The incentives are not as needed with the older children, as they are generally motivated from their hearts to have daily personal devotions with the Lord.

6. Control your time on the job. This requires balance. I know a Christian author who traveled all over the country speaking. He and I were on a radio program together one time, and the host asked us, "How do you balance your family and your ministry?" This man's response was a simple "You don't," which he said with a chuckle. It showed. Approximately six months later, his wife and children left him. He had become married to his ministry and neglected nurturing his own children as he encouraged others to nurture theirs. If your job is keeping you away from your family too much, you need to change it. God will honor those who honor Him. God will enable you to be faithful as you fulfill your role as father if you simply trust Him. Furthermore, you must never worry more about material goods than your children's spiritual training. It must remain a top priority.

7. *Create tapes for your children.* Another way to train our children spiritually is to create tapes for them. Chapter 6 provides step-by-step instructions on how any father can become a storyteller. Simply pick out a family, name three or four fictitious children, and have those children interact in the story you make up. Buy a decent tape recorder and a pack of sixty-minute tapes. Pick out a geographical location, a time period, and a particular spiritual lesson you want to teach. As you tell the story, it'll simply come together. Your children love tapes. They'll listen to them over and over again. This is a way fathers can train their children spiritually while they're at work or on trips.

It's particularly humorous to walk around your house at night and hear your voice echoing from two or three rooms simultaneously. Many times my children will remind me of a story I told and what they learned, even though I've long since forgotten the story. Another option is to read good storybooks with spiritual lessons on tape so your children can listen to them.

8. *Sing Scriptures to songs.* It is helpful to set Scriptures to songs. What I mean by this is to take a familiar tune and simply sing a Bible passage. For instance, consider the song: "Seek ye first the kingdom of God and His righteousness and all these things shall be added unto you. Alleluia" (from Matt. 6:33 KJV). We have added five more verses to that same tune. "All things work together for good to those who love God and who are called according to His will. Alleluia" (from Rom. 8:28). Another verse is "Be ye steadfast and unmovable, always abounding in God's work. Knowing your labor is not in vain. Alleluia" (from 1 Cor. 15:58 KJV). Still another one is, "Confess with your lips that Jesus is Lord, and believe in your heart that He rose again from the dead. Then you shall be saved" (from Rom. 10:9).

This is an easy way for children to memorize Scripture and hide the Word of God in their hearts so they do not sin against God (Ps. 119:11).

9. *Hang Bible verses on the walls all around your home.* Deuteronomy 6 commands us to teach the Word of God to our children in a comprehensive way—when we rise up, when we lie down, when we walk along the way, we tie it to our foreheads, we tie it to our doorposts, on our wrists (6:7–9). In

other words, the Word of God should be before our children at all times. It is not hard to frame Bible verses that have been written in calligraphy or have been purchased at Christian bookstores. My wife has taped Bible verses on cards over every door and by every sink and light switch so that the Word of God is constantly before the eyes of our children and ourselves.

It is also a wonderful testimony to visitors. They can never leave with the impression that we do not love the Lord because it is apparent from the Bible verses all over our house.

10. Record answered prayers. As a father, I believe it is important that we record answered prayers in our family and review them periodically with our children. Many of my children were too young to remember when various miracles occurred in our lives. Even our twins need to be reminded of the wonderful miracle God performed to save them alive in the womb. I've made a practice of writing down these instances of answered prayer in my organizer under a section called *Answered Prayer.*

Periodically, I read portions of this to my children so that they can be reminded of God's faithfulness. Scripture makes it very clear that it is our responsibility as fathers to "tell their children about your faithfulness" (Isa. 38:19 NIV).

11. Go through Proverbs with your children. I believe this is the best method of spiritual training and instilling moral values. As fathers, you should be in charge of teaching Proverbs to your children. If you're unable to do anything else mentioned in this chapter, teach your children Proverbs. They will learn wisdom and life skills from the Book of Proverbs.

12. Lead your family in evangelism. It is important to show your children that Jesus *really* means everything to you. Our children need to understand that the good news cannot be kept inside—it is not just for your family—but it needs to be proclaimed throughout the world. It is important that you lead in family evangelism by passing out tracts together, visiting neighbors, and inviting them to church. Another activity is to have your children write a tract. When we go to a restaurant, I have my children fan out in pairs to deliver tracts to people sitting at various tables.

In chapter 12, I explain many practical ways you can share the gospel as a family.

Do You Feel Overwhelmed Yet?

I do not know about you, but being a godly father seems quite overwhelming. You might be saying to yourself, *There is no way I can do this.* You are right. You can't. I can't. But God can.

You also need to ask yourself, *How bad do I want it? How bad do I want to be a godly father?* Then put forth the effort, planning, prayer, and emotion to make it happen. I will repeat what I have said often in this book—never-dying souls are at stake.

When it comes to being sold out for Jesus Christ in the training of my children, I think of a quote from Dick Bliss, a creation scientist. He gave a sermon at a church one morning during his travels. He said in part:

> "The door is open for us. God is saying, 'Here, I've given you all the scientific evidence. I've given you all the tools to tell others about Jesus Christ. I've given them all to you. Now, get out there and testify for me.'

> "I want to read something to you that epitomizes where I am, as I leave you this day. A pastor in Africa who had endured severe persecution for his faith, stapled this on his door. I'm just going to read the last two paragraphs from this, because this is where I want Dick Bliss to be. And I want to ask you the question, 'Where do you want to be for Jesus today?' Are you just going to sit in the pew, or are you going to go out and work and be a testimony for Him? What are you going to do?

> "This young pastor's testimony reflects my own:

> "'I will not flinch in the face of sacrifice—hesitate in the presence of the adversary—negotiate at the table of the enemy—ponder at the pool of popularity—or meander in the maze of mediocrity. I won't give up, shut up, let up, until I have stayed up, stored up, prayed up, paid up, and preached up for the cause of Jesus Christ.

> "'I am a disciple of Jesus. I must go till He comes—give till I drop—preach till all know—and work till He stops me. And when He comes for His own, He will have no problem recognizing me. My banner will be clear.'

"I want to tell you in testimony today, dear friends, I want my banner to be clear should Jesus Christ call for me today. I want Him to see Dick Bliss, and I want my banner to be clear. How about your banner?"

Thus ended the morning worship service. After lunch with the pastor and an afternoon of preparation, Dick Bliss failed to respond to the knock on his hotel door to go to his evening engagement. Inside, it was discovered that Jesus Christ did indeed call for him that day. No doubt, his banner was clear (From *Impact* newsletter, February 1995, Institute for Creation Research, El Cajon, Calif.).

Fathers, let us commit together to make certain our banner is clear. Let us run the race to win. Let all who see us know we truly love our children and are committed to nurturing their souls in the Lord. Let us stand out in the midst of a culture of fathers who selfishly seek their own way and ignore keeping God's standards.

A Closing Quiz and Commitment

In conclusion to the issues and ideas discussed in this chapter, I ask you to turn to Appendix I and take the quiz for fathers. Answer each question as accurately as possible. After you complete the quiz, give it to your wife, with your answers, and have her answer the same questions from her perspective. You may be a little surprised!

Your wife also needs to answer the question about what is the most important thing you can do for her as a home schooling mother. Take careful note of her answer and put it into practice. Not only will you bless her, but God will bless you.

This little exercise can help you put feet to your convictions and start you on the road to become a more faithful home school father.

How to Be a Storyteller: Spiritual Lessons on Tape

W e know God desires that home schooling be a joint effort by both the mother and father. A father who works outside the home, however, has limited time to dedicate to teaching his children, especially the younger ones. I understand the predicament because I work at an office thirty miles from our home for forty-five hours a week, travel at least twelve times a year to speak at home school conferences in various states and countries, and testify before legislatures. Although I sometimes take one of my children with me to the office and rotate them to accompany me on some trips, I, like most fathers, am away from home a large portion of each week. Since we fathers are given the command in Ephesians 6:4 to "bring up our children in the nurture and admonition of the Lord," how can we spiritually nurture our children when we are away from home?

I've discovered one practical way we as fathers can use to maximize our time with our children and to shape their characters. I use the simple technology of a tape recorder. I tell my children stories on tapes to teach spiritual lessons.

Some of you are probably thinking, *Me? A storyteller? Impossible. I'm not a good public speaker. I can't talk more than a few minutes at a time.* Please do not give up before you start. I was never a good storyteller either, until I became really motivated and discovered this simple formula for storytelling that I will describe in this chapter. I am convinced every father can be a good storyteller and can capture those stories on a cassette tape.

CHAPTER SIX

Why Storytelling?

Jesus told stories. People hung on every word of His parables. Jesus did not tell empty, useless stories as do TV sitcoms and most modern movies. Rather, His stories had a purpose. He wanted to teach a spiritual lesson and share God's wisdom.

The Bible tells us we are to be conformed to the image of His Son. We can imitate Jesus in how He communicated God's truths by repeating His parables or stories and by creating our own.

Have you ever noticed your children's faces when they watch a movie? Have you seen their complete attention while listening to a good story being read aloud? Children who normally jabber or fidget are suddenly quiet and attentive.

When we sit around the table for dinner, my children beg my wife Tracy or me to tell a story about when we were children. They sit completely mesmerized, eagerly listening to every word. Children love stories.

When our children learned to read, they fell in love with nonfiction stories, historical fiction, and biographies. Although they enjoy learning from other books, stories are still their favorites.

Most of us do not have time to write children's stories, biographies, or historical fiction, but we can find time to talk with our children. We can find time to relate a story we heard or read, an experience, or the result of our own imagination. If we do this on tape, we can significantly impact our children.

In my experience, children between the ages of two and fourteen love to listen to cassette tape recordings of stories. At this time the market is flooded with Christian tapes of stories and songs. There are so many tapes from which to choose that it can get expensive. Also, the message on many tapes available in the marketplace is too often shallow and redundant. The most important value of a father making his own taped stories is that the content of the tape can be trusted. Some of the Christian story tapes available leave much to be desired.

The influence of cassette tapes is easily understood when you simply take time to watch your children. Children will turn on a tape and listen to it over and over and over again. They will play tapes while they are playing in their rooms. My wife will turn on a tape for our younger children while she is finishing home schooling the older children. My children will know the characters in the story inside and out, and they seem to never tire of listening to the tape one more time. Tapes are a part of their lives.

Fathers can make tapes that will have a tremendous impact on their children. They can simply tell stories, ad lib, on tape. As I mentioned before, the concept may seem a little frightening to some fathers. However, you will find that not only will you do a good job but also your children will love to listen to their daddy's stories on tape again and again. This will enable you to help mold their characters and give them instruction in many areas of life.

At the same time, Dads, you'll be helping your wives in an important way in the training of your young children and in fulfilling God's command in Ephesians 6:4.

The Equipment Needed for Storytelling

Obviously, there are sophisticated ways for you to make taped stories for your children. You can have background music, sound effects, special sound equipment, splicing, and editing.

However, I suggest a very simple method that takes no more time than the telling of the story. All you need is:

- A basic, good-quality tape recorder with a microphone, and
- Some high-quality sixty-minute tapes.

The tapes need to be high quality because your children will listen to them repeatedly. It is very disappointing when one of the tapes breaks and the story is lost forever. As a precaution, I have made copies of most of my tapes in case one breaks or is lost.

Although not a prerequisite, I also bought a few large tape jackets where the children can store up to twelve of my tapes at a time. I have done approximately thirty tapes, and each tape has at least two stories on it. I average about one new tape a month. It helps to have a schedule written down in your organizer so you do not forget. You can build up your children's expectation a few days before you are going to do a *Daddy Tape*.

By the way, you may be able to think of timesaving ways to do stories for your children. I, for instance, have a long commute to work, so I occasionally tell my children stories on tape during this time. Although the sound quality is not as good, the children still enjoy them. Also, from time to time I do a story on tape while I am in a hotel on a trip. I mostly tell stories in one of the children's rooms at bedtime in the dark.

Benefits of Storytelling to Your Children

The benefits to your children are many. First of all, you can minister to your children's souls. You can teach them, through the characters in your stories, that they need a Savior and that a close daily walk with the Lord is important.

Second, dads have the opportunity to teach children key character qualities and how to develop them in their lives. As all fathers know, repetition is essential for children to develop godly character qualities. As your children listen to your tapes again and again, they are being grounded in God's Word.

Third, children grow closer to their dads when they listen to the tape repeatedly with their brothers and sisters. My daughter Bethany, when she was six years old, said one of the reasons she liked my taped stories was because it showed I cared about her!

Fourth, your children gain more knowledge—from how to do something to the consequences of disobedience and from historical truths to biblical principles.

Fifth, these tapes provide an opportunity for moms and dads to put the children to bed early, turn out the lights, and let them listen to the tapes. This gives moms and dads some extra time to themselves to work (such as writing this book, for instance!) or to talk.

Have you ever noticed how children become focused at night when the lights are out and they are in bed? I have found that this is the time when the children are most willing to speak of spiritual things and their personal feelings. I have some of the best talks with my children when I put them to bed at night. It is an opportunity to shepherd their hearts and draw close to them. Similarly, I have found that the children will listen intently to a tape in their rooms at night, absorbing and even memorizing every word.

Of course, these tapes give moms an opportunity during the day to let the children calm down and occupy themselves by listening to a tape. This frees her to get some other work done or to spend time teaching the older children. An unexpected benefit is that the practice of telling stories helps fathers to articulate better, to avoid the ah's and um's so common in modern conversation.

I have discovered that it also instills the desire and ability in my children to be storytellers. Bethany, my oldest child of seven children, has been a master storyteller since she was seven years old. She writes down the names and ages of the fictitious characters of her story and lets her imagination, past experiences, and books she has read be her guide in creating a wonderful story. Megan, Jesse, and Susanna are all following their dad's and big sister's example and are becoming good storytellers themselves. They will be able to use their talents in training children in Sunday schools, vacation Bible schools, various ministries, and eventually in training their own children. There is no doubt storytelling is generational.

Last, if your job requires you to travel, like mine does, the tapes give your children a chance to hear your voice and not miss you quite so much. Besides the telephone, it is the next best thing to being there!

Main Ingredients of a Good Story

So how does a father tell a story? The main ingredients for a good story are:

- Voice inflection (You cannot tell a good story in a monotone..),
- A specific moral lesson and a character quality to teach your child,
- A historical setting (such as Roman times, frontier days, the Civil War, or the Depression),
- A geographical location (For instance, set the story in Italy, on the Oregon Trail, in the Rocky Mountains, Sudan, or Boston. I often pick a place I have visited or studied about in my reading of history. Traveling to Alaska, South Africa, Japan, and many states gives me vivid pictures in my memory to recount on tape..),
- Instructions about how things work (such as a gun, covered wagon, car, airplane, sailboat, bank, or factory), and
- Imagination!

Since you deal with your children on a regular if not a daily basis, you will know what important spiritual lessons, character qualities, or skills they need to learn. Therefore, once these few ingredients are settled in your mind, you simply need to start talking! It only takes me a few minutes to think of a starting point; then off I go, almost letting the story tell itself. If my story is to be of a historical nature, I may pick up a biography or history book for a few minutes earlier in the day to remind myself of some specific dates or places.

For instance, I will often begin my story by explaining to my children when and where the story is taking place. I might explain that it took place in Bible times or in the days of the frontier in our country or perhaps in modern times. Of course, a historical setting opens up thousands of options for you to describe the type of transportation used back then, the type of clothing, or the type of work people did during that time period. This also gives you the opportunity, if you so choose, to recount some historical facts that occurred during the American Revolution or the Civil War or during the exodus from Egypt. There are limitless opportunities for you to teach your children history, science, geography, and cultural information as you tell a story.

After I have established the setting, I identify the particular family around whom the story will revolve. I'll generally have a mother, a father, and three or four children of various ages. I will name each one of them. My children become very attached to these characters and remember them long after they have listened to the tape. You might use the same family throughout various tapes if you are using the same geographic and historical setting. If you switch time periods, as I often do, you'll need to start with a new family and children with new lessons to learn.

As you tell the story, be sure to have the children, parents, and other characters interact. This can be done by slightly changing your voice and identifying who is speaking to whom. My kids love to hear me recount conversations between the characters in the story.

For example, you should have conversations like this: "Samuel said to his friend, 'Remember, my dad said I should never cross the road without an adult.' His friend Johnny responded, 'Aw, we won't be gone long. Your dad will never know. Besides, the little creek over there is really neat and filled with crayfish and stuff to catch. Let's go, Samuel!'" In this scenario, you introduce your children to an important lesson and to the consequences of disobedience. You are also making them aware of negative peer pressure and the dangers of traffic on a busy street.

Building Your Children's Character through Stories

As you tell your story, you can move the story toward a particular lesson. For instance, we lived by an outdoor pool for a time, so I told my young children a story about a child who was disobedient to her parents and ended up going too close to the pool and falling in. I recounted all the horror involved in not knowing how to swim and nearly drowning. Another example would be to tell a story that explains what happens when a child lies, how one lie leads to another lie, and how other members of the family get hurt. I have told stories about little children disobeying their parents by using matches, falling through ice, or getting lost in the woods or in a store. I have told many stories about children who find themselves in circumstances where fellow peers are pressuring them to do something that is against the Bible or their parents. When my children went through a stage of trying to excuse their disobedience by saying, "But Charity was doing it," I told a story that showed how all disobedience had to be punished. I was able to clarify in their young minds that God holds each person responsible for his or her actions.

I regularly have the characters in my stories pray, praise, and give thanks to the Lord. My characters often read the Bible, too. This helps my children see the importance of developing godly habits and a consistent life of service to the Lord.

Other stories involve children interacting with their dad about who Jesus Christ is and what He has done for us. Sometimes the children tell a neighbor about Jesus, and the neighbor comes to the knowledge of our Savior. Other times the children in the story tell someone about Jesus and are rebuffed or are questioned hard by the other person. All this enables my children to become comfortable with the problems they will face in this world and the types of people who will try to convince them not to follow Jesus.

If you notice that your children have been fighting with one another or have been disrespectful to their mother, this would be the perfect opportunity for a story involving children who engage in that same behavior. You can, of course, interact with Scriptures and the consequences of such behavior in your story. Obviously, the possibilities are limitless.

To guide your creativity, you may want to write down a few lists that cover various moral and spiritual lessons, geographical locations, historical accounts (Oliver Cromwell, Custer's Last Stand, Paul Revere's ride, Lewis and

Clark, Bible stories), and how certain things work (car engines, sailboats, computers, pulleys, and levers).

Making a Story Exciting

I suggest that you give your stories an exciting aspect in order to keep your children's attention. That excitement could be in the form of a shipwreck, a child getting lost, or the family finding a hurt dog and nursing it back to health. Other types of excitement that you can insert in your story can involve a farm family fighting off a wolf, or a child who disobeys his parents and causes some major catastrophe. Many times I will make sound effects to enhance the action.

I once told a story about three window washers on the top of the Empire State Building in New York City. All of a sudden a storm hits, and the men are left dangling in a damaged scaffolding. The father of the children in the story witnesses to the two men. One accepts Christ and the other does not. The one who scoffs at God ends up dying, and I explain the consequences of dying without God's forgiveness. The children are sitting on the edge of their beds as the lesson hits home and is imbedded in their minds and hopefully in their souls.

I have told true, courageous, and miraculous accounts of persecuted Christians in China and the Sudan using a fictitious reporter and father of four. In the story the reporter recounts his adventures to his children after he returns.

I have told of avalanches in Colorado, Indian attacks on the frontier, mountain climbing, Civil War battles, rattlesnake attacks in New Mexico, French Huguenots during St. Bartholemew's Massacre, and the Battle of Blood River in South Africa when God answered the prayers of the Afrikaners who were fighting against the Zulus. The children enjoy the excitement while they learn valuable lessons, history, and geography.

Teaching Your Children Skills through Your Story

Additionally, as you describe a particular family, you can spend a certain amount of time explaining the type of work the father does. The work might be carpentry or training horses or working on a computer. This will give you

75

an opportunity to give your children a basic understanding of certain types of jobs and skills. You can introduce them to the work a lawyer does or all the responsibilities and tasks of a mother. Maybe the father in your story is a policeman or a fireman or is a candidate for a government office. In another story, the teenager in your story could learn some basic skills in the area of mechanics or excel in a sport. You can talk about how electricity works or how to track an animal in the woods.

When I get the chance, I will read a G. A. Henty Christian adventure book (Mill Hall, Pa.: Preston/Speed Publications) or a biography and then recount a condensed version of the story on tape in my own words while it is still fresh in my mind.

Read Stories on Tape

If you don't feel particularly creative one night, read a really good short story on tape by flashlight in your child's room. A perfect resource would be *Courageous Christians* by Joyce Vollmer Brown. Another source would be Rudyard Kipling's short stories such as "Rikki Tikki Tavvi" or "The Maltese Cat." I have also read some of my favorite Christmas stories on tape.

As a father, you have a wealth of knowledge to share with your children. You have traveled, read books, learned skills, observed God's work in your life, and much more. Telling your children stories transfers this knowledge to them. It gives them an opportunity to see how a particular skill works in real life and how attitudes and obedience to their parents can directly affect people's lives. You can essentially teach your children the difference between good and bad behavior and whet their appetites for learning more about certain periods of history or certain skills.

Above all, storytelling gives the father a perfect opportunity to train his children in the nurture and admonition of the Lord (Eph. 6:4). Furthermore, your children will have an opportunity to grow closer to you as they see the desire in your heart to spend quality time with them through storytelling.

The Home
Schooling Husband:
Ways to Show
Unconditional Love

T hree home school fathers whom I thought I knew, all professing Christians, shocked me by abruptly leaving their wives and families. Only a few years earlier, one of these men had had tears in his eyes after I spoke on the subject of home school fathers loving their wives and children. Now he was divorcing his wife and emotionally torturing his children. Another father outwardly walked the Christian life in every respect, but inwardly he was gradually losing his love for his wife and looking for love in other places. He ended up walking away from his five children, his wife, his church family, and God, simply to enjoy an adulterous relationship. A third home school dad left his wonderful wife and three little children. It was discovered that he had had several affairs over the years. All three of these experiences helped me realize that even Christian home school husbands are not immune to the temptations in our culture that destroy marriages at a rapid rate.

There is a divorce revolution taking place. Our culture will lie to us and tell us to look out for our selfish desires, assuring us that our children will not be affected by a divorce. A massive study conducted by psychologist

Judith Wallerstein reveals the opposite result. Her book *The Unexpected Legacy of Divorce: A 25 Year Landmark Study* (New York: Hyperion, 2001) documents the devastating effects of divorce. Since 1971, Dr. Wallerstein has interviewed and followed the lives of sixty divorced families in affluent Marin County, California. She has also counseled over six thousand children with divorcing parents in the facility she established, The Judith Wallerstein Center for the Family in Transition in California.

Dr. Wallerstein found that the children of divorce suffer in many ways.

- These children do not have a healthy role model. When they become adults, they have no guide for healthy marital partnerships.
- Children of divorce have a significantly smaller chance of entering college. For children with intact families, 90 percent of them had fathers who contributed to college expenses, whereas only 30 percent of children of divorce got help from their fathers.
- There is much more substance abuse. Children of divorce use drugs and alcohol before age fourteen more often than children of intact families.
- Girls were much more likely to commit fornication.
- Children of divorce had less social confidence; only 40 percent functioned well in social relationships. One third went to therapists regularly to straighten out their personal lives.

Even more condemning in demonstrating the casualties in the divorce revolution are the national statistics. More than one million children a year have experienced parental divorce since 1970. One quarter of Americans between the ages of eighteen and forty-four are the adult children of divorce. Some 40 percent of all married adults in the 1990s have been divorced. Married couples with children currently represent only 26 percent of all households. About 45 percent of new marriages will end in divorce. About 60 percent of remarriages will end that way.

These statistics from Dr. Wallerstein's research are alarming and frightening. Who bears the greatest responsibility for this national tragedy? I am convinced that the fault lies primarily with the husbands. Why? It is very simple. Husbands are not unconditionally loving their wives as commanded by God the Creator. Without such love, marriages will fail. "The buck stops here" with us husbands.

The Command: Husbands, Love Your Wives

In Ephesians 5:25, the command is clear: "Husbands, love your wives, just as Christ also loved the church and gave Himself up for her." This straightforward command is repeated in Colossians 3:19, where God says, "Husbands, love your wives and do not be embittered against them." Additionally, the Bible says, "Husbands, likewise, dwell with them with understanding, giving honor to the wife, as to the weaker vessel, and as being heirs together of the grace of life, that your prayers may not be hindered" (1 Pet. 3:7 NKJV).

Home school husbands, loving your wife is not an option; it is a command! You must make a conscious decision to love your wife even though you do not always feel like loving her. Your wife is a sinner, and she will disappoint you. Your wife will often disagree with you and even hurt you with things she does and says. In many ways, she will not live up to your idealistic expectations.

When the hard times come and disagreements surface, these supposed "irreconcilable differences," many husbands will respond selfishly by withdrawing their love or simply leaving the relationship. Divorce has become an easy escape. Popular culture provides virtually no incentive for husbands to do the hard work that will keep their marriages together.

Ephesians 5:25 gives a very different picture: Husbands are to love their wives unconditionally. There are no biblical exceptions other than adultery and abandonment. Does this sound radical? Not really. God has decided, in His perfect will, to hold marriage as sacred. Marriage represents the permanent union that Christ has with us, the church.

A few years ago I was on a plane flying to speak at a home school convention. As providence would have it, I sat next to a lady who was clearly a feminist. A few minutes of conversation confirmed it, and I was beginning to feel she was hopelessly bitter. However, as our conversation continued, I began trying to steer her to an opportunity to share the gospel. As I explained how easy it is to die, she agreed and related a recent near-death experience of her employer in a plane that had mechanical difficulty. God gave me my cue, and I began to explain the Word of God to her.

She immediately recoiled. She said that the Bible simply tells husbands to treat their wives as doormats. All she knew was that wives had to submit to their husbands and that husbands nearly always abuse their authority.

I calmly responded by turning to Ephesians 5:25, and I told her how her understanding was completely inaccurate. I read the passage "Husbands, love your wives, just as Christ also loved the church and gave Himself up for her." I explained to her what Christ did for the church, and how He gave His own life for her. I recounted how He died for us even though we were His enemies. The church represents all of His people whom He loves unconditionally. I told her that is how a husband is to love his wife. It is a complete dying to self and an unconditional love. Tears welled up in her eyes when she heard this truth for the first time.

After that major breakthrough, her demeanor completely changed, and for the next hour she willingly drank in the Word of God. I left her with a Gideon New Testament and a huge smile on her face. Her heart was now open to the gospel.

God's ways are beautiful and right. His laws are perfect. As we home school husbands practice this command to unconditionally love our wives, God will bless us. Our love must not be dependent on our wife's submission to us. Our love must not be conditional on how well our wives organize their day, home school the children, or lead in discipline.

Certainly Christ's love for us is not dependent on our submission or obedience: "While we were enemies we were reconciled to God through the death of His Son" (Rom. 5:10). Since the love of Christ is an undeserved gift, and since husbands are called to imitate Christ in the way they treat their wives, is it right for our love for them to be based on works? We need to ask ourselves, *Are we making our wives earn our love?*

As husbands, we must die to ourselves. We are to love our wives just as Christ loved the church and gave Himself up for her. Christ was happy to die for us (Heb. 12:2). Are we willing to die over and over again for our wives so that they may come more and more to both life eternal and a life of joy here on this earth? The command is unequivocal. We are to love our wives the same way that Jesus loves us. This is a permanent commitment.

Christian home school husbands are without excuse. We know better than the world about the precious gift of children and how God commands us to train them as I reviewed in chapter 2. We know the sacred place marriage has in the heart of God. To whom much is given, much is required (Luke 12:48). We have a clear responsibility to be faithful in unconditionally loving our wives.

80

How Can We Love Our Wives Unconditionally?

You might be thinking, *But you do not understand. My wife is not easy to live with.* In the power of your flesh, it is impossible to love your wife unconditionally. But with God, all things are possible. God gives us enough grace in Christ for us to have all the joy and hope and encouragement that we need, no matter how difficult our circumstances. We can do all things through Christ who strengthens us (Phil. 4:13). We can love our wives even when we feel we are not loved in return.

Men, let us take responsibility for our own actions, words, attitudes, and feelings toward our wives. God will hold us responsible one day before the judgment seat for our faithfulness—or lack of faithfulness—in dying to ourselves and loving our wives. I truly believe that whatever extent we fail to love our wives is a result of our own sin. This is similar to the truth that whatever extent we do not reflect Christ in our lives is a result of our own sin. We cannot wait for our wives to change before we love them unconditionally. That is nothing more than a sinful excuse.

Recognize Your Wife as a Weaker Vessel

How often do we become impatient with our wives over home schooling? How often do we blame our wives if our children are not learning as well as we think they should? How often do we ignore how our wives feel about their lives or a particular situation? If we are doing these things regularly, we need to repent. God wants us to treat our wives in an understanding way. We husbands are to live with our wives in an understanding way as with a weaker vessel, since she is a woman (1 Pet. 3:7). This is a command.

In creation, God made woman as a weaker vessel. In His sovereign wisdom, He ordained for our wives to be more fragile and delicate than we are. How does that apply to home school husbands, and how we must treat our wives?

For a moment, let us consider the weaker vessel analogy. Stronger vessels would include pots and pans, rainwater barrels, and trashcans. You do not worry about protecting these types of vessels. They can be used for strenuous jobs and can handle a great deal of pressure. In many ways, these stronger vessels represent men.

Weaker vessels, on the other hand, are teapots, vases, china dishes, or heirlooms. These vessels are fragile and often easily broken. They need to be well cared for and handled gently. They often need attention and must be kept safe from harm. These weaker vessels are a picture of our wives.

Therefore, to fulfill this command, you need to temper your strength when you are dealing with your wife. You should regularly ask her how she feels. You must really listen and try to understand her problem rather than gruffly telling her the solution. You should come alongside her to provide emotional support when she is tired and overwhelmed. Home schooling is overwhelming, and you are the key to her success in overcoming the challenges she faces.

Recognize Your Wife as a Fellow Heir of Salvation

If those illustrations are not enough to cause us to change our attitude toward our wives and remove all harshness in our tone of voice when addressing them in public or private, we must remember they are also adopted children of God, bought with the blood of Jesus Christ. 1 Peter 3:7 commands us husbands to "show her honor as a fellow heir of the grace of life."

Spiritually, we stand as equals before God as heirs of His salvation. We are no better than our wives simply because we are men. When we consider our spiritual heritage, there is no difference between male and female. In essence, we are called to treat our wives in the same loving way that Jesus Christ treats us: with compassion, kindness, and sensitivity. We need to show concern for our wives' problems, fears, hurts, needs, and struggles, even if we think they are little or silly.

We need to take an active and sincere interest to show we love our wives for who they are in Christ. This builds on the point we discussed earlier: we must not make our wives earn our love. Our love must be without condition. If we focus on who our wives are in Christ, we will encourage them in the Lord and build up their faith. It is important that we remind them to put their whole trust in God and to stand on the promises of the gospel when the road is difficult. We also must share with them the joy of the Holy Spirit. In other words, husbands, we need to be the spiritual heads of our wives and our households.

Marriage Is under Attack

The strategy of Satan is to separate wives and husbands and thereby destroy families. The Christian community throughout our country is beset with marriage problems and divorce. In fact, the divorce rate among Christians is almost the same as the divorce rate in the U. S., where two-fifths (43 percent) of first marriages end either in divorce or separation within fifteen years (federal study of 10,847 women, Centers for Disease Control and Prevention, 1995). Something is wrong for sure.

The home school movement is also suffering from marriage infidelity and divorce because husbands are not loving their wives. Some home school husbands are being tempted by pornography on the Internet. I know two home school leaders who recently have been exposed for addiction to pornography. Their marriages and families are teetering on the brink of collapse. Pornography is just as evil in God's eyes as adultery because Jesus warned, "But I say to you that everyone who looks at a woman with lust for her has already committed adultery with her in his heart" (Matt. 5:28).

Husbands are not guarding their hearts. They should do as Job did: "I have made a covenant with my eyes" (Job 31:1) to keep his integrity. Husbands are not keeping their hearts pure by immersing themselves in God's Word (Ps. 119:9). Too many home school husbands are wrongly assuming that they are immune to the divorce revolution. They are growing complacent. They are not diligent in building a close walk with the Lord (as outlined in chapter 3) and loving their wives unconditionally.

There is a survey that presents stark evidence that establishes these and other factors as the bases of failed Christian marriages. This survey conducted by Dr. Howard Hendricks gathered information from 246 men involved in full-time ministry who had been unfaithful to their wives within the two-year period of the study. All 246 were involved in sexual immorality. All the men had started strong; they had strong marriages and a strong commitment to full-time ministry for God. Nonetheless, they fell to sexual temptation one by one.

Dr. Hendricks found four common traits among these 246 men that indicate why they fell into sin.

First, none of these men had a personal daily time with the Lord in prayer and Bible reading. They had ceased to nurture their own souls. They had quit spending time with God in private. The Word of God says, "Your word I have hidden in my heart, / That I might not sin against You" (Ps. 119:11 NKJV). Jesus said, "Man shall not live by bread alone, but by every word that proceeds from the mouth of God" (Matt. 4:4 NKJV). Satan wants to cut us off from the Word of God as he tried to do with Jesus in the wilderness.

Second, these men were accountable to no one. They isolated themselves from other people and had no authority in their lives to which they were accountable. Some home schoolers are so independent that they do not even get involved with a local church. They may attend church but do not join. Or they may join a church that does not provide accountability. Some home schoolers are so dissatisfied with the lack of perfection in the churches that they establish churches in their own homes with only their families. They are accountable to no one. These are all dangerous positions to be in because God wants us to have accountability through both the church and fellow believers (see James 5:16 and 19–20).

Third, 86 percent of the men counseled women privately. They put themselves in temptation's way. How often do you meet alone with women for business appointments or lunches? Do you travel with women or stay late at the office with female assistants? You are setting yourself up for a fall.

Last, every one of these 246 men said they thought it would never happen to them. Proverbs tells us that "Pride goes before destruction, /And a haughty spirit before a fall" (Prov. 16:18 NKJV). We should never think, *It will never happen to me. I am immune to sexual temptation.* Rather, each day we should humbly beg for God's mercy and His strength to stand firm. We should pray the prayer that Jesus taught us, "And do not lead us into temptation, but deliver us from evil" (Matt. 6:13). Without His hedge of protection around us, we will fall. This should serve as a warning to us, along with other examples from the Scriptures where great men of God, like David and Solomon, fell into sexual sin.

Home school husbands, it is not so important how you start in your marriage and your home school, but how you finish. The goal is to finish strong. "Do you not know that those who run in a race all run, but only one receives the prize? Run in such a way that you may win. Everyone who competes in the game exercises self-control in all things. They then do it to receive a perishable wreath, but we an imperishable. Therefore I run in such a way, as not without aim; I box in such a way, as not beating the air; but I discipline my body and make it my slave, so that, after I have preached to others, I myself will not be disqualified" (1 Cor. 9:24–27).

The three friends that I described at the beginning of this chapter all started out their marriages and their home school strong. But they did not finish the race. They cheated and finally quit. They spiritually failed, and they need to repent from their adultery (see Prov. 5:5 and 20–23, 6:23–29, and 9:18).

Home school husbands, we need to run to win in our marriages. We need to be faithful to the end, or we will be disqualified. We need to avoid opportunities to be alone with other women—at church, at work, or when we travel. At HSLDA, we have adopted a policy that women employees cannot travel with men. We not only want to avoid temptation but also the appearance of evil. When it comes to this area, it is much better to be safe than sorry.

When the temptations come—on television, movies, the Internet, billboards, women we see in public, pornography, our imaginations, meeting alone with women, emotional attachments through friendships, or blatant adultery—we need to instantly beg God for strength and say with Joseph when he was tempted by Potiphar's wife, "How then could I do this great evil and sin against God?" (Gen. 39:9). God will give us instant delivery and drive the evil from our thoughts.

Also maintain a godly physical relationship with your wife to further protect you. As the Bible commands, "Rejoice in the wife of your youth. / As a loving hind and a graceful doe, / Let her breasts satisfy you at all times; / Be exhilarated always with her love" (Prov. 5:18–19). I can truly say my wife is becoming more beautiful to me every year. I only have eyes for her.

Most important, we need to have a lifelong commitment to unconditionally loving our wives. No matter how many of our expectations are not met, we must be faithful to God, who specifically ordained our marriage. We must never forget that it is not how we start that counts—it is how we finish. We must finish strong in the Lord.

Why do so many Christians fall short of winning the race and lose their marriages? It is because although we know what we should do, we do not love our wives as Christ loves the church. In the remaining part of this chapter, I will give a number of practical tips on how you can fulfill this command. A book that will be beneficial for you to read that deals with our responsibilities as husbands in much greater depth is *The Complete Husband: A Practical Guide to Biblical Husbanding* by Lou Priolo (Amityville, N.Y.: Calvary Press, 1999).

Twenty-Three Practical Tips for Home School Husbands

God has blessed me with a wife—a truly wonderful wife. She considers herself low maintenance because she is truly content with whatever the Lord gives her. She is not demanding. I could easily slack off and act more selfishly because she can take it. This only means I have to discipline myself even more to love my wife as Christ loved the church.

Since we were married in 1984, God has given me greater and greater insight into how to really love my wife. He has opened my eyes to what a treasure she is. I have found that the more I die to myself and love her, the lovelier she has become in every way. This is the way God intended marriage to be. It is a beautiful process whereby two people become more and more united.

Remember, loving our wives unconditionally is not an option. It is our responsibility before God Almighty. Below are twenty-three practical tips that God has shown me on how I can love my wife unconditionally. As we love our wives in these ways, I believe God will bless our marriages, our children, and our home schools.

Cultivate and Nurture a Close Walk with God

If you're unhappy in your marriage, it is likely because your relationship with Jesus Christ is weak. Nurturing your own soul is the most important thing you can do for your wife. In chapter 3, I explain both the importance of nurturing your own soul and practical steps you can follow to do it. Take time to discipline yourself in this area no matter how busy you are. Write it down in your organizer, if you have one, in order to keep your appointment with God.

Lead Your Family in Family Devotions

Surveys show the number one desire of home school moms is for their husbands to assume the leadership of family devotions. Not only does this show the Lord how much you love Him and demonstrate to your children that He has first place in your life, but it is one of the best ways to love your wife. Chapter 5 gives many practical suggestions on how you can be faithful in family devotions.

Be an Example of Submission to Christ

Your fear of God makes a big difference in your marriage. If your wife sees you submitting to Christ, she will want to submit to you. You must respect and love God if you want to be respected and loved by your wife.

Help Your Wife Build a Closer Relationship with the Lord

I try to facilitate a daily time (at least thirty minutes) that my wife can be alone to spend time with the Lord. The easiest way to do this is for me to get the children up and operating in the morning while she spends time with the Lord. During good weather, she takes a walk in the morning to pray alone with the Lord. Your wife needs time with her Father, and you are ultimately responsible for helping make it happen.

Be Sensitive, Affectionate, and Understanding of Your Wife

We must treat our wives as weaker vessels and live with them in an understanding way as commanded in 1 Peter 3:7. We need to stop taking our wives for granted and start listening and supporting them. Home schooling is hard work, and this increases her need for your understanding and love.

Give Your Wife Your Time

"Most married couples only spend about twenty minutes a week inter-acting face to face, particularly once there are children," notes Georgia Watkins, Director of the Stress Program at Mount Sinai School of Medicine in Manhattan. She explains that couples married twenty-five years or more tell her that it's not quality time that is key. It is quantity time (*Reader's Digest*, July 1999, 142).

It is important that you make your wife and your marriage relationship a priority. Your time with her must take precedence over time with your children. As a home school dad, you understand the importance of nur-turing your children in the Lord, but it cannot be at the expense of your relationship with your wife. You need to cooperate to maintain time for each other. Often, your time disappears as your children absorb more and more of it. Your children need to see your visible commitment to spending time with your wife. Make and write down appointments with her in your calendar. Set up regular uninterrupted evening meetings at least three times a week.

Communicate with Your Wife

There is no replacement for regular and specific communication with your wife about your work, feelings, her work, spiritual growth of the chil-dren, and other events in your lives. She is your best friend, and you should not keep anything from her. Remember, God wants you and your wife to be one. Your wife wants and needs this communication to feel truly loved.

Pray with Your Wife

It is a good idea to pray every night for a few minutes on your knees with your wife before you go to bed. Tracy and I have found this to be the best conclusion to a busy day and a time to clear out any frustrations with one another by the power of God. There is no better way to start a night of rest than praying to our Father.

Protect Her Time

One important way to love your wife is to protect her from demands on her time and emotions. If your wife is anything like mine, she is a virtuous woman with many diverse talents. These types of women are often in demand for home school support group activities, church ministries, and many other good works. Believe it or not, home schooling itself could even become excessive. As an example, in our home school, my wife wanted to teach our thirteen-year-old Latin. Latin is a fine subject to learn, and I reviewed my wife's teaching load. Our fifth child had just been added to the formal teaching schedule, and I concluded it would be too much for her. Although disappointed, my wife consented. It was not long before time proved my concerns were well founded. Latin would have put her under.

Let me share one other example that demonstrates how we must protect our wives from over-committing themselves. The local crisis pregnancy organization asked her to join their board. It was quite an honor to serve directly in such an important cause: saving the unborn. After seriously considering this tempting offer, I counseled her to not go on the board, and the Lord confirmed it in her heart too.

Give Your Wife Time Alone and Overnights

After nearly fifteen years of marriage, I finally discovered that my wife needs some time alone. During the first few years of marriage, I was blinded to this fact because I am so opposite. I was an only child and spent much time alone. Now I love to be with people—especially my wife and children. When I am not at work, I want to be with my children or my wife all my waking hours. I love it.

My wife, however, is different. She is with the children every day. Her schedule is constantly interrupted. Even though she loves time with me, she also wants time away. At first, I took her desire to be alone personally. I could not understand why she did not want to be with me during her extra time. God finally opened my eyes to see her need.

I decided to give her a budget to spend one night away each month. Two times she went away with friends to a bed and breakfast to work on photo albums. Four times she simply stayed by herself at a nearby bed and breakfast where she worked on lesson plans, read, or added pictures of our family to her photo albums. One time she traveled with close friends to a Christian mothers' conference, and still another time she stayed with her mother. What a blessing and refreshment those times have been to her! What a breakthrough it was for me. Now she loves me all the more because I am willing to let go of our time in order to meet her needs.

Every time she goes away, I stay with the children, and we have wonderful and meaningful time together. These times, when it is just my seven children and me, are some of the most memorable, fun, and focused times we have together. Even though I miss my wife at these times, I am blessed because I am blessing her.

Do Simple Things for Her
That Show You Are Dying to Yourself

Sometimes showing love to your wife can be demonstrated in simple ways. For example, do a chore that she usually does. Better yet, discover a chore she really hates to do, and do it for her. Ever since we were married, I committed to always do the dishes for her. I figured she could make better meals if she did not have to worry about doing dishes afterward. It has worked too! Now I have built-in helpers whom I can direct to make sure the kitchen is cleaned up for her.

Read Inspirational Books with Her

One way to grow closer to your wife while growing closer to the Lord is to read good books or the Bible together as least two evenings a week. One book we recently read together that changed our lives was *When God Weeps* by Joni Eareckson Tada. We wept together as God showed us more of His heart. This quiet time at night spent reading together before bed helps us wind down and enjoy some peace after our long, hectic day.

Praise Her

Proverbs 31:28–29 states, "Her children rise up and bless her; / Her husband also, and he praises her, saying: / 'Many daughters have done nobly, / But you excel them all.'" You need to make a habit of praising your wife as often as possible, when she is not around and when she is. Complimenting and praising her before her parents will be particularly meaningful and supportive. Also, do not hesitate to praise her before friends and coworkers. This will build her up and build up the marriages of others as they see your close relationship and are blessed.

Pastor Steve Schlissel of New York, speaking at HSLDA's National Christian Home School Leadership Conference, said it best this way, "Praise your wife even if it scares her at first!"

Also, teach your children to praise their mother. You need to help your children verbally appreciate their mother. They will automatically take her for granted otherwise. This will probably bless your wife in a major way since she spends most of her time investing in your children.

Provide for Her Physical Needs and Beyond

Give her whatever she needs to run the household. Do not skimp if you can help it. Better equipment in the kitchen, a better vacuum, bigger shelves, and more freezer space will help her run her house more efficiently and better serve you and your children. It will also free up her precious time.

If she has aches, pains, and tight muscles, massage her to help her relieve stress and enable her to sleep better. I found this to be a wonderful treat for my wife. Even though I am tired at night, I always ask her if it hurts anywhere. A majority of the time it does, and I gladly massage her for twenty to thirty minutes while we talk in bed. One important tip is to buy some massage oil and use it every time you massage her. I did not learn the importance of massage oil until about ten years into our marriage. The massage is so much more effective, and it prevents chafing your wife's skin. Massaging is a guaranteed blessing to your wife. Both you and your wife will grow physically closer in the process as well.

Seek Your Wife's Advice

It is important to show your wife how much you love her by seeking her advice. I have often said my wife is my best counselor, and her advice is always helpful. She enables me to make wise decisions on many matters. In this process you also need to be vulnerable with your wife and admit your own weaknesses. Show her that you truly trust her and confide in her completely. There should not be any secrets.

Admonish Her

As we have said, you are her spiritual head and are responsible before God. However, always admonish her privately, never in front of others. The goal is not to embarrass her, but to build her up. Keep in mind as you admonish her that you must respect her as a fellow heir of salvation.

Verbally Tell Her That You Love Her Every Day

This is both obvious and easy. Of course, you need to support your verbal communication of love for her with action. But do not forget to say it when you leave for work, say goodbye on the phone, and other spontaneous times.

Take a Lead Role in Your Home School

You need to be committed to your home school and take a lead role in encouraging your wife. Remind her of the bigger vision when she loses heart. Be involved in choosing the curriculum for your children and interact with your children as to what they are learning. Most important, be in charge of your children's spiritual growth. Chapters 4 and 5 give you many practical ways you can be a committed and effective home school father.

Perform All Discipline

When you are home, you should be in charge of the discipline of your children, not only to give your wife a break, but also to show her and the children that you completely support your wife. In chapter 4, I discuss at length the home school father's role in the area of discipline.

Schedule Regular Date Nights and Getaways

Your wife and your relationship will profit when you spend time alone with her away from the children. This facilitates communication. Your wife spends a majority of her time with her children. She needs time away from them, and you can provide her a needed break and some adult conversation.

Another way to demonstrate your love to your wife is to plan periodic getaways to a nearby bed and breakfast. Spending one hundred dollars three or four times each year is worth the invaluable benefit these times are to the health and strength of your marriage. Make an arrangement with another home school family or two who will watch your children. (In our case, three or four families!) In return, you care for their children when they go on getaways as well.

My wife and I find the most peaceful and enjoyable times are when we simply rest and read together. This shows her how much I truly enjoy her company. In a relaxed setting free from interruptions, we are able to cultivate and deepen our relationship. I cannot overemphasize the value of these times as you work to build a closer relationship with your wife.

Be Honest

Be a man of your word. Be trustworthy and carry out your promises to your wife. Always keep you wife informed of where you are going and what you are doing. Our wives need the security of knowing that we are open books to them and that they can depend on us.

Hold Regular Family Meetings

It is helpful to arrange regular family meetings to plan the schedule, focus on problems, and encourage the diligent efforts of our children and wives. This can send a message to our wives that we truly care about our families. We often hold planning meetings at work with our employees in order to get everyone on the same page and to run the business more efficiently. These should be some of the same goals of a family meeting. Certainly our families are more important than our work, so we need to make time to care for its successful daily operation.

Always Practice the Fruits of the Spirit with Your Wife

If you do nothing else as a home school husband for your wife but consistently exercise the fruits of the Spirit in all your interaction with her, you will be doing a great deal for her. This means to love her; have joy and peace in your heart; be patient, kind, and good to her; be faithful; always be gentle; and have self-control (Gal. 5:22–23). What a tremendous support you will be to her if you live by and practice these fruits! I believe the more you practice the fruits of the Spirit, the more your heart will change and your love will increase for your wife. You will also find yourself wanting more and more to implement the practical ways to love her as listed above.

Are You Ready?

- Are you ready to intensify your love for your wife and love her unconditionally?
- Are you prepared to die to your own selfishness and love your wife as Christ loves the church?
- Do you feel the call to be a more faithful home school husband?

Our marriages are sacred in the eyes of God. Our wives are the exact wives God wants us to have and the wives we need. God has ordained our marriages. Let us be found faithful as we focus on truly and deeply loving our wives.

Furthermore, I think we must not forget that there are consequences if we fail to love our wives as God demands. "Do not be deceived, God is not mocked; for whatever a man sows, this he will also reap. For the one who sows to his own flesh will from the flesh reap corruption, but the one who sows to the Spirit will from the Spirit reap eternal life. Let us not lose heart in doing good, for in due time we will reap if we do not grow weary" (Gal. 6:7–9). Our wives may not always respond to us the way we want. They may be stubborn at times. But we cannot lose heart because God promises that in due time—His perfect timing—we will reap. Our responsibility is that we sow to the Spirit and not to the flesh as we deal with our wives. Ultimately, our reward is with our Father in heaven. This knowledge and His strength enable us to love our wives unconditionally.

In 1994, I learned that I had a degenerative disease called multiple sclerosis. God has used and continues to use this disease *to shake me and wake me* on how important my wife is to me and to Him. From the time of my diagnosis, I changed and began trying to make every day count in my relationship with my wife. I began to understand her more and to die to myself. Her value in my eyes has grown ever since.

I would have been unable to share the information in this chapter with you before the diagnosis of my multiple sclerosis. God has used it, by His grace, to mold me more into His image. I've learned to submit my life more to Him. He showed me how I could love my wife more like Christ loves us. Many of these practical suggestions above originate from my struggle with multiple sclerosis.

If I can love my wife more even though my physical strength is less, surely God can give you the strength to love your wives in the ways described in this chapter. In my weakened condition, God has enabled me to run the race with greater strength than ever before. I still have a way to go, but my eyes are clearly fixed on the goal, and I better understand His perfect rules. *I am committed to run strong and finish strong. How about you?*

May God bless your marriage and secure its foundation on the Rock of Jesus Christ. And may your home school thrive as your marriage grows and you and your wife work more closely as a team in training your children for His glory!

The Home Schooling Mother: God Is My Strength

BY TRACY KLICKA

Have you ever reached the end of a long day home schooling and felt that you did not get anything done? The children did not cooperate, and you had to spend more time disciplining them than anything else. The teaching that took place just did not seem to sink in. Your designated time in the afternoon for filing projects and paying bills did not happen.

Do you feel you do many things that do not last? You tell your children to clean up the family room, and ten minutes later it is messed up again. You spend half the day straightening up the pantry, and two days later everything is out of place. You drill certain character qualities in your children only to be disappointed when you need their help most. Your seven-year-old is still having trouble reading,, and your thirteen-year-old still has difficulty spelling.

Maybe you think you spend more time as referee than as mother? One child grabs another child's toy out of his hand, leaving him screaming. Then you rush over to two other children who are fighting because one was teasing the other. A child comes to you for the fourth time complaining that no one will play with her. Your littlest one falls down and scrapes his knee—apparently another careless child bumped him.

Do you ever start to despair when a spelling test for your ten-year-old is interrupted . . . for the fifth time? You wonder if your child will be intellectually marred for life. You also wonder once again if home schooling works.

CHAPTER EIGHT

Or you doubt that you are organized enough to make your home school successful.

Do you often feel like you are being blown out of control by a hurricane or you are in the eye of the storm helplessly watching your home school unravel? You wonder if true peace and unity can ever be achieved in your home because all you seem to see is disunity and chaos.

Do you feel like your spiritual life has stagnated because you are always busy with endless activity?

Welcome to the life of a typical home schooling mother! These experiences, fears, and times of confusion are common to the average home schooling mom. Peter wrote, "But resist [Satan], firm in your faith, knowing that the same experiences of suffering are being accomplished by your brethren who are in the world" (1 Pet. 5:9). These troubles are difficult to avoid completely. God never promised us that home schooling and nurturing the souls of our children would be easy. In fact, He never promised that serving Him in any area of this life would be easy.

God, in His great love, gives us difficult times to teach us to trust Him, not to look at the circumstances. We do not walk in the strength of our flesh, but by the power of His Spirit at work in our hearts. He wants us to walk by faith, not by sight (2 Cor. 5:7). That is what the Christian life is all about: faith. "Faith is the substance of things hoped for, the evidence of things not seen" (Heb. 11:1 KJV).

To Home School Requires Faith

Home schooling requires faith—faith to believe that God will honor those who honor Him in training their children in the nurture and admonition of the Lord. Faith that God will provide the resources to home school effectively. Faith that God will give you wisdom and the right words to say. Faith that God will enable your children to learn and apply what they learn. Faith to believe that when you train your children in the way they should go, when they are old they will not depart from it (Prov. 22:6). Faith to believe that God will give you peace in the midst of the turmoil and challenges. Faith to hold on to the promise that you can do all things through Christ who strengthens you (Phil. 4:13).

I believe our faith is meant to be tried. One of my favorite authors is Charles Spurgeon. He explained the testing of our faith this way, "Scripture never says that he who believes will not have his faith exercised. Your faith will be exercised. An untried faith will be no faith at all. God never gave men faith without intending to try it. Faith is received for the purpose of developing endurance."

Spurgeon is simply summarizing this truth that appears in the Book of James: "Consider it all joy, my brethren, when you encounter various trials, knowing that the testing of your faith produces endurance. And let endurance have its perfect result, so that you may be perfect and complete, lacking in nothing" (James 1:2–4).

The trials we experience in home schooling build endurance. If we can keep home schooling when the going gets tough, it demonstrates our faith is real. Many times we mothers will be treated harshly by our children, and our extensive labors will not be appreciated. We still should not give up because we know God gives the reward. "For what credit is there if, when you sin and are harshly treated, you endure it with patience? But if when you do what is right and suffer for it you patiently endure it, this finds favor with God" (1 Pet. 2:20).

God uses the difficult times and the testing of our faith to conform us more to the image of His Son. Is not that our heart's desire: to be more like Jesus? Suffering, though hard, is actually a blessing! In chapter 11 my husband deals with this truth extensively. In the midst of these trials, our main goal must remain constant. Our never-changing goal must always be that God gets all the glory. He is the One who redeems us, changes us, and does a new work in our hearts.

As we glorify Him with our obedience, faith, and trust, He enables us to do His will in training our children. He teaches us the way we should go: "Good and upright is the LORD; / Therefore He instructs sinners in the way. / He leads the humble in justice, / And He teaches the humble His way" (Ps. 25:8–9). "Who is the man who fears the LORD? / He will instruct him in the way he should choose" (Ps. 25:12).

An Ordinary Mom

You might be thinking, *But you do not understand. I am just not cut out to continue home schooling. I am not a supermom. In fact, I am not even organized. My faith is not as strong as other mothers. I can't even find time to spend communing with God. Sending them to school seems so much easier.* Those feelings and doubts are real. But God will provide. Consider my home school mother credentials.

I was not raised in a Christian home. My biological father sexually abused me. I never had the opportunity to be around babies. I never learned how to cook or manage a household. I never supervised children or taught children at school or even Sunday school.

I was and still am quite ordinary. I have no special talents that equip me to be a good mom, much less a supermom. All I have is God. But that is enough. I laugh when some people come up to me after they find out I have seven children *and* I home school them, and say, "Can I touch you? You must be a saint!" No, I am not a saint. I am just a poor sinner like anyone else. It is God's grace and His grace alone that enables me to run the race and stay the course. And He will complete the good work He has begun and give me the strength to finish the race.

I was saved when I was a teenager and came to know Jesus personally as my Lord and Savior. I wanted to glorify and love Him with all my heart. As I spent time growing closer to Him, He gave me the strength and faith to walk in His ways.

About a year before I married Chris, God made it clear to me that public schools were no place to fulfill God's command to bring up our children in the nurture and admonition of the Lord. Chapter 2 describes the biblical commands to parents concerning the training and educating of their children. In fact, the public schools were, and are, doing quite the opposite. God gave me the assurance that He would give me the strength to home school whatever children He decided to give me in the future.

God was leading me down the path of faith and trust in Him. As I explained earlier, living by faith is what the Christian life is all about. Little did I know what He would bring me through to strengthen my faith: seven children, affliction with an incurable disease, near death of my twins, a husband with multiple sclerosis, and much more. Chapter 11 explains some of these trials and how God has sustained us, enabling us to keep home schooling our children.

So what is the secret to staying the course in our home school and having peace no matter how trying the circumstances? The secret is to nurture our own souls.

Looking Out for Number One

The most important thing we can do for our home school and the means to achieve true peace is to take daily time to nourish our own souls. Our pastor Jack Lash, a home school father of seven children, has said that the success with which you do anything for your family depends in great part on the condition of your own soul.

Busyness, hardships of life, our sins, and the pleasures of this world all tend to distract us from a proper focus on the Lord and building our relationship with Him. We need a *daily renewal* of His love and provision to sustain us. We must cry out to Him for His strength and wisdom. We must surrender our whole hearts to Him each day. "The eyes of the LORD move to and fro throughout the earth that He may strongly support those whose heart is completely His" (2 Chron. 16:9). We must say with the psalmist, "Teach me thy way, O LORD; I will walk in thy truth; unite my heart to fear thy name" (Ps. 86:11 KJV).

In chapter 3, my husband shares many principles and commands from the Word of God that clearly show that nurturing our own souls must be our number one priority. If this priority is not first, everything in life will suffer, including our home school.

I will build on Chris's chapter and give more practical tips to nurturing our own souls from a home school mother's perspective.

Roadblocks to Spiritual Growth

First of all, I think it is necessary to identify common roadblocks to our personal spiritual growth. We need to know the enemy's strategy so we can combat it more effectively. I have listed below five key areas of sin that lead to soul starvation.

Performance or Surrender? Beware of the Barrenness of a Busy Life

At the beginning of this chapter, we discussed the overwhelming busyness that is a common occurrence among home schoolers. Busyness can be one of the biggest roadblocks to our spiritual growth.

We often think we are indispensable. As we face our home school responsibilities and other tasks each day, we feel the pressure to perform. We begin to act and sometimes believe that it won't get done without us. We take comfort in the thought that we are engaging in good works. We are not wasting time. My husband will sometimes say in exasperation after a very busy day, "We are too busy! But everything we do is good, so how can we cut anything out?"

This is a big problem for many home school mothers. We get caught up doing so many good deeds; we do not know how to say no. Eventually all those good works can dampen our personal relationship with Jesus.

In the hubbub of life, we forget 1 Chronicles 29:14–16, "But who am I and who are my people that we should be able to offer as generously as this? For *all* things come from You, and from Your hand we have given You." Without God's mercy, we are nothing and can accomplish nothing.

The psalmist teaches us which sacrifices God wants from us: "For You do not delight in sacrifice, otherwise I would give it; / You are not pleased with burnt offering. / *The sacrifices of God are a broken spirit; / A broken and a contrite heart*, O God, You will not despise" (Ps. 51:16–17). *He wants our hearts!*

Jesus tells us that the greatest commandment and foremost commandment is to "LOVE THE LORD YOUR GOD WITH ALL YOUR HEART, AND WITH ALL YOUR SOUL, AND WITH ALL YOUR MIND" (Matt. 22:37). We are disobeying this commandment if we treat our busyness and daily good works as a greater sacrifice than simply communing with Him. "Has the LORD as much delight in burnt offerings and sacrifices / As in obeying the voice of the LORD? / Behold, to obey is better than sacrifice" (1 Sam. 15:22).

In Whom Do We Trust? Ourselves

God wants us to build our faith in Him, not in ourselves. We must not think that the success of our home school depends upon us and our special talents and organizational abilities. If we think this for very long, we will quit when the chaos hits and the storms come.

These four Scriptures summarize far better than I can where we must always put our trust.

- In the fear of the LORD there is strong confidence, / And his children will have refuge (Prov. 14:26).
- I will cry to God Most High, / To God who accomplishes all things for me (Ps. 57:2).
- But we have this treasure in earthen vessels, so that the surpassing greatness of the power will be of God and not from ourselves (2 Cor. 4:7).
- "For My hand made all these things. / Thus all these things came into being," declares the LORD. / "But to this one I will look, / To him who is humble and contrite of spirit, and who trembles at My word" (Isa. 66:2).

Treasures of the Heart: Loving This World More Than God

As we discussed above, our relationship to the Lord is more important than anything else. It is more important than all the good things we do and even more important than our children, marriages, relatives, or local churches. None of these things can save us. Only our relationship with God will bring us to heaven.

We all know the first commandment. In Exodus 20:3 and 5, God says, "You shall have no other gods before Me. . . . You shall not worship them or serve them; for I, the LORD your God, am a jealous God."

For home schoolers, there is a great temptation to put your children before God. We do not do it intentionally. We simply end up taking our beliefs and commitment to train our children a little too far. We start allowing the time with our children, teaching and protecting them, to claim a bigger part of our hearts than our relationships with God. We hang on to our children a little too tight. We work so hard on doing everything right for our children, in sharp contrast to the world, that we start acting like our efforts will save them. Our children become our treasure.

But God warns us, "Do not lay up for yourselves treasures on earth . . . but lay up for yourselves treasures in heaven. . . . For where your treasure is, there your heart will be also" (Matt. 6:19–21 NKJV). Also, we are told, "And He will be the stability of your times, / A wealth of salvation, wisdom and knowledge; / The fear of the LORD is his treasure" (Isa. 33:6).

We need to say with David, "Whom have I in heaven but You? / And besides You, I desire nothing on earth" (Ps. 73:25). Being closer to God must be the deepest and strongest desire of our hearts. I know this is easy to say and hard to live. But we must.

Looking at the Things That Are Seen: Looking at Our Circumstances Only

Since we are creatures on this earth, it is easy to get swept away by the things on this earth. The circumstances in which we find ourselves become everything that matters to us because we can see them with our eyes. We cannot see God and the spiritual world around us with our physical eyes, so we do not take these as seriously as our circumstances.

This is why we often permit the busyness of home schooling and life to squeeze out our personal quiet time with God. Or we allow ourselves to despair or be overwhelmed by the hardships that we face.

God wants us to have eyes of faith, "looking unto Jesus, the author and finisher of our faith" (Heb. 12:2 NKJV).

We cannot rely on our circumstances, but we must rely on God's Word that endures forever. The psalmist reminds us, "You, O LORD, will not withhold Your compassion from me; / Your lovingkindness and Your truth will continually preserve me" (Ps. 40:11). God assures us, "And God is able to make *all* grace abound to you, so that *always* having *all* sufficiency in *everything,* you may have an abundance for *every* good deed" (2 Cor. 9:8). We have everything we need in Christ! He is all-sufficient.

We need to ask God to help us understand just how short our lives are. Our lives are like a vapor—here today and gone tomorrow (James 4:14). We need to see our lives, our home schooling, and our struggles in light of eternity. "We do not lose heart. . . . For momentary, light affliction is producing for us an eternal weight of glory far beyond all comparison, while we look not at the things which are seen, but at the things which are not seen; for the things which are seen are temporal [suffering, hardship], *but the things which are not seen are eternal* [our salvation, the riches of our inheritance in Christ in the saints]" (2 Cor. 4:16–18).

When we get to our eternal reward in heaven one day, we will look back on our lives on earth as nothing more than a flash. This larger view helps us keep our struggles and our daily home school challenges in the proper perspective and not become overwhelmed.

Under Authority: Lack of Submission to our Husbands Will Hurt our Spiritual Growth

This last point is not easy for a woman to make. We must make ourselves vulnerable when we submit to our husbands. God is very clear: "Wives, be subject to your own husbands, as to the Lord" (Eph. 5:22); "You wives, be submissive to your own husbands" (1 Pet. 3:1); and "Wives, be subject to you husbands, as is fitting in the Lord" (Col. 3:18). Yet this requires faith, too, because we do not see the immediate results. It is hard to submit our lives to a sinner at such a personal level. But God is telling us, from the beginning to the end of the Bible, to trust Him. Wives, we need to trust God to guide and control our husbands. We need to trust our Father that He "causes all things to work together for good to those who love God, to those who are called according to His purpose" (Rom. 8:28). Our responsibility as wives is to respect and honor our husbands. It is God's responsibility to take care of our husbands.

Our pastor, Jack Lash, often reminds our congregation that our spouses are perfect for us: even with all their sins and shortcomings. Their problems are what God uses to build our faith and conform us to the image of His Son. For example, if your husband does not notice all the things you do and seldom praises you, maybe God is dealing with your pride. God wants to build humility and self-denial into your character. He wants you to be faithful, not for an earthly reward, but simply because you know it pleases your

Father: "knowing that from the Lord you will receive the reward of the inheritance. It is the Lord Christ whom you serve" (Col. 3:24).

Submitting to our husbands in obedience to God is humbling. But that is exactly what God, in His great wisdom, wants us to do. "Humble yourselves in the sight of the Lord, and He will lift you up" (James 4:10 NKJV).

God also wants us to submit to the authority of our husbands so that He can work in us to accomplish the necessary spiritual growth in our hearts. Remember God's assurance in 1 Peter 3:1–6, that our husbands can be won without a word by our respectful behavior and our gentle and quiet spirit which is precious in God's sight. Adorning yourself with a quiet and gentle spirit doesn't come automatically, easily, or quickly. It can only come as we cry out to the Holy Spirit in prayer and repentance, patiently waiting on God. First Peter 3:6 tells us to follow the example of Sarah and other godly women who subjected themselves to their husbands with a gentle and quiet spirit but without fear.

So why can we submit to our husbands without fear? It is because we trust in our Sovereign Lord on a daily basis. As we obey God in this area, we *will* grow closer to Jesus.

How to Look Out for Number One

I have discussed some things we must avoid in order to nurture our souls and grow spiritually. What are some practical ways to discipline ourselves into a close walk with the Lord in the midst of our busy home schooling life? How do we make certain that our relationships with God are *number one?* Here are some suggestions.

Pray and Study the Bible Each Day

When we pray to God, we are talking to Him. When we read His Word, God is talking to us. These are the two main ingredients of any relationship. There must be regular two-way communication with someone you love if you truly want to know them and be close to them.

I think many of us purpose to pray and read God Word's each day, but we just do not get it done. We need to get serious and deal with the common obstacles.

First, we must search our hearts and make a commitment to God. Then we must discipline ourselves to keep our daily appointment with God, much like we keep our other appointments. Prayer takes work! We must discipline our bodies and make them our slaves (1 Cor. 9:27).

Remember, the greatest obstacle to prayer is often ourselves! J.C. Ryle in *A Call to Prayer* (Laurel, Miss.: Audubon Press, 1996) emphasizes the importance of battling our sin natures when he recounts the prayer of a Hottentot native of South Africa: "Lord, deliver me from all my enemies, and above all, from that bad man—myself." Amen!

Second, be realistic. If we set our expectations too high, we will often fail. Ultimately, God wants our hearts. It is better to spend a little time with Him each day than to set aside an hour or two once a week because we miss so many days in between. Whatever you do, do not give up! God wants us to persevere in prayer to Him.

Third, be sure to guard your time. Protect it at any cost. In chapter 3 my husband gives several tips on how you schedule a quiet time with the Lord and avoid distractions. I will add a few more thoughts.

As a home schooling mom of seven children, I know distractions come very easily and often. In spite of the circumstances, we must stay focused.

I often think of Susanna Wesley, who had nineteen children. She loved the Lord, but she sometimes found her best-laid plans to pray to the Lord destroyed by the invasion of her children. So when those chaotic times came, she would simply stop and pull her apron over her head and pray!

Although the apron method works, the best time is always at a quiet time of the day when you are most alert. I alternate between early morning and during the children's rest time during the afternoon. As often as I can, I mix exercise with prayer. I like to take a vigorous walk two or three times a week in the early morning before my husband leaves for work. It is a wonderful time to be alone with the Lord.

Of course, the Bible commands us to "pray without ceasing" (1 Thess. 5:17), so be sure to develop a habit of praying throughout the day. I pray *bullet* prayers to make every moment count. For example, we can easily pray when we are doing menial tasks such as dishes or washing the floor since such tasks do not require much mental effort. We can't always wait for blocks of time to pray because many times they won't come.

I also recommend that you create a prayer list that you keep in your organizer. Be sure to include yourself, each child, and your husband. If you do not pray for them, who will? God uses your prayers to shape the hearts of your family members. It is important to engage in intercessory prayer for extended family, friends, missionaries, church leaders, neighbors, special groups, and political leaders. Like my husband, I try to keep track of answered prayer as well. This gives me encouragement during times of difficulty and doubt.

Meditate and Feed on God's Word

Our daily Scripture reading helps keep us from sin. "Thy Word have I hid in mine heart, that I might not sin against thee" (Psalm 119:11 KJV). Sin, of course, is the biggest obstacle we have to growing spiritually.

Meditating daily on the Word of God helps us to keep our eyes focused on the things that are unseen, the eternal things. It enables us to walk by faith: "Behold, as for the proud one, / His soul is not right within him; / But the righteous will live by his faith" (Hab. 2:4 NKJV). It builds our trust in God, who is a Spirit that we cannot see, so we can say with David, "Our soul waits for the LORD; / He is our help and our shield, / For our heart rejoices in Him, / Because we trust in His holy name" (Ps. 33:20–21).

The Word gives us hope in the midst of tough times and prepares us for the day's challenges. Psalm 27:13 NKJV says, "I would have despaired unless I had believed that I would see the goodness of the LORD in the land of the living." I know that dealing with my own disease of ulcerative colitis as well as my husband's multiple sclerosis and what it is doing to him would have driven me to despair many times if it were not for this promise.

Meditating on God's Word is food for my soul, so I have learned to create a *Scripture log* in my organizer. I write down verses to encourage me and to help me conquer my own personal sins. I have also kept a log of special verses to minister to me during times of need, and I regularly share my list of verses with friends and acquaintances who may be experiencing hard times. This way the verses I meditate on become a double blessing—to me and to others. My verses are a tool that I use to evangelize the unsaved who are suffering. Remember, the Lord promises us that His Word will not return void. See chapter 12 for more information on evangelism and home schooling.

What about Fast Food? I do not mean McDonald's or Burger King! We avoid the kind of fast food that is better known as junk food. I am referring to *God's fast food*. Several years ago, I took Deuteronomy 6 seriously and put up framed Bible verses all around our home and Bible verse cards on every doorway and by every light switch. This has proved to be a way for our family to receive constant Fast Food for our souls throughout each day.

I give our family Fast Food in other ways. We keep a Bible in every bathroom and play Scripture music and hymns in the house and car. I often find myself singing in the car with my children, and we grow together in the Lord.

Of course, you can always devote some time to reading devotionals— another Fast Food source of both short teaching and encouragement. Spurgeon's *Morning and Evening* (New Kensington, Pa.: Whitaker House, 1995) and the Institute for Creation Research's daily devotional "Days of Praise" are some of my frequent readings.

I generally keep longer devotional works by my bedside. There is no hurry to get through them, so I chew them slowly to gain the most benefit from the meaty content. In Appendix II, I have provided a list of resources through which God has richly blessed me.

My husband and I have tried to discipline ourselves to spend a little time each night in bed reading a devotional book for at least twenty minutes before we turn the lights out. It is a time for us to be at peace, feed on the Lord, and be close to each other. Sometimes Chris will read out loud something God is teaching him. Other times we will read a book together or read separately. It is a restful time after the turmoil of the day, and it also has the side benefit of helping us become closer soul mates.

Sunday Worship

Sunday is one of the most delightful days to focus on the Lord, but it can also turn out to be one of the most frustrating days. With seven children and a husband who cannot move quickly because of his disability, I know how chaotic Sunday mornings can be! If we do not guard against it, Sunday mornings become hectic and disorganized instead of focused on our Father.

To truly honor the Lord, Sundays should be a day of peaceful rest and extra worship.

I have learned to protect the Sabbath by preparing ahead of time. On Saturday night, I create a list of things that we need to take to church: items to return to people, personal notes, or ministry items. I go to each of my children's rooms at night and choose their clothes for the next day. Now that I have a fourteen-year-old daughter, she assists me in this preparation. Everyone has a bath or shower, and the children go to bed early. We avoid staying out late Saturday night so we can be fresh to receive God's Word the next day.

We also get the breakfast food ready, usually something simple, and set the table. I gather as much as I can, like diaper bags and Bibles, to put by the door so everyone is not running around frantically the next morning trying to locate these necessary items.

I play Christian music on the stereo at home, and we often sing a Scripture song in the van on the way to church. When I had babies, I never knew for sure if I could make it to church every Sunday, but I always planned to be there. I usually spend a few minutes in mental preparation and make a cup of *leaded* tea or coffee if I was up late with one of the children. I often pray beforehand for the Lord to prepare my heart.

If for some reason you can't go to church, have extra sermon tapes or teaching videos at home, devotionals to read (I keep a Sunday pile), and a hymnal and/or copies of praise and worship songs on hand to use.

In the afternoon, after a simple meal, the children must rest, read, or play with toys that point them to God. We have a special time for extended devotions in the evening.

Other Considerations to a Strong Spiritual Life

Do not neglect physical rest. Don't deprive yourself of sleep on an ongoing basis just so you can get more done. My husband often uses the excuse when he is pushing himself too hard: "I have to keep up this pace because the harvest is great and the workers are few." He will be the first to admit that though the harvest is great, his body is also the temple of God and he needs to be a good steward of it.

Lack of sleep will catch up with you; the more tired you are, the more likely you will become discouraged and sin by having a bad attitude. This will impact your Christian testimony to your family and to others. It will also affect the quality of your home schooling.

Sometime, of course, you will miss sleep due to situations out of your control: sick children, feeding babies, and emergency projects. At those times you must simply trust God to provide the strength and energy you need. Be patient with your weakness as a result of losing sleep. I was up every night for more than a year and a half feeding and caring for my twins. This was necessary because these babies needed special attention due to medical circumstances. I noticed before long that I was experiencing short-term memory loss. I could have gotten angry, but I tried to wait on the Lord.

It is important to eat healthy foods to help avoid depression and fatigue that get in the way of your service to the Lord. I believe you need to eat healthy foods even when you don't think you have the time.

We always have a salad ready to eat in the refrigerator. We have a salad for dinner every night. We avoid, by my husband's orders, having any desserts during the week—unless it is a special occasion. The children look forward to having dessert on Sunday. This discipline helps me with my health and weight. We always have fruit, carrot sticks, nuts, and seeds on hand for snacks instead of junk food. I grab one of these instead of a handful of chips or a cookie.

I also make carrot juice, take a spoonful of Barley Green, or drink ginseng tea when I need extra energy. Now that my husband has multiple sclerosis and I have ulcerative colitis, we can see the direct impact diet has on our health. We want to spare our children these trials when they get older, so we firmly keep good eating habits. We have noticed that our children are among the most healthy in our church and home school support group.

Hand in hand with good eating is exercise. Some of you are probably thinking, *Exercise? Are you crazy? That is a luxury I do not have time for! Besides, it is what is on the inside that really counts.* It is true, as I have explained in this chapter, that our hearts are what God wants. That must be our first and foremost priority. However, God did give us bodies with which to glorify Him, too. We must be good stewards of our bodies and take care of them. One important way to do so is to exercise regularly.

There are both physical and mental benefits from exercise. You will have better stamina to take care of your family. We all agree home schooling is hard work, and keeping up with your children's endless energy takes effort. We need all the help we can get, and a little exercise can go a long way toward increasing our energy level.

If we exercise, we will also look better. This is important to husbands. It is the way God made them. My husband never pushes me in this area, and he is very understanding. But because I know he appreciates when I am in good shape, I try to exercise because I love him. In addition, keeping ourselves in at least minimal physical condition helps protect our husbands from temptation. The world, from every direction—billboards, the media, stores, and the Internet—is bombarding our husbands with physical temptations. Keeping ourselves in shape all the more strengthens our husbands.

By exercising, we also feel better mentally. It releases endorphins, creating a chemical reaction that helps fight depression and builds our immune system.

Of course, you do not have to go overboard. Thirty minutes of biking or walking three days a week and controlling your eating habits will do wonders. My best friend makes exercise part of their home school physical education program. Each child chooses one half-hour activity each day. They take turns walking, riding a bicycle, following an exercise video, or jumping rope. They all participate in this activity together.

There is no doubt in my mind that feeling strong and having our health helps us to cope better with the unpredictable pressures of home schooling. It helps us be more alert to do the Lord's service.

It is also important to have *recharge times.* These times bring a little refreshment to our hearts and offer a welcome change of pace. Some activities I especially recommend are date nights or an overnight with your husband once a quarter at a local bed and breakfast. These getaways not only strengthen your relationship with your husband but also enable you to enjoy needed rest.

I try to have a regular planning day when my husband stays home with the children. I go to a local library to prepare lesson plans, write, or prepare projects. A periodic breakfast or lunch out with a friend to share my heart and ideas is always a blessing. Also, I try to have an evening out once a month for a home school support group meeting or to put together photo albums with a friend.

And of course there is E-mail. What a wonderful time to minister to friends and be ministered to! After family devotions, my husband puts the children to bed and gives me time to get on the computer and send a few notes to friends or visit Elisabeth Elliot's Web page. It is so quick and easy to do this, and it is a great blessing. Like anything else, you need to do E-mails in moderation—you can end up spending so much time on-line that you lose special times with your older children and your husband.

Try to look at these things as necessities and *not* luxuries! The additional considerations I have reviewed will only enhance your home schooling and improve your attitude. God wants us to serve Him with joy, and doing these things can help us to overcome the routine and bring good balance to our lives.

Conclusion: Glorify God and Enjoy Him Forever

The bottom line is that we should not exist for our families; we exist for God. He made us for Himself. We exist to glorify and enjoy Him forever. Remember, "Whatever you do in word or deed, do all in the name of the Lord Jesus, giving thanks through Him to God the Father" (Col. 3:17), and "Whatever you do, do your work heartily, as for the Lord rather than for men; knowing that from the Lord you will receive the reward of the inheritance. It is the Lord Christ whom you serve" (Col. 3:23–24). This must always be our attitude toward our home schooling, our children, and our husbands.

Our families are a tremendous blessing that He gives us and a means by which we may love Him more and more.

May God help you and guide you as you diligently seek a closer walk with Him. May you serve your family faithfully in His name. He promises He will draw closer to us as we draw closer to Him.

Teaching a Biblical Worldview: How to Train Christian Warriors

The term *biblical worldview* is often used in Christian circles, but do we really understand what a biblical worldview is? The Scripture says in Ephesians 4:14–15, "We are no longer to be children, tossed here and there by waves and carried about by every wind of doctrine, by the trickery of men, by craftiness in deceitful scheming; but speaking the truth in love." God wants us to know His truth. He wants us to view the world looking through His eyes. God wants us to apply His heavenly blueprint to the world. Where can we obtain this heavenly blueprint? It is in His Word.

God's Word commands, "Whether, then, you eat or drink, do *all* to the glory of God" (1 Cor. 10:31). To truly glorify God, we need to do all things *for* Him and do all things *His way*. If we do things our way instead of His, we are acting like humanists. Our views and opinions become the measure of all things. This is a major error that plagues Christianity today. Christians believe as Christians, but many do not apply God's Word to every area of their lives. They are either consciously or unconsciously thinking they can follow God on their terms rather than God's. They say they love God, but they ignore His teachings: "For this is the love of God, that we keep His commandments; and His commandments are not burdensome" (1 John 5:3). They think they know God, but they do not know His commandments. How can this be? "By this we know that we have come to know Him, if we keep His commandments" (1 John 2:3).

CHAPTER NINE

God makes it clear, "If we live by the Spirit, let us also walk by the Spirit" (Gal. 5:25), and "Faith, if it has no works, is dead" (James 2:17). To do good works, walk by the Spirit, and keep His commandments, we must know the Bible well. We cannot know it in simply a superficial way. We must "hunger and thirst after righteousness" (Matt. 5:6 KJV). We must desire to think God's thoughts after Him. If we are commanded to do all to the glory of God, we need to look at all things through the lens of God's Word. Not only must we develop and apply a biblical worldview, we must teach our children to do the same.

Definition of a Worldview: What Kind of Glasses Are You Wearing?

But you might be wondering, *What exactly is a worldview?* One illustration that helps us understand is to imagine our worldview to be a pair of glasses. Ask yourself the following questions:

- Are you wearing rose-colored glasses that make everything look all right and any type of belief or opinion acceptable? Such a worldview is called *relativism.*

- Do you look through a pair of lenses that is multicolored and nothing in the world is to be taken seriously? You look for ways to avoid responsibility and to simply have fun. The main goal of your worldview is to satisfy yourself. This selfish philosophy of life—all too common in our country—is called *hedonism.*

- Are you wearing the lenses of science? You won't believe it until you see it. Everything must pass the experiment of the scientific method: you must be able to replicate an experiment you have performed. As a result, religion and faith cannot be true. Such a worldview is labeled *rationalism.*

- Do you look through dark glasses at the world? You have no hope. You are cynical. You believe things will only get worse and there is nothing you can do about it. You live like the rich man, thinking: *Eat, drink, and be merry, for tomorrow I die.* This worldview is called *cynicism.*

Looking through the Lenses of Scripture: A Biblical Worldview

Are you wearing Bible glasses? Are you looking at the world and how to make decisions through the lenses of Scripture? As you read the Word and apply it to your life, you can truly understand that God made the world and that He controls and sustains all things. You see that God is the sovereign Lord of the universe. Christ Jesus is the "image of the invisible God, the first-born of all creation. For by Him all things were created, both in the heavens and on earth, visible and invisible, whether thrones or dominions or rulers or authorities—all things have been created through Him and for Him" (Col. 1:15–16).

You also understand, by looking through the lenses of Scripture, that God sent His Son to be our Redeemer so that we have everlasting hope. You have joy in the knowledge that God is preparing a place in heaven for all those who love Him. You understand that "God causes all things to work together for good to those who love God, to those who are called according to His purpose" (Rom. 8:28).

From the Bible, you learn that in Christ "are hidden all the treasures of wisdom and knowledge" (Col. 2:3), and that "the fear of the LORD is the beginning of knowledge" (Prov. 1:7).

As you look through the lenses of Scripture, you begin to see that God has something to say about economics. As you search the Scripture, you find many examples of economic principles that God teaches, such as the concept of private property, the importance of tithing, or the need to pay a fair wage.

As you peer through the lenses of Scripture, however, you see that God has ordained all of history. His providence personally guides every detail toward the ultimate consummation when His Son Jesus Christ will return to this earth. You understand that nothing happens by accident or by chance, but that God is in control.

As you look through the lenses of Scripture at science, you see that God made the world and that His laws of gravity, entropy, and many other laws harness the earth. You can see the glories of God's creation as you study a small insect or a huge volcano. You see the power of God throughout creation; you see how all creation gives glory to Him.

You can begin to understand why atoms hold together and do not burst apart even though they are made up of electrons and protons that repel each other. Since all matter is made of atoms, why doesn't everything simply blow apart? The Bible gives us the answer: Jesus holds *all things* together! "He is before all things, and in Him all things hold together" (Col. 1:17).

You gaze upon the principles of mathematics and see that God has ordained the numerical orders. You see the Trinity explained through the mathematical principle of 1 x 1 x 1= 1.

You understand the importance of diligently working as long as God gives you strength. Government welfare is not an option for healthy men: "If anyone will not work, neither shall he eat" (2 Thess. 3:10 NKJV). In Exodus 20:9–10, God clearly commands, *"Six days you shall labor and do all your work, but the seventh day is a sabbath of the LORD your God; in it you shall not do any work."* This doctrine of hard work to the glory of God is often referred to as the "Protestant work ethic."

Your biblical worldview is your *map* through life—a map drawn by the Architect of the world, the God who made us in His image. Are you going to follow the map of the world or of some vain philosophy, or will you follow the map that is laid forth in the Word of God that shows how we should live? Are you following the biblical map that steers us clear of abortion but leads us to the truth that life begins at conception? The biblical map shows us that men must be the head of their wives and family: "For it was Adam who was first created, then Eve" (1 Tim. 2:13, see also 2:11–12). Paul counseled men: "Love your wives, just as Christ also loved the church and gave Himself up for her "(Eph. 5:25). This means we need to steer clear of the feminist and chauvinist worldviews.

This map leads us to train our children in the nurture and admonition of the Lord (Eph. 6:4 KJV) and to avoid schools that teach our children that God does not exist. As we follow the biblical map, we must walk on the path of disciplining our children rather than avoiding discipline as the world would tell us (Prov. 13:24).

As we study this biblical map, we find that we must help the poor, the widows, the orphans, and die to our own selfishness as we journey through this world on the narrow path to heaven.

These principles are no doubt elementary, but we need to think about them and teach them to our children. This requires that we find a curriculum that applies God's principles to every area of life. There are many secular books that Christian schools simply baptize and pray over, but children who use them are still learning the way of the world. We want our children not only to *believe* as Christians but also to *think* as Christians. We do not want our children to believe as Christians but to think like the pagans. Jesus commands us to "'LOVE THE LORD YOUR GOD WITH ALL YOUR HEART, AND WITH ALL YOUR SOUL, AND WITH ALL YOUR MIND.' This is the great and foremost commandment" (Matt. 22:37–38). We cannot separate our children's minds from their hearts. We need to train their minds to love the Lord: that is why teaching them and helping them adopt a biblical worldview is a necessity.

Thus, we must be self-conscious in how we teach our children academic subjects. We must teach them from the foundation of God's truth: His Word. As one of the most important tools for providing your children with a biblical worldview, I strongly recommend that home school families obtain the *Encyclopedia of Bible Truths for School Subjects* (Ruth Haycock, Colorado Springs, Colo.: Association of Christian Schools International, 800/ 367–0798). This is an invaluable resource that demonstrates how biblical principles apply to virtually every academic discipline. Each chapter in this book covers a different subject: e.g., art, math, science, grammar. The biblical principles are clearly outlined and thoroughly supported by hundreds of Scripture passages. This book serves as an index to the Bible as to what God says about the academic subjects that you are teaching your children. This will give your children a sound understanding of the biblical foundations for most areas of life. This will help them see the relevancy of Scripture to society and describe to them, in practical terms, how the Bible is the source of all knowledge and wisdom. Your children will learn the standard (the Bible) by which they must live and judge all things. I think the *Encyclopedia of Bible Truths for School Subjects* is especially helpful for home school students who are in the junior high and high school levels.

Another good resource is from David Quine, who has recently written a book called *Let Us Highly Resolve* and has created a biblical worldview curriculum called the Cornerstone Curriculum. Information on his biblical worldview materials can be obtained from the Cornerstone Curriculum Project in Richardson, Texas, at 972/235–5149 or www.cornerstonecurriculum.com.

If you want to provide your high schooler with some intensely practical biblical worldview training, contact Summit Ministries at 423/775–7599 or 719/685–9103 or www.summit.org. You can also obtain *Understanding the Times* by David Noebel from Summit Ministries. It compares the reasonableness of the biblical worldview to three other prominent worldviews, covering theology, philosophy, biology, ethics, ecology, sociology, politics, economics, law, and history. This is a must for every home school library.

Another important resource is *American Christian History: The Untold Story* by Gary DeMar, which you may obtain through American Vision at 800/628–9460 or at www.americanvision.org. This provides a thorough review of the history of our country from a Christian perspective. American Vision also offers a wonderful biblical worldview magazine. I highly recommend that you subscribe to it and have your children read it. Also, his excellent three-book series called *God and Government* will enable you to teach your children government from a biblical perspective.

I recommend *Proverbs for Parenting: A Topical Guide to Child Raising from the Book of Proverbs* by Barbara Decker (Boise, Idaho: Lynn's Bookshelf, 1989). This excellent resource for the Book of Proverbs provides a practical biblical worldview instruction for your children. *Shepherding a Child's Heart* by Ted Tripp (Wapwallopopen, Pa.: Shepherd Press, 1995) is an insightful book for teaching your children in the Lord and providing godly discipline. His brother David Tripp has written *Age of Opportunity: A Biblical Guide to Parenting Teens* (Phillipsburg, N.J.: P&R Publishing, 1997). This book provides an excellent resource for training your teenagers in the Lord. Parents with children of any age will benefit from this book.

A professionally designed magazine for keeping yourself and your family up-to-date on current events is *World* magazine, 800/951–6397. This weekly magazine looks at the world's events from a biblical perspective. You might assign various articles for your teens to read and summarize. This exercise helps them practice analyzing issues from a biblical perspective.

A biblical worldview is foundational. Make certain that a consistent biblical worldview is incorporated in your home school. We want our children to be well equipped with God's answers so they will be able to lead.

The Home Schooling Teenager: Standing against the Tide

What in the world is a home school teenager? Home schooling itself is considered strange in our modern-day culture. That must mean that a home school teenager is *really* strange. What teenager in his or her right mind would want to be home schooled when he or she has the opportunity to attend public schools, where—according to modern culture—they can have a really good time?

In public school teenagers have few limits. They often engage in free sex and experiment with drugs and alcohol without major repercussions. In the public school setting, teenagers expect to hang out with their friends every day, spending all of their free time goofing around in activities that show total disrespect for their parents or any authority.

These activities and attitudes of the youth in our culture are rooted in the sin of selfishness. Public school teens, for the most part, are primarily focused on themselves. The pervading philosophy that influences these young people is to do what feels good for them. God, the giver of all truth, and His Word, the blueprint for how we all must live, are reliably excluded from public school classrooms.

The Evidence of the Moral Decay of Our Youth

As the youth of today sow the wind and reap the whirlwind, the consequences are obvious. One simply needs to review the statistics. For example, crime among youth has reached its highest level in the history of our

CHAPTER TEN

country. The National Crime Survey, released by the U.S. Department of Justice's Bureau of Justice Statistics, showed that almost three million violent crimes and thefts occur on public school campuses each year. This equals approximately 16,000 incidents per school day or one every six seconds. The survey indicated that about sixty-seven students of every thousand teenagers or 1.9 million are victims of violent crime, including rape, robbery, assault, and murder each year. The survey estimated that a third of violent crimes are not reported, making the actual figures much higher.

The Surgeon General expressed shock at the findings of a survey of high school students that revealed that nearly 20 percent of all girls and 40 percent of all boys thought it was OK to force sex if a girl was drunk. Another survey showed that approximately 500,000 U.S. teenagers in grades seven to twelve habitually do binge drinking (taking five or more drinks in a row). The survey showed that nearly 14 percent of the nation's eighth graders are already binge drinkers.

In a federally funded study by the Guttmacher Institute, it was discovered that among fifteen-year-olds, 33 percent of boys and 27 percent of girls were sexually active; among sixteen-year-olds, 50 percent of the boys and 34 percent of the girls were sexually active; and among nineteen-year-olds, 86 percent of boys and 75 percent of girls were sexually active. These are all unwed teens.

The Centers for Disease Control and Prevention did a school-based survey designed to produce a nationally representative sample of risk behaviors of students in grades nine to twelve. The study found that 18.3 percent of the students carried a weapon during the thirty days preceding the survey, and 7.4 percent of high school students were threatened or injured with a weapon on school property during the twelve months preceding the survey. Approximately 32.9 percent of the students nationwide had property stolen or deliberately damaged one or more times during the twelve months preceding the survey. Meanwhile, the survey found that the numbers of multiple homicide victims in public schools had tripled in the last few years.

On the academic front, the statistics are terrible. A recent survey of colleges found that one-third of the students coming to the universities need significant remedial help in reading, writing, and math. No longer does a high school diploma from a public school signify that a child knows how to read and write.

Home School Teenagers Are Different

Yes, home school teenagers *are* strange when defined from the perspective of our modern culture. Home school teenagers are different. However, home school teenagers can be proud of and thank God for this difference.

The Temptations Will Come

Yet the road is not easy. The world and our modern culture seek to mold teenagers into its image. There is a tide flowing through our country that sweeps many young people away. This tide is in the form of many temptations. These temptations include:

- Skipping daily quiet time and study of God's Word because your schedule is too busy,
- Allowing yourself to engage in premarital sex because you reason that you will marry the person anyway,
- Dressing immodestly to get attention and because of your pride,
- Listening to music and entertainment that fills your mind and heart with thoughts far from the Lord, and
- Abandoning the biblical principles you learned at home and thinking like the world in order to create and implement solutions to problems around you.

James Dobson estimated that 50 percent of Christian youth walk away from Christ after they graduate from college. The pressure of the world is intense. The world persecutes those who refuse to be molded into its shape. The rebellion of youth today is reflected in their preferred music. A quick look at the lyrics reveals a preponderate emphasis on satisfying one's own desires and pleasures and a general disrespect for authority. You will not find lyrics to any modern songs that say, "I really love to obey my mom," or "Dying to ourselves is where it's at."

Biblical illiteracy is rampant today. America's teenagers are ignoring the Word of God and, as a result, are not living or thinking according to His Word. A dramatic shift has taken place. Our culture once reflected a biblical mind-set. The founders of our nation, even if they didn't all have a personal relationship with Jesus Christ, applied God's principles to every area of life. Alexis de Tocqueville once said, "Among the Anglo-Americans, there are some who profess Christian dogmas because they believe in them, and others who do so because they are afraid to look as though they did not believe them. So Christianity reigns without obstacles by universal consent." In the 1700s and 1800s in our country, there was intense peer pressure, but it was peer pressure that influenced teenagers toward the Bible rather than away from it. In our modern culture, the biblical mind-set has been replaced by a human mind-set. Christians are thinking like non-Christians. Christian teenagers are being taught in public schools to think like non-Christians and to come up with humanist solutions. The teenagers of our country are biblical illiterates. They are missing out and messing up. They are living like people did in the time of the judges in the Bible, when "everyone did what was right in his own eyes" (Judg. 21:25). These changes have caused the fabric of our nation to unravel before our eyes.

God Honors Those Who Honor Him

By this time, you are wondering, *OK, OK, I know things are bad . . . but is home schooling still worth it?* You are thinking, *Will I get a job? Couldn't I have had more friends if I wasn't home schooled in high school? I'm supposed to have fun in my youth, because I'll be able to work my whole life when I graduate. What about marriage? Does courtship really work?*

These are all common questions that occupy every home school teenager's mind at one point or another. You are yelling, *But what are the answers? I need the answers!* The answer is surprisingly simple. It is found in the Word of God, where God promises, "Those who honor Me I will honor" (1 Sam. 2:30). The road to get there is more complicated because it requires discipline and endurance.

Home School Teenagers Need to Be Lifetime Students of His Word

The challenge to the home school student is to aspire to a much higher standard of excellence than our culture has to offer. In fact, the challenge is to reach to the highest standard. You need to become masters of God's Law, His holy Word, the Bible. You need to be lifelong students of His Law, a Law that endures forever. God's Word is the path to life. You need to saturate and immerse yourself in the Word of God so completely that everyone who knows you will know that you are a disciple of Jesus Christ. Charles Spurgeon once wrote of his favorite author John Bunyan that Bunyan was so filled with the Word of God from continuous Bible study that if he cut himself, God's Word would spring from his veins.

We need to take advantage of the privilege to know the Word of God. In countries like China, where many Christians are tortured and persecuted for their faith, there is only one Bible for every hundred Christians. Here in America, the Bible is everywhere. The Word of God states, "From everyone who has been given much, much will be required" (Luke 12:48).

You are without excuse.

As home school teenagers, it is important for you to *internalize* the instruction of your father and mother concerning the Word of God. *Your mom and dad can't save you.* Your mom and dad cannot make decisions for you as you grow into adulthood. You must discipline yourself to know God's Word so that you will have the right answers when you must make decisions and face hard times. You need to make a decision to have a personal relationship with Jesus Christ in order to have eternal life in heaven with God. Remember that your teenage years are the *launching pad* for the rest of your life. You must redeem the time, not only by studying the Word of God, but also by doing it.

When I was a teenager, I knew many other young Christians raised in Christian homes. We all heard the Word of God and learned its importance to every area of life. We all started out strong. However, when we graduated, I saw several of my friends drift into major sins because they let the world mold them and shape them into its image. They gave in to the temptations. They did not fully internalize the Word of God in their lives. They hid the Word of God in their hearts at one time, but they let it slip out. This shows how important it is to have a daily time to study and meditate on the Word of God.

One of these young Christians dated a non-Christian. He thought he could handle dating a non-Christian, but he got her pregnant. He did right by marrying her, but the damage was done. Years later, she divorced him. Two other young Christian men became overly obsessed with the outward appearance of both themselves and girls around them. One of them caused his girlfriend to become pregnant. She subsequently couldn't handle the shame and, over his objections, aborted the child. The other got married, but he was unfaithful to his wife. A few other young Christians I knew began to experiment with drinking and smoking. For one of them, smoking led him to experiment with marijuana.

Each of these Christians had started out strong, but they did not stay strong. They let the influence of our worldly culture overtake them and push them into these sins. They all knew better. They knew the Word of God, because they heard it so many times, but they did not apply it to every area of their life. All of them stayed true to Christian principles of government and orthodox biblical theology. However, when it came to their personal lives, they rejected God's way of holiness for the way of their own self-centered pleasure. They stopped building a close daily walk with God through prayer and reading His Word.

I thank God for His mercy to me. By His grace He helped me to stand against the tide. I was trained the same way as these other young Christians. I heard the same teachings. I, too, knew how biblical principles applied to every area of life, and I adopted a solid biblical theology. However, God helped me to go one step further to develop a closer walk with the Lord. So when I was faced with the temptations, the words of Joseph, when he was tempted by Potiphar's wife, would always come to mind, "How then could I do this great evil and sin against God?" (Gen. 39:9). There are more practical tips on building a close walk with the Lord in chapter 3.

If you have been raised in a solid Christian home and attended a strong Christian church, you are no more secure from the temptations of the world than my friends were. However, if you have loved the Lord with *all* your heart, *all* your mind, and *all* your soul, then He will protect you. It is interesting to review the lives of the kings of Israel as recorded in 1 and 2 Kings and 1 and 2 Chronicles. The Bible tells us that every king who fell by the wayside and sinned greatly against God sinned because they only loved God with *part* of their hearts, *part* of their souls, and *part* of their minds. God wants *all* of your heart, soul, and mind (Matt. 22:37). Studying God's Word and applying it to your life is the solution to standing tall in the midst of an overpowering culture.

God's Plan for How You Can Stand against the Tide

Let's examine the Word of God to help us understand this battle against our culture and how you can stand firm.

How do we know the difference between right and wrong? The answer is found in Romans 3:20, "Through the Law comes the knowledge of sin." As I have said, we need to know God's Law. But some of you will say, I heard that we don't have to follow the Law since Jesus came and we are simply under grace. We are indeed saved by grace and grace alone, but true salvation requires us to obey God. As Jesus Himself said in John 14:15, "If you love Me, you will keep My commandments." Again Jesus says, "He who has My commandments and keeps them is the one who loves Me; and he who loves Me will be loved by My Father, and I will love him and will disclose Myself to him" (14:21). And finally, "He who does not love Me does not keep My words" (14:24). Paul reemphasizes, "Do we then nullify the Law through faith? May it never be! On the contrary, we establish the Law" (Rom. 3:31). Loving God in a fuzzy, sentimental way is not the type of love that God requires. Such touchy-feely love will not enable you to stand against the tide.

How well should we know God's law? Well enough to love it and obey it, to meditate on it all the day. David, under inspiration from the Lord, said,

> O how I love Your law!
> It is my meditation all the day.
> Your commandments make me wiser than my enemies,
> For they are ever mine.
> I have more insight than all my teachers,
> For Your testimonies are my meditation.
> I understand more than the aged,
> Because I have observed Your precepts.
> I have restrained my feet from every evil way,
> That I may keep Your word.
> I have not turned aside from Your ordinances,
> For You Yourself have taught me.
> How sweet are Your words to my taste!
> Yes, sweeter than honey to my mouth!
> From Your precepts I get understanding;
> Therefore I hate every false way.
> —Psalm 119:97–104

The culture today makes false promises. God's Word in the above passage tells us to hate everything false. Earlier we considered whether or not you, as a home schooler, could make it in the world. The simple remedy is to be a student of God's Word. Psalm 119 tells you that if you meditate on God's Word, you will become wiser than your enemies, your teachers, and the aged. The Word of God helps you avoid every evil way. To study, learn, and apply the Word of God is the best tutorial program available. Psalm 119:102 says, "I have not turned aside from Your ordinances, / For You Yourself have taught me." The Word of God is His letter of love to you. It is God speaking personally to you. God, who made the whole universe and everything that is in it, is personally tutoring you.

What a privilege it is to be taught by God! This is the God of Isaiah 40. In that chapter we learn that in comparison to the greatness of God, we are nothing but grass and grasshoppers. In fact, the nations are like a drop in the bucket; yet this God desires to have a personal relationship to tutor us in His ways, which are always the best. In fact, the Word of God is sweet, sweeter than honey. Why is it sweet? Because ultimately it points us to our Savior. We realize that as we try to keep the law, we fall short. And since the punishment of any sin is death, we need a Savior. The Word of God leads us to our Savior. This means the Law of God is sweet. What can be sweeter than living in eternal bliss with God in heaven forever?

> The law of the LORD is perfect, converting the soul;
> The testimony of the LORD is sure, making wise the simple.
> The statutes of the LORD are right, rejoicing the heart;
> The commandment of the LORD is pure, enlightening the eyes;
> The fear of the LORD is clean, enduring forever;
> The judgments of the LORD are true and righteous altogether.
> More to be desired are they than gold,
> Yea, than much fine gold;
> Sweeter also than honey and the honeycomb.
> —Psalm 19:7–10 NKJV

But some will tell you that the Law of God, His Word, is some ancient document for a people of long ago. A passage from the New Testament sets us straight: "For the word of God is living and powerful, and sharper than any two-edged sword, piercing even to the division of soul and spirit, and of joints and marrow, and is a discerner of the thoughts and intents of the heart" (Heb. 4:12 NKJV). Is your sword sharp, or is it rusty from lack of use? Remember, there is power in the Word, and the Bible is a living document that changes lives.

You have probably seen the bumper sticker or T-shirt that teenagers like to wear that says, *No fear.* I guarantee you that those teenagers fear many things. That expression is only words with no meaning. However, if you belong to the Lord, if you learn and apply His Word, if you carry the sword of the Lord—which is more powerful and sharper than any two-edged sword— with you, you can know no fear. You are secure through all eternity; you can be bold and courageous.

One of the most important verses in the Bible that will help you understand your priority as a home school teenager and as a Christian is found in the Sermon on the Mount, "Seek ye first the kingdom of God, and his righteousness; and all these things shall be added unto you" (Matt. 6:33 KJV). When I was in college, I allowed myself to be sidetracked by a dating relationship, and I lost my focus. Through the breakup with that girl, God brought me back to this verse, and I resolved to take this verse seriously for the rest of my life. I began to seek first the kingdom of God by using my position as editor of the weekly college newspaper, *The Collegian,* to preach God's Word and to apply biblical principles in every discipline at the college. Things began to change. I also sought first the kingdom of God in ministering to the twenty-eight freshmen under me in my role as an R.A. (resident assistant). I spent much time discipling these young men and working about twenty-five hours a week on the college newspaper.

Last, I sought God first by throwing myself into my studies so that I could improve my GPA and establish a better standing for law school. Although the road was hard, the hours were long, and the persecutions were intense from fraternities and sororities that challenged my Christian stand at the college newspaper, the blessings began to flow. First, I met the girl who would become my wife. Second, my grades climbed higher than they had ever been. Last, students were influenced by my work on *The Collegian* and in the Bible studies I had with the freshmen.

You do not need to worry about whether you will get a job or if you'll have enough money to provide for a wife. You do not need to be anxious about whether home schooling will prepare you sufficiently to be successful in this life. Instead, you need to focus on what really matters, seeking first the kingdom of God and His righteousness in your life. Then, and only then, will these things be added unto you. And the most wonderful aspect is that you won't have to waste time in worrying. Worry is a sin.

What is God's greatest commandment to us? It is, "'YOU SHALL LOVE THE LORD YOUR GOD WITH ALL YOUR HEART, AND WITH ALL YOUR SOUL, AND WITH ALL YOUR MIND.' This is the great and foremost commandment" (Matt. 22:37–38). The most important commandment God gives us is to nurture our souls and build a relationship between ourselves and God Almighty. Ultimately, it will affect everything else.

As a home school teenager, you are commanded to be godly in your youth and to follow your parents' instruction as they seek to be faithful to God's Word. Proverbs 4:1–2 says, "Hear, O sons, the instruction of a father, / And give attention that you may gain understanding, / For I give you sound teaching; / Do not abandon my instruction." Another passage from Proverbs instructs,

> Hear, my son, and accept my sayings
> And the years of your life will be many.
> I have directed you in the way of wisdom;
> I have led you in upright paths.
> When you walk, your steps will not be impeded;
> And if you run, you will not stumble.
> Take hold of instruction; do not let go.
> Guard her, for she is your life.
> —Proverbs 4:10–13

This is serious. God makes it clear that we cannot have a half-hearted commitment. We need to be fully and completely committed to following the Word of God as taught by our parents. Proverbs 6:20–23 states:

> My son, observe the commandment of your father
> And do not forsake the teaching of your mother;
> Bind them continually on your heart;
> Tie them around your neck.
> When you walk about, they will guide you;

> When you sleep, they will watch over you;
> And when you awake, they will talk to you.
> For the commandment is a lamp and the teaching is light;
> And reproofs for discipline are the way of life.

The world is in darkness. The Word of God is the light. You must master it so you can share it with the people of the world so they will no longer stumble, but know the way to eternal life.

As Paul wrote to young Timothy, he gave advice for all youth when he said, "Flee from youthful lusts and pursue righteousness, faith, love and peace, with those who call on the Lord from a pure heart" (2 Tim. 2:22). Today's youth culture screams out for you to come and partake of its lusts. God commands you to do the opposite: to flee evil, to pursue righteousness which is found in the Bible, and to walk by faith, not by sight. This passage tells you to love when the world will tell you to hate and to harbor that peace that passes all understanding. This power comes from within. It comes from a pure heart that is focused on the Lord.

In 1 Timothy 4:8 and 12, we are reminded not to get hung up on our bodies—like the friends of my youth who were involved in bodybuilding—but to focus on what really matters. In this passage, God says, "For bodily discipline is only of little profit, but godliness is profitable for all things, since it holds promise for the present life and also for the life to come. . . . Let no one look down on your youthfulness, but rather in speech, conduct, love, faith and purity, show yourself an example of those who believe." This is no time to goof off. Don't give anyone an excuse to look down on your youthfulness, but let the Lord's Spirit mature you and draw you close so that when you talk, people will know the depth of your spiritual walk. Your conduct, love, faith, and purity will speak of the Holy Spirit who lives within you.

Psalm 119:9 sums it up: "How can a young man keep his way pure? / By keeping it according to Your word." The Bible says that we must hide the Word of God in our hearts. Why? So that we will not sin against God. Your life's goals should be the same as the goals God lays forth in Psalm 119:44–47:

> So I will keep Your law continually,
> Forever and ever.
> And I will walk at liberty,

> For I seek Your precepts.
> I will also speak of Your testimonies before kings
> And shall not be ashamed.
> And I shall delight in Your commandments,
> Which I love.

Only when you walk in the liberty of obedience to God's Law will you find true freedom, freedom from the many vices and the slavery that Satan has to offer through the culture of our modern-day youth. God's yoke is not heavy, but light. Since you are all made in the image of God, the only way you can be happy is when you are walking according to the Word of God.

My life verse is found in 1 Corinthians 15:58 NKJV, and God has never let me down: "Be steadfast, immovable, always abounding in the work of the Lord, knowing that your labor is not in vain in the Lord." You need to be rock solid, standing solidly on the rock of Jesus Christ. Once again, God reminds us not to worry about the future, what we will wear, what we will eat, or if our home schooling is going to pay off. First Corinthians 15:58 indicates that your labor is not in vain in the Lord. The most important part is to remember to do it for the Lord. Do you remember the passage quoted earlier? "Those who honor Me I will honor" (1 Sam. 2:30). As you honor God by following His standards in a proper courtship, as you dress modestly to not give anyone a reason to sin, as you strive to live a holy life and seek God with all your heart, soul, and mind, and as you study His Word and apply it to every area of your life, God will honor you. You cannot go wrong. Your prayer and desire must be the same as Jesus Christ: "Not my will, but thine, be done" (Luke 22:42 KJV). Surrender completely. Stop rebelling. Be sold out for Jesus Christ.

Remember, your parents can't save you. The fact that you started out strong ultimately does not matter. What matters is that you finish strong.

I want to leave you with a practical nine-point test that will enable you to stand against the tide and make certain that your decisions and the positions you take honor God. The man who had the greatest godly influence on my life, John Vouga, headmaster of Christian Liberty Academy, gave me these points. I have them written in the front of my Bible to this day.

You can apply this nine-point biblical test to all things:

- *Does it violate any part of the Scripture?* "But examine everything carefully; hold fast to that which is good; abstain from every form of evil" (1 Thess. 5:21–22). "But each one must examine his own work" [test your own works] (Gal. 6:4; see also 2 Tim. 3:15, 1 Pet. 1:24–25, and Col. 3:16).

- *Does it weaken my testimony as a Christian?* "To this end also we pray for you always, that our God will count you worthy of your calling" (2 Thess. 1:11). Are we living holy lives so as to be counted worthy of our calling by God? See Lot's weak testimony in Sodom and Gomorrah (Gen. 19:14). Can people tell you have Christ living in your heart? Does the light of Jesus shine from you and dispel the darkness around you? "Let your light shine before men in such a way that they may see your good works, and glorify your Father who is in heaven" (Matt. 5:16).

- *Can I ask God's blessing on it?* "You belong to Christ; and Christ belongs to God" (1 Cor. 3: 23). We must do all to the Glory of God! (1 Cor. 10:31–33, Col. 3:17, 23, and Eccles. 12:13).

- *Is it a stumbling block to someone else?* Will your action lead a weaker Christian astray? If so, you are sinning against Christ Himself! (Rom. 14:17–21; see also 1 Cor. 10:24–33).

- *Does it harm me physically?* Your bodies are the Lord's too! Keep them from filth and injury, for they are the temple of God (1 Cor. 6:19; see also 1 Cor. 3:16–17 and 1 Thess. 4:4).

- *Does it edify me spiritually?* (1 Cor. 10:23). Not all things do! (1 Cor. 3:1–15).

- *How does it advance the cause of Christ?* "Act as free men, and do not use your freedom as a covering for evil, but use it as bondslaves of God" (1 Pet. 2:16; see also Col. 1:10, 1 Cor. 15:33, and Matt. 10:38).

- *Does it give opportunity to the flesh?* "For you were called to freedom, brethren; only do not turn your freedom into an opportunity for the flesh, but through love serve one another" (Gal. 5:13).

- *Do I use the freedom to serve, love, and share the gospel with others?* (1 Cor. 9:19–25, Gal. 5:13, Rom. 15:2, and 1 Cor. 10:33).

As I travel around the country, I find many people who made a decision for Jesus Christ, but they do not live for Him. They are not sold out. As a result, on Judgment Day they will explain, "But Lord, I did this in Your name, and I did that in Your name." And Jesus will say, "I never knew you; depart from Me, you accursed, into the lake of fire" (Matt. 7:22–23 paraphrase). Do not be like the five virgins in Matthew 25 who were not prepared.

I am just a regular guy. All my life I've been average. I was an average student in high school. I was average in college. I took my LSAT, which is the law school entrance exam, and achieved one of the lowest scores possible. I took it a second time and achieved a very high score. But the law schools to which I applied for admission averaged the two scores together, and I was mediocre. When I was finally accepted at the O. W. Coburn School of Law, which is now called Regent University School of Law, God made it clear that it was not by my own merit, but by His. When I was selected to be on the law review, which is a coveted position in law school, I knew it was by God and God alone, since I didn't even know what they were talking about in my law classes. When I graduated, I took the bar exam and failed the first two times, suffering untold emotional anguish. God once again made it clear to me that it was not by my might, nor my power, but by His that I would be a lawyer.

Since then, through my weakness, God has used me to change laws in many states through the courts and legislatures—laws that bring about freedom for thousands and thousands of parents to train their children in God's ways. Can I claim that I have incredible talent? Can I claim that I am above average and one of the best litigators in the country? No. I can only boast in the Lord, because He is the one who has made me what I am.

It is no different for you. God and God alone is the one you must rely on completely. He will direct your path in spite of the plans that you make. One of the passages of Scripture that means a lot to me is applicable here. It is 1 Corinthians 9:24–27, "Do you not know that those who run in a race all run, but only one receives the prize? Run in such a way that you may win. Everyone who competes in the games exercises self-control in all things. They then do it to receive a perishable wreath, but we an imperishable. Therefore I run in such a way, as not without aim; I box in such a way, as not beating the air; but I discipline my body and make it my slave, so that, after

I have preached to others, I myself will not be disqualified." I urge you to run that race to heaven. I urge you not to walk or waste your time in your youth, but apply yourself and buffet your body so that you will not only learn the Word of God but also apply it. You will find that God will open the right doors and enable you to succeed.

Already we're beginning to see the results of godly home schooling in study after study of home school students. One study was done by Dr. Gary Knowles, assistant professor of education at the University of Michigan. He surveyed fifty-three adults who had been taught at home. He found that two-thirds of them were married, which is normal for adults their age. None were unemployed or on welfare. He found that 75 percent felt that being taught at home had helped them interact with people from different levels of society. More than 40 percent of them had attended college, and 15 percent of those completed a graduate degree. Nearly two-thirds were self-employed. Ninety-six percent of them said they would want to be taught at home again. Dr. Knowles said, "That so many of those surveyed were self-employed supports the contention that home schooling tends to enhance a person's self-reliance and independence."

God's blessings are upon the home school movement. As long as you, the next generation, can carry on this torch of godly training of your children, a revival will continue in our land.

Now, run that race to win!

Understanding Suffering in the Midst of Home Schooling

There are no crown-bearers in heaven
who were not cross-bearers on earth.
—Charles Spurgeon

Suffering is something we all experience. Times of suffering in the midst of home schooling can cause us to give up on home schooling. Often we are discouraged by the suffering and may even question God.

Over these last few years, God has brought my family through major periods of suffering. The hardest trials have been: my car accident, my kidney stones, my wife's incurable ulcerative colitis (which she almost died from in 1989), deaths of very close friends, the near death of our twins, and my diagnosis with multiple sclerosis. The Lord has helped us to understand our suffering in light of His total sovereignty. He taught us that He is in control! His sovereignty is our *only* security because everything else is temporary and fleeting.

Through the fire of our trials, God also helped us understand why we are home schooling our seven children. We are not home schooling merely for home schooling's sake—it is not the end in itself. Rather, home schooling is simply the means to an end: bringing our children up in the nurture and admonition of the Lord so they will love and obey God all the days of their lives. Home schooling is the best vehicle we as parents can use to fulfill the commands God has given us to train our children. (See chapter 2 for a

CHAPTER ELEVEN

detailed review of appropriate passages throughout the Word of God, especially Deut. 6 and Eph. 6:4).

In short, God has shown us that suffering is actually a blessing! At this point, you are probably thinking, *Sure it is. Right. I can't wait. Send some hard times my way so I can be blessed too!*

I do not think any of us wants to suffer. It is against our human nature. We generally want to avoid suffering at all costs. I also believe we should not look for trouble. What we should do is prepare our hearts and souls and entrust our lives to His perfect care.

It is true, however, that suffering is a blessing. God uses suffering to shake us and wake us up. Times of suffering are times God draws us closest while He molds us, shapes us, and conforms us to the image of His Son. It is an opportunity to see our priorities clearly and to set them straight. We learn to concentrate on what really matters: living holy lives, sharing the gospel, advancing His kingdom, and training our children to love God with *all* their heart, *all* their strength, and *all* their mind. Suffering is a blessing. It is OK to suffer. I can say that with my whole heart.

Types of Suffering

We all suffer. Psalm 34:19 says, "*Many* are the afflictions of the righteous, / But the LORD delivers him out of them all." Everyone reading this book has suffered in some way. The great man of God, Augustine, being very familiar with difficult times, once wrote, "God had one Son on earth without sin, but never one without suffering." As the Suffering Servant, Jesus was no exception. As God's adopted children, we share in that suffering.

Some of you have suffered various types of persecution. Since 1985, I have been an attorney fighting in the legal trenches alongside home school parents. We are fighting for their freedom to train and educate their children. I have witnessed thousands of examples of innocent home schoolers being persecuted for their beliefs. Many home schoolers still face prejudiced public school officials, hostile social workers, aggressive prosecutors, or statist judges. Other persecution comes at the hands of relatives, neighbors, friends, or even churches that do not understand home schooling. Remember that the disciples, after being beaten and imprisoned, counted it all joy to be considered worthy to share in the suffering of Jesus Christ.

Some of you suffer in the form of diseases or various physical infirmities: cancer, back problems, intestinal diseases, multiple sclerosis, heart problems, and all types of chronic diseases. Sometimes God uses short-term illnesses to shake us up and get our priorities straight.

Many of us have experienced the death of a loved one, and all of us will some day. The sorrow never completely disappears. On May 29, 1994, my legal assistant, Kimberly Wray, was tragically killed in a car accident along with Angela Yerovsek, another legal assistant at HSLDA. Kimberly and Angela were in their mid-twenties. They were both beautiful Christian girls. They were killed by a man under the influence of drugs. Kimberly had worked with me for three years. She was a close friend to my family and me. Her death was a total shock, and it was hard to take. Yet despite my tears, I knew she had finally won the race and crossed the finish line. She went where she always wanted to be, and she did not want to come back. She is experiencing joy beyond our imagination. Both Kimberly and Angela are with their Savior, Jesus Christ. But it still hurts those left behind.

God used this tragedy to build my faith. I saw Him at work in the circumstances. He worked this tragedy together for good for those who love Him. He lovingly and sovereignly used their deaths to bring others to Christ. I had the privilege of sharing the gospel with one of Kimberly's close friends, Dana, who worked for our travel agent. I asked her if she knew where Kimberly was. She said without hesitation, "She is in heaven." I asked, "Do you know where you are going when you die?" She said, "No." I asked her if she wanted to know and she said, "Yes." I then told her about Jesus being the only way to heaven. I soon led her to pray to ask the Savior into her heart! I asked some girls in the office to help disciple her by having a Bible study. Dana has been living for the Lord ever since. In fact, we hired her to work at my office at HSLDA. Meanwhile, Angela's father, who had been a nominal Christian, also came to the Lord through this terrible loss.

Financial hardships are another difficult area of suffering. Losing one's job and wondering if you will have enough money to make ends meet is always difficult to bear.

Other types of suffering include having a spouse reject God and sue for divorce, or various marriage problems.

We all face routine types of trials of one kind or another: broken down cars, job hassles, children who are sick in the night, costly mistakes, accidents, moving, or losing close friends.

As I travel and speak on this topic at state home school conferences around the country, many home school parents have shared all of the sufferings listed above with me. Some tell stories of God's power in the midst of suffering. Others explain the relief and peace they feel after they allow the Scripture verses and story I shared to penetrate their hearts.

The Question Is:
How Will You Handle the Suffering?

We all will suffer. So, the big question is: How will we handle suffering?

- *Will we become angry with God? Will we question His love for us?* I spoke at a home school conference recently, and a mother came to me fighting back the tears. She said, "I was going to have twins, too, but one of them did die. I have been shaking my fist at God ever since, demanding why He allowed one to die. After hearing what God has taught you, now I understand how wrong I was and how much God truly loves me."

- *Will we grow bitter and begin to resent others around us who do not appear to be suffering as much as we are?* That is an all-too-common response. At another home school conference, a couple approached me with tears in their eyes. They said, "We want to confess a sin to you and before God." I responded, "What do you mean? I don't even know you." The home schooling couple continued, "We have been resenting all these home school speakers who have perfect families, perfect jobs, and all the money they need. Bitterness crept in. After hearing you tonight, we realize that appearances are not what they always seem to be. God has convicted us of our sinful attitude and how much we need to be filled with thankfulness. We have to trust Him more and accept that He's in control and will see us through."

- *Does our faith begin to wane and our hope in God die in the midst of suffering?* Some home schoolers at conferences have confided in me that they were beginning to doubt God and their own faith because they were not being healed. They had begun to realize that God is not bound by any name-it-and-claim-it magic words. Rather, He is the awesome, all-powerful God who loves us first and works all things together for good for those who love Him and are called according to His purpose (Rom. 8:28).

- *When we suffer, do we simply begin to whine and complain and feel sorry for ourselves? Do we take out our suffering on those around us?* One home school dad came to me after I spoke and, with an expression of relief and thankfulness, said, "Thanks for what you shared. It was a blessing to hear that someone who has had it worse than me is not complaining but rejoicing in the Lord. You see, I have had two heart bypass surgeries, and I was depressed that God was not blessing me like others. I was feeling sorry for myself, but now I am beginning to see God's hand in all this, working for my good!"

- *Do we give up on home schooling and stop pursuing what God has called us to do?* One of the first things that comes into our minds when we are sick is to cut back so that we can rest more. We begin to reason that maybe we should just send our children to school. It is too hard to continue. We need to focus on ourselves. We forget the call of God on our lives to home school. We forget that when we are weak, then we are strong. We must abandon ourselves to God's promise that He will give us sufficient grace and that we can do all things through Christ who strengthens us (Phil. 4:13). It was never our strength in the first place. We must realize that He wants us to home school by faith and surrender all to Him. God will honor those who honor Him, and He will enable us to fulfill the calling He gives us to home school.

- *Or, in reaction to suffering, do we honor and glorify Him and humble ourselves in the sight of the Lord, knowing He will lift us up?* (1 Pet. 5:6). Do we seek the awesome face of God, realize His sovereignty, and say with Job, "The Lord gave and the Lord has taken away. Blessed be the name of the Lord" (Job 1:21). Do we focus on the Lord and grow closer to Him? Do we look for new opportunities to share the gospel? Do we consider whether God is chastening us and that we must repent of our sins? (We always need to do this to some extent.) Do we see our priorities in a clearer light, concentrating once again on training our children's souls in the Lord and daily thanking them for the privilege of home schooling them? Do we simply thank God and look for the new opportunities He has given us to glorify Him?

One of my favorite hymns that captures the proper attitude God wants us to have in the face of life's trials was written in 1675 by Samuel Rodiguso. A man I always admired greatly, Greg Bahnsen, shared his love for this hymn. He was a pastor, theologian, and author. He suffered through many heart problems and surgeries in his short life. On his last Sunday on this earth, he led the worship with this hymn, knowing his next surgery was to be on Tuesday and that the surgery was high risk.

What ere my God ordains is right
Holy His will abides
I will be still, what ere He does
And follow where He guides
He is my God though dark my road
He holds me that I shall not fall
Wherefore to Him I leave it all.

What ere my God ordains is right
He never will deceive my soul
He leads me by the proper path
I know He will not leave me
My God is true each morning new
Sweet comfort, yet shall fill my heart,
And pain and sorrow shall depart.

What ere my God ordains is right
Here shall my stand be taken
Though sorrow, need, or death be mine
Yet am I not forsaken
My Father's care is 'round me there
He holds me that I shall not fall
And so to Him I leave it all.

Greg Bahnsen died in surgery a few days later at the age of forty-seven; and he went straight to the arms of His Savior, whom he trusted so completely. What God ordained for Greg's life was right.

God Is Good All the Time

"God is good all the time. All the time God is good." "God never promised it would be easy." This message ministered to me recently as the ten-man Liberian A Cappella Choir sang at our church. Some spent the night in our home. Six of the young men were blind and had suffered much hardship in their homeland. Yet you could not take away their joy in knowing Jesus. In fact, the words from another of their songs are, "We still have joy!"

My life has become much harder as I struggle to walk with multiple sclerosis. The cane has become my third leg. Ever since a bout with chicken pox two years ago, the strength in my legs has slowly slipped away. Walking used to be basic and natural, but now climbing the stairs is like climbing a mountain for me, and walking in my own house and office is a chore and a challenge. I am learning to die to my self-effort and my own pride to get things done. I have begun to understand that "I have been crucified with Christ; and it is no longer I who live, but Christ lives in me" (Gal. 2:20). I am learning to choose joy even though simple tasks like putting on my socks and shoes are a struggle, and my future looks bleak. God tells us to "rejoice always"(1 Thess. 5:16) and "count it all joy when you fall into various trials, knowing that the testing of your faith produce patience" (James 1:2–3 NKJV). Another passage exhorts, "We also glory in tribulations, knowing that tribulation produces perseverance; and perseverance, character; and character, hope" (Rom. 5:3–4 NKJV). I am slowly learning, "In *everything* give thanks, for this is God's will for you in Christ Jesus" (1 Thess. 5:18). I am thankful for so much—even multiple sclerosis.

God is faithful. This whole struggle with multiple sclerosis has helped mature the faith of my children to know God better and to be better prepared for the hardships of this life. They are learning by my experience how they must walk by faith and not by sight. While reading the Book of Mark with Charity and Amy, we came to the account of Jesus healing the paralytic and forgiving his sins. I said, "See, Jesus can heal my legs too because I'm kinda like that man." Charity, reflecting on her understanding of the sovereignty of God, responded instantly, "Remember Daddy, Jesus might not heal you this instant. He may want to heal you a little later." She is right.

God also performed a miracle in December 1999, as my tongue and some of my face was going numb. As I anguished before Him to keep my ability to work, speak, train my children, sing to Him, and evangelize, He restored my tongue and face completely!

The Suffering Saints

Suffering and hardship are common to everyone; this includes home school families. To continue home schooling in the face of a tremendous difficulty is hard. The temptation is to abandon home schooling and send the children to school. We reason, "We need to get our children away from the situation and make sure their education is not interrupted." As a result, the bond is broken, and the education of our children in the school of life is damaged.

Marianne Lash, the wife of our pastor Jack Lash at Gainesville Presbyterian Church, has experienced many times of suffering as a home school mother of eleven. Nine of the children are her own biological children, and two are adopted. Once their house burned down, and she has endured countless other pressures and stresses of maintaining a large family as well as a vibrant ministry at the church. Through it all, she has been suffering for years with a chronic condition called fibromyalgia. During a Bible study, when everyone was sharing various lessons that God had taught them during the past year, Marianne recounted some of her family's hardships and simply said, "Suffering is our curriculum for sanctification."

Marianne Lash is right. We home schoolers understand the importance of a good curriculum. The curriculum that God uses for our instruction is the best. Oftentimes, the deepest lessons and the most important truths are best learned when we have a bout with, or continually experience, hardships and suffering.

A quick look at the Word of God demonstrates that our Father in heaven, out of great love for His people, has repeatedly used suffering as a means to mold His children more into the image of His Son. He has used it to increase their faith and prepare them for His work, and He has also helped them to long all the more for their heavenly home with Him.

Jacob

Let's look a moment at Jacob. He endured twenty-six years of servitude to his uncle Laban. Laban swindled him out of his wages. Laban tricked him regarding his beloved Rachel. Then Rachel died while giving birth to his child Benjamin. Jacob is later told that Joseph, his favorite son, met a violent death. Jacob lived for decades with this sorrow. His thigh was dislocated by an angel, causing him to limp. In his old age, he had to take an arduous journey to Egypt and start over. That is just a small part of the suffering Jacob endured.

Abraham

Jacob's grandfather, Abraham, had been led by God to leave his homeland to wander in the wilderness for many years. He received a promise early on that his descendants would be like the sands of the seashore and the stars of the sky, and yet his wife was barren. When he finally did have a child, God told him to sacrifice his only son. He was engaged in wars with evil kings, who kidnapped his nephew, Lot. He and his people were constantly in danger. Never did he have a permanent roof over his head.

Joseph

Joseph is another example. Through no fault of his own, his brothers hated him. In fact, he was nearly murdered by them and eventually sold into slavery. Joseph had no rights. He had no hope. He was lonely being raised and trained in a pagan land that worshiped false idols. He couldn't see his family and those he grew up with. He received tremendous injustice after being falsely accused by Potiphar's wife. He experienced endless postponement of the dreams that the Lord had given him. He spent years in prison, forsaken and with no hope. Yet Joseph remained firm. When he was tempted by Potiphar's wife, he said, "How then could I do this great evil and sin against God?" (Gen. 39:9). Then when he met with his brothers, who had done him such harm and caused him such suffering, he forgave them and said, "You meant evil against me, but God meant it for good" (Gen. 50:20). Joseph had unwavering trust in God and His sovereignty that all He ordained was right and that all things would work together for his good because he loved God and was called by Him.

Hebrews 11: Unnamed Saints

All the disciples and the saints mentioned throughout the Bible, particularly in the New Testament, suffered greatly. Hebrews 11 is filled with examples of the faith that these saints had in spite of their circumstances. It also tells about the innumerable people who were faithful to the death, even people whose names are now unknown.

Paul

Of course, there is the example of Paul. He went hungry and suffered many beatings. He was shipwrecked. He experienced physical weakness. He had a thorn in the flesh that God never removed, even though He was able. God, in fact, told Paul that the thorn was there to keep him from getting too prideful. He experienced nakedness and financial want. He was persecuted in town after town and stoned. He experienced years in bondage in prison, waiting for the death sentence. Yet he continued to boldly proclaim the Word of God wherever God took him. If he was shipwrecked and ended up on an island, he shared the gospel there. If he was in prison, he shared the gospel with the Praetorian guard. If he was sick, he shared the gospel where he had to rest.

This should be our attitude as well. We should look at each hardship and each suffering as an opportunity to share God's good news with someone new or to let our light shine so people can see how we handle suffering by God's grace. People will see that we have joy in the midst of the suffering and will be amazed and pointed to God for their only hope of salvation.

God is telling us over and over again that He is completely sovereign. He is in control. That is our greatest hope as we go through the suffering. We know there is purpose, and it will be for our good.

James and Peter

Another example of the suffering of God's people is found in Acts 12, the story of James and Peter. Herod wanted to please the Jews, so he captured the apostle James. This is the same James who was specially trained by Jesus Himself. He was also part of the privileged three who attended some events that the other disciples did not, such as the Transfiguration. James was ready. He was prepared to do a great ministry for the Lord—a lifetime of ministry. Yet in verse two, we find that James was captured by Herod and killed by the sword. That's it. There was no miraculous deliverance. God didn't answer his prayer or the prayers of the other apostles and believers to deliver him from jail and protect him. James was killed, and his life of ministry was cut short.

Peter was captured as well. Because Herod knew that the death of James would please the Jews so much, killing Peter would please them even more. Yet God miraculously delivered Peter. He opened his cell door and the prison gates, dropped the chains off of his feet so he could walk out, and made everyone in the prison unaware of what was even happening. The other apostles were meeting with a group of believers to pray fervently for him. Peter went to that house, and he knocked on the door. When Peter told Rhoda who he was, she ran back to tell the others, but they did not believe her. They were praying, but they did not believe that Peter would be delivered.

So what's the difference? Did Peter have more faith than James? Did more people pray for Peter than James? Was James just not as good as Peter? No. What we find from this passage is simply the working of God's will. What we think would be the better way to do things, such as delivering James in a miraculous way by making the jail fall down through an earthquake, is not what God had planned. Instead, we see that God simply wanted James home. James had glorified God in his life. God was done with James. Peter still had more work to do. God sovereignly ordained the lives of each of these men for His glory, and He did what was best for each of them. "Therefore, those also who suffer according to the will of God shall entrust their souls to a faithful Creator in doing what is right" (1 Pet. 4:19). Also, the Scriptures say, "For to you it has been [graciously given] for Christ's sake, not only to believe in Him, but also to suffer for His sake" (Phil. 1:29). It is a privilege to believe in Christ, but it is also a privilege to suffer for Christ. God has promised us that it is "through many tribulations we must enter the

144

kingdom of God" (Acts 14:22). Fervent Christians can expect persecution: "Indeed, all who desire to live godly in Christ Jesus will be persecuted" (2 Tim. 3:12).

We all need an attitude like the attitude of Jesus Himself when He asked for the cup—the great suffering He was facing on the cross—to be passed from Him. But He ended with a humble reliance on God's sovereignty and love. In the Garden of Gethsemane, He prayed, "Not my will, but thine, be done" (Luke 22:42 KJV). As the musician Scott Rowley said in a song he wrote about this prayer of Jesus, "With these seven simple words, the victory is won."

We are not alone in our suffering. We are in good company! "How great a cloud of witnesses!"

Jesus Understands Our Suffering

As we face the hardships and sufferings, we wonder why we don't immediately get delivered the moment we pray. If God is sovereign, then His ways are not our ways. But what we do know is that not only does He work all things together for our good, but He understands. Jesus is not like "a high priest who cannot sympathize with our weaknesses, but One who has been tempted in all things as we are, yet without sin" (Heb. 4:15). In another passage Jesus told Saul on the road to Damascus, "Why are you persecuting Me?" (Acts 9:4). He identifies with our suffering. He Himself was persecuted. When we hurt, He hurts. He is a man of sorrows and is acquainted with grief. "During the days of Jesus' life on earth, he offered up prayers and petitions with loud cries and tears to the one who could save him from death, and he was heard because of his reverent submission. Although he was a son, he learned obedience from what he suffered and, once made perfect, he became the source of eternal salvation for all who obey him" (Heb. 5:7–9 NIV). Jesus set the pattern. God is chipping away at us, molding and shaping us to be more like Him as we go through the hard times. God is working more and more each day to unveil Christ in us.

Paul understood when he prayed, "Three times I pleaded with the Lord to take [the suffering] away from me. But he said to me, 'My grace is sufficient for you, for my power is made perfect in weakness.' Therefore I will

145

boast all the more gladly about my weaknesses, so that Christ's power may rest on me" (2 Cor. 12:8–9 NIV). The suffering and hurting process will not end until we become completely holy. That, of course, won't occur until we're in heaven one day. But we have that hope and promise of heaven, where there will be no more tears and no more sorrows.

In the meantime, until we get to heaven, God is with us. He is giving Himself. He is constantly holding us, comforting us, never giving us more than we can bear. He becomes a father to the fatherless, the husband to the widow, our counselor, healer, and deliverer. He can do no more than give Himself to us.

And what greater love, what more amazing and incredible love, can there be than that God, who created the whole universe, would be pleased to have His own Son die for us while He watched. No greater grief has anyone experienced than God over the death of His Son. Yet He did this because He loves us.

Joni Eareckson Tada wrote a book called *When God Weeps: Why Our Sufferings Matter to the Almighty* (Grand Rapids, Mich.: Zondervan Publishing, 1997). This is absolutely the best book I have ever read about the hard questions of suffering. The book is filled with Scripture references of how God uses suffering. Joni explains how God uses suffering in the lives of His people. One friend of hers named Carla was suffering from a severe case of diabetes. She already had both legs and some fingers amputated. Life was hardly worth living. Carla had read a verse from her Bible, "For to me, to live is Christ and to die is gain" (Phil. 1:21 NIV). Carla really wanted to die, especially after she found out she had uterine cancer. However, Joni asked her to finish reading the passage: "If I am to go on living in the body, this will mean fruitful labor for me. Yet what shall I choose? I do not know! I am torn between the two: I desire to depart and be with Christ, which is better by far; but it is more necessary for you that I remain in the body" (Phil. 1:22–24 NIV). Joni pointed out that this half-blind, legless, ailing woman had to realize that it was more necessary that she remain alive (*When God Weeps*, 98–101).

You see, when we go through times of suffering as mothers, fathers, children, home schoolers, and ultimately, as Christians, we are billboards for Jesus Christ. The world is looking at us with complete amazement. How we handle our suffering is a testimony to the world of the power that is within us. Humanly, there is no way that we could still have the fruits of the Spirit in the midst of the suffering, but God's supernatural strength can enable us to be gentle and kind and to have self-control, to still be faithful and loyal and patient. Non-Christians do not understand, but they want to understand, and this is our opportunity to share the gospel of Jesus Christ with them.

Furthermore, Joni points out that having a family at church that is going through hard times pulls the church together and helps members to get their eyes off selfish, petty problems. These members die to themselves and help others in need. This prevents church splits (*When God Weeps*, 112–13).

Paul actually says that we should boast in our weaknesses. Joni quotes a poem by Liz Hupp that summarizes the power of the example of a person going through hard times.

> I saw the woman in the chair; she was in the church again today. Someone said they have sold their house; they are going to move away. 'No,' I cried, 'they cannot go, they cannot move away!' I didn't get to know her; there's something I need to say: Please tell me your secret; I want to sit at your feet, I need to know how you handle the pain that is your daily meat. How do you keep on smiling when each day your health grows worse? How do you keep depending on God when you're living with a curse? Every time I see her; her smile comes from deep within. I know her fellowship with God isn't scarred by the chair she's in. She admits her health is failing; she knows she's fading away. How can she remain so calm, when I'd be running away? My friend, can you tell me how you can trust the Lord, how you can stay so gentle and sweet when He seems to wield His sword? You are to me a promise that even in the midst of pain, God is near and faithful if I will turn to Him again (*When God Weeps*, 101–2).

After Paul explained that it was more necessary that he remain, he added, "I know that I will remain, and I will continue with all of you for your progress and joy in the faith, so that through my being with you again your joy in Christ Jesus will overflow on account of me" (Phil. 1:25–26 NIV).

Furthermore, there are special rewards for all of us as we face suffering according to God's ways and not our human reactions. Romans 8:17 NIV, says, "We are heirs—heirs of God and co-heirs with Christ, if indeed we share in his sufferings in order that we may also share in his glory." We will share in Christ's highest glory. Second Corinthians 4:17 KJV says that affliction "worketh for us a far more exceeding and eternal weight of glory." Joni Eareckson Tada states, "It is not merely that heaven will be wonderful in spite of our anguish; it will be wonderful because of it. Suffering serves as a faithful response to affliction, accrues a weight of glory, a bounteous reward. God has every intention of rewarding your endurance. Why else would He meticulously chronicle every one of your tears? 'Record my lament; / list my tears on your scroll— / are they not in your record?' (Ps. 56:8 NIV)." Paul reinforced this thought: "I consider that our present sufferings are not worth comparing with the glory that will be revealed in us" (Rom. 8:18 NIV). Joni ends by saying, "It has been said that something so grand, so glorious is going to happen in the world's finale, something so awesome and wonderful that it will suffice for every hurt. It will compensate for every inhumanity and it will atone for every terror. His glory will fill the universe and hell will be an afterthought compared to the resplendent brightness of God's cosmos and the Lamb who gives it light" (*When God Weeps*, 210–11).

In heaven, we will see all this pain disappear. All the crippled people who know Jesus will be made whole. All the amputees will have restored limbs. We sinners will have our sin cleansed from us, and we will shine with the light of Jesus. Joni also points out that we will see "what lessons the angels and the demons learned about God from observing Him at work in our afflictions." We will see the influence our sufferings and how we handle them had on untold numbers of people whom we didn't even know were watching. We may even hear the angels say to those who suffered most, "Enter into the joy of the Lord." What a glorious day it will be!

Suffering will come to all, but as Psalm 30:5 KJV states, "Weeping may endure for a night, but joy cometh in the morning." We have an eternal home waiting for us that God has prepared. We must never forget that God is with us as we go through our times of hardship.

Yes, God has lovingly taught us so much through suffering. Let me give you a small glimpse of what we have been through.

God Is Our Only Security

It all began in August 1994, when Tracy and I learned she was pregnant with our fifth child. The prospect of a new baby initially seemed overwhelming. We already had four children: Bethany, seven; Megan, four; Jesse, two; and Susanna, only five months old. Yet, we trusted in God, confident that we were in His will.

Diagnosis of Multiple Sclerosis

Within the month, I began suffering from various symptoms of numbness in my lower body, particularly my legs. Soon the numbness affected my balance and my strength. It wasn't long before I had to walk with the assistance of a cane. After a spinal tap, various MRIs, and other electrical tests, the neurologist told me I had multiple sclerosis. The doctor diagnosed me with the type of multiple sclerosis that progressively gets worse. I was steadily losing control of my body, getting worse with each passing week for six months. Knowing that multiple sclerosis is a degenerative disease that causes many to end up in a wheelchair or worse, my first thought was, *How long will I be able to provide for my growing family?*

The trauma and emotion I went through after receiving the diagnosis was, at first, difficult to bear. I announced my diagnosis at our church at the Thanksgiving service. The church body literally surrounded my wife and me and tearfully prayed for us. For the first time, I realized that even though we cannot see Jesus directly, He has chosen to manifest Himself through His people, the body of Christ. God was giving us a huge hug through His people. I will never forget the love of God that was poured on us at that time and how we felt the overwhelming presence of God. My condition did not change, but the reassurance that God was by our side and that we were not forsaken calmed my soul.

My church family at Gainesville Presbyterian Church held a day of prayer and fasting, the elders anointed me, and they prayed for my healing. Members of my church pitched in with practical help for my family as my strength level rapidly decreased to about one-fourth of my normal strength. Our assurance was simply, "God is in control." We knew we were not.

Twins!

During this time, we learned that we were going to have twins! Now we were really wondering what the Lord had in store for us: six children, seven and under! The prospect of one baby was a lot to deal with; the thought of twins and me with multiple sclerosis seemed almost impossible. During a sonogram visit a few weeks later, we learned that the smaller baby was at least three weeks behind her twin in size. We were also told that they were identical twin girls, and we named them Amy Grace and Charity Anne.

Because of the complicated nature of the pregnancy, we were referred to specialists at the University of Virginia (UVA) Hospital in Charlottesville. These doctors are specialists in difficult and at-risk pregnancies, and as the weeks passed, the news became more grim. Amy's growth fell farther behind. Dr. Ferguson, our primary physician, informed us that in situations like this, the smaller baby usually dies. He gave Amy nearly no chance of survival, and he tried to prepare us for a very premature birth in which even Charity might not survive. Since they were identical twins, they could not be born separately. If Amy died, Charity would have to be born. We repented from our initial lack of faith. We began to pray just for the twins to be born alive. The prayer chain was regularly used on our behalf.

My condition worsened over the next six months. In addition, I assumed new responsibilities at the Home School Legal Defense Association (HSLDA) when I became the executive director of the National Center for Home Education. I had to restructure many aspects of the Center, lobby regularly on Capitol Hill, oversee state legal and legislative action, manage seven employees and five interns, and master many new tasks. Keeping up with my new responsibilities required long hours and late nights. Our lives were unsettled in every area. I knew God alone was my strength—mine was virtually gone.

During my daily devotions, I came across a passage that became one of Tracy's and my greatest comforts: "Therefore we do not lose heart, but though our outer man is decaying, yet our inner man is being renewed day by day. For momentary, light affliction is producing for us an eternal weight of glory far beyond all comparison, while we look not at the things which are seen, but at the things which are not seen; for the things which are seen are temporal, but the things which are not seen are eternal" (2 Cor. 4:16–18).

More and more we began to understand that this life is temporary, and so our hope is in the eternal life that Jesus Christ purchased for us on the cross. The affliction we were experiencing was really only momentary and *nothing* compared to heaven that awaits us where there are no more tears and no more sorrow. God, in His sovereignty, was blessing us with these afflictions to conform us more to the image of His Son. We found ourselves walking by faith and not by sight (2 Cor. 5:7). This is exactly what God has called all of us to do. We tend to think we are safe because we have so many blessings, yet when we do not walk by faith, we are in danger of later becoming overwhelmed by our circumstances.

We knew there was a purpose in this: to bring glory to God. We knew that God loved us. We could say with Job, "The LORD gave and the LORD has taken away. Blessed be the name of the LORD" (Job 1:21).

Sharing God's Love

The apostle Paul wrote, "But you know that it was because of a bodily illness that I preached the gospel to you the first time" (Gal. 4:13). Suddenly this verse had new meaning to Tracy and me. Paul became ill and had to stop in Galatia. It probably was not on his agenda. However, he preached the gospel to the Galatians, many came to the knowledge of Christ, and a church was born. We were experiencing the same opportunities for ministry. Every time I visited the neurologist or met with another technician, the Lord gave me an opportunity to share the gospel and give testimony of His love and power. I was able to hand out Bibles, gospel tracts, and other materials to encourage and persuade those in the medical community to turn to the Lord.

The same opportunities were arising concerning the twins. We were able to tell doctor after doctor and nurse after nurse that people were praying for Charity and Amy. Tracy and I were able to share the gospel with our doctors and give them Bibles and materials to show them the way to eternal life. We learned that God's ways are not our ways. We learned to pray with Jesus Christ, who asked the Father if His cup of suffering could pass from Him, but ended His prayer with, "Not my will, but thine, be done" (Luke 22:42 KJV).

God was impressing on us the importance of souls. We were learning to redeem the time He has given us and use every opportunity to share His gospel. The more we shared the gospel with strangers, the easier it became. Soon, virtually everyone we would speak to heard what God was doing in our lives and what He could do for them if they only believed and completely surrendered their lives to Him.

Our friends from church and other Christian brethren told us that our testing was helping to build their faith. It stirred them to pray more often and change their priorities, even as it caused us to change ours. We realized that our children are here temporarily, and they are a huge yet wonderful responsibility. We need to make sure that we train them up in the Lord, so that they know the Savior and will walk in righteousness all their days.

Some of our friends began praying for the first time. God was using our suffering to encourage and strengthen the faith of people everywhere. Word of our situation went out to 45,000 families through HSLDA's *Home School Court Report*. Letters began pouring in. People were praying for us. Their churches were praying for us. As you will see, God used the prayers of His people to move mountains on our behalf. The kindness and love shown by God's people toward us humbled us.

God gave us another passage: "Blessed be the God and Father of our Lord Jesus Christ, the Father of mercies and God of all comfort, who comforts us in all our affliction so that we may be able to comfort those who are in any affliction with the comfort with which we ourselves are comforted by God. For just as the sufferings of Christ are ours in abundance, so also our comfort is abundant through Christ" (2 Cor. 1:3–5).

God enabled us to comfort friends and strangers alike: two women who were experiencing premature labor, multiple sclerosis patients near and far, a lawyer on a plane whose mother was dying of cancer, a young soldier whose father was in a coma, nurses with marriage problems, friends struggling with illnesses, and on and on. God opened doors to share the gospel.

In fact, I had the privilege of leading that young soldier, Joe Fish, to the Lord! I found out that he was from my home state of Wisconsin. He was rushing home to see his dad, who had been in a bad car accident that morning. His father was not expected to live. I related to him my own suffering with the twins and my multiple sclerosis and how God was sustaining me.

Because of my hardships, he opened up. He said, "I have been taught the Indian religions but did not believe them. I knew God was out there but did not know how to find Him. Now I met you." I carefully explained the gospel and reviewed the tract "This Was Your Life" with him. He gave his life to the Lord right on the plane. I left him with a Gideon New Testament.

Suffering is a blessing! What could be more important than souls being saved for all eternity? There is power in prayer!

Meanwhile, God brought a godly Christian home school family from Pennsylvania to us, whose daughter, Elizabeth Smith, was led of the Lord to live with us and minister to our family for eight months. God the Father provides for His children. She was to become another of our many miracles!

Premature Labor

After visiting friends during the first week of January, we learned that their children had come down with chicken pox the very next day. Our four children and I had been close to these children all day long. Since neither the children nor I had ever had chicken pox, it was almost certain that we were infected. We stayed home from church for two weeks during the incubation period. Providentially, God in His mercy spared us all this extra trial at such a difficult time. But this was not the end of chicken pox—God knew that it was more than we could bear at that time—but it would return when we were stronger. His timing is always perfect.

When Tracy was twenty-seven weeks pregnant, she went into premature labor. When we checked into the hospital, the doctor put her on medication and successfully stopped the labor. But a side effect of the medication was a rapid heart rate that was very uncomfortable for Tracy. The doctor sent her home on modified bed rest, but after a week the negative side effects did not improve. In addition, the babies seemed to be growing rapidly and causing significant pressure on Tracy's back and kidneys. We thanked God for Elizabeth, who took over the running of the household and helped care for the children during this time.

After just one week, the doctor ordered Tracy to discontinue her medication because of the negative side effects. She went into labor again at twenty-nine weeks. This time, in our local hospital, the doctor put her on a second medication, magnesium sulphate, that caused her to become violently ill and rendered her immobile. Knowing she could not continue on this medication much longer, yet fearful they would not be able keep the labor stopped, the doctors sent her by ambulance to the University of Virginia Hospital, an hour and a half away.

The magnesium sulfate had stopped the contractions, but the side effects were horrible and the doctors discontinued the medication. An ultrasound revealed that Charity was at a normal twenty-nine weeks of development but that Amy was nearly eight weeks behind. There was virtually no amniotic fluid in Amy's sac, her head was caved in, and her spine was twisted. Dr. Ferguson turned to me and said, "If Amy lives, and I do not bet on it, she will be a vegetable." From a human standpoint, he was right. It was hopeless.

Meanwhile, Charity had a huge excess of amniotic fluid. This condition was not only causing premature labor but also endangering the lives of the twins. We prayed for God's mercy and prayed He would have the doctors remove the fluid rather than put Tracy on magnesium again. The doctors at UVA decided to draw off fluid from Charity's sac, just like amniocentesis is done. In the middle of the night, risking instant childbirth, infection, or sudden tearing of the placenta from the uterus, the doctors at UVA removed a gallon of amniotic fluid during a painful five-hour procedure. Immediate relief came to Tracy. The painful pressure on her organs and back finally ended. After her release three days later, Tracy returned two more times to have fluid removed—a total of another gallon. The doctors said this fluid would keep building up until the babies were born. It was hard for us to contemplate continuing this painful and dangerous procedure. Then suddenly, God answered the prayers of His people, and the fluid buildup stopped. There was no medical explanation! It was a miracle.

Miraculous Improvements

Subsequent sonograms showed that Amy was growing again. She had not grown for eight weeks. Again, there was no medical explanation! Her head rounded out, and her spine began to look fine, another miracle! The doctors had been hoping to delay labor for just a few more days when Tracy had been at twenty-seven weeks, but God enabled her to go another ten weeks in this high-risk and unstable situation. God was answering the prayers of His people and was literally keeping Amy alive against all odds! Dr. Ferguson said he would not have bet on Amy surviving and was amazed at the change. When Dr. Bell, one of our local doctors, learned that Amy was still alive, he blurted out, "This is a miracle, truly a miracle!" Many families at church were providing meals and running errands for us. God blessed us in countless ways throughout this situation.

Meanwhile, prior to the twins' positive developments, I was slowly losing ground with my multiple sclerosis. I was exercising by riding a stationary bike for twenty minutes on hard resistance. Each week it became harder and harder, and I could ride fewer minutes each time. I asked the Lord for a fleece. I asked that if I could ride for twenty minutes once again, it would be a sign that my condition would not get worse. God answered my prayers in His mercy, and I was able to barely go for twenty minutes before my legs lost all feeling and slipped off the pedals, virtually paralyzed. While some strength would return each time, I still required the use of a cane to walk.

Two days later, after riding for only ten minutes and feeling I could go no further, I looked up to heaven and prayed that God would give me His strength because I had none of my own. It was God and God alone. I prayed Isaiah 40:31 NKJV:

> But those who wait on the LORD
> Shall renew their strength;
> They shall mount up with wings like eagles,
> They shall run and not be weary,
> They shall walk and not faint.

At that moment, He also gave me a vision that Amy would be born alive! Within minutes, my legs began getting stronger and stronger, enabling me to pedal the bike for thirty minutes! I was so excited I yelled to Tracy to come downstairs. She thought I'd fallen off the bike and couldn't believe that I was moving and doing so well. We gave God all the glory. That marked a turning point for my condition.

During this same time, many people were giving me information on treating multiple sclerosis nutritionally. The mainstream medical community offered little hope; it was basically all doom and gloom. Doctors do not know the cause or the cure. They don't know what causes the disease to get better or worse. The nutritional community, on the other hand, was filled with testimonials and logical analysis about how our immune system works and how we can build it up to fight the disease through diet, vitamins, enzymes, and drinking a lot of water and carrot juice. I prayed daily that God would give me the wisdom to determine which path I should take. He brought all these things together as I began to find a common thread running through all the information, and I radically changed my diet. Through the prayers of God's people, my condition began to change. The stress of Tracy's difficult pregnancy no longer incapacitated me as it had previously done.

Work stress also no longer affected my multiple sclerosis, and there was a lot of stress. At one point God again revealed His great love for me. I had moved my office from one part of the HSLDA building to another, creating total chaos. This, in addition to everything else, seemed overwhelming. One morning, I told my wife, "I'm on the edge. I can't go on." At the end of the day, I dumped one of my moving boxes on the floor in frustration. Out tumbled a note from Beth Bowen that I had stuck in my drawer back in 1986. Beth had worked for me for eight months and had given me the note when I had a couple of major briefs due and was feeling overwhelmed. The note simply read, "Come unto me you who labor and are heavy laden, and I shall give you rest." Immediately, a calm swept over me that never left. I had peace that passes all understanding. I began praying and praising God. The message was exactly what I needed—it was straight from heaven. Beth had died of cancer a few years earlier while still only in her mid-twenties. God works in powerful ways.

Through all our trials, God was with us, comforting and strengthening us. Nothing we did was of our own strength. He continues to uphold us by His mighty hand. His mercies know no end!

Our Children Were Blessed as We Continued to Home School through the Hard Times

During this time, each of our four children grew in the Lord in mighty ways. Megan, who was four years old, met with the elders and clearly confirmed her faith in Jesus Christ as her Lord and joined the church! Bethany, our seven-year-old at that time, struggled with negative attitudes concerning some of her home school subjects. The Lord used our vulnerability in all this to also teach her to lean on Him for all things. Her attitude improved and so did her work. God works in a powerful way through suffering! Although Tracy taught from bed, home schooling was *still* the right choice. Sending our children off to school or day care would have been a disaster. Times may get difficult, but God will see us through.

Our children experienced our pain and wept with us. They prayed diligently. They learned that everything we own, including our lives, belongs to God. They learned that God gives and takes away. They learned God was in control and still loves us, even if Daddy ends up in a wheelchair and the twins die. It was OK. God would take care of us. Complete healing would come and all sorrow will end one day when we reach heaven. Our lives on this earth are very, very temporary in light of eternity.

The Twins Are Born!

On April 28, 1995, we drove to UVA Hospital and waited for Tracy to be induced the next morning. When the contractions started, the mildest of them were too much for Amy, and her heart rate dropped. The doctors decided a cesarean was necessary. Tracy and I were completely at peace with the decision. No less than eighteen medical personnel were assembled in the delivery room to help us. To comfort us during the procedure, God gave us the verses from the Psalms that I read to Tracy:

> For the LORD is a sun and shield;
> The LORD gives grace and glory;
> No good thing does He withhold from those who walk uprightly.
> O LORD of hosts,
> How blessed is the man that trusts in You!
> —Psalm 84:11–12

I looked up from Tracy just in time to see the doctors pull Charity out. She cried immediately and appeared healthy. Even so, a team of doctors whisked her away. Within seconds, the doctors pulled out Amy, half Charity's size and looking very frail.

A second team of doctors quickly took Amy away. She made no sound. Tracy and I were uncertain of her condition. We learned that Charity was a healthy six pounds, and I was able to hold her soon thereafter. As I looked worriedly over at the other team of doctors, all wearing masks, working on Amy, one of them noticed me. I'll never forget what happened then. He turned to me and gave me a hearty "thumbs up." I told Tracy. Tears came to our eyes. God had saved both our babies!

Amy was then rushed off to intensive care. Her lungs were fine, however, and there was no indication of any type of handicap. She was breathing on her own, a significant miracle considering her size: two pounds and thirteen ounces! A week before her birth, the doctors had estimated her weight to be just two pounds and three ounces. God had given her ten more important ounces during that last week! The Lord had given Tracy a verse from Psalm 36: "How precious is Your lovingkindness, O God! / And the children of men take refuge in the shadow of Your wings" (Ps. 36:7). How true His Word is, and by His mercy and grace He delivered us. Psalm 34:19 says, "Many are the afflictions of the righteous, / But the LORD delivers him out of them all."

When we saw Amy that evening, she was a bundle of wires and tubes. It was hard to look at such a small, frail baby. But she was alive! She remained in intensive care for five weeks. Our church family prayed us through a couple of infections, three blood transfusions, a heart problem, and several other complications. Amy's thyroid was not working properly, and the doctors told us she would probably be on thyroid medication the rest of her life. God worked another miracle—after eight months, she completely came off the thyroid medication. Now she is walking, talking, learning, and acting like any other child her age, although she is noticeably smaller than her twin sister. Charity is growing fast and is helping her twin learn just about everything. The close, loving relationship between Charity and Amy is a blessing to behold.

At times, the complications of life were nearly overwhelming. The pressure of caring for the twins and our four other children sometimes seemed impossible to bear, but God continued to give us a peace that passed all understanding; He gave us His grace. He had mercy on us and is using these children as a testimony around the country and throughout the medical community. A few days after the birth, Dr. Ferguson admitted that these were miracle babies. "God had a lot to do with it," he finally acknowledged.

My multiple sclerosis improved. For the next four years I was restored from 20 percent of my strength to 85 percent, and I put away my cane. I continue to follow a strict diet, completely avoiding all saturated fats, fried foods, white flour, white sugar, white rice, and so forth. I am also taking enzymes and many key vitamins and herbs. All of this works together to build my immune system to fight back against the disease. I am convinced God led me to learn about nutrition and change my diet to partly heal me. (I have written a twenty-four-page booklet entitled *Multiple Sclerosis: What Can You Do?* which summarizes my diet, the supplements I take, and why. You can E-mail us at klickaclan@erols.com to receive a copy.)

Chicken Pox Causes a Setback

By God's grace, He has continued to use me with my multiple sclerosis. My witnessing for Jesus Christ intensified as God sent me opportunities to share the gospel an average of twice a week. The multiple sclerosis has made me credible, and people listen. I have spoken to an average of fifteen thousand home schoolers at conferences each year and successfully directed many major legislative battles to protect home school freedoms on Capitol Hill. I traveled throughout South Africa to help home schooling become legalized. I spoke throughout Canada and in three cities in Alaska. I ministered in the extreme heat to home schoolers in Mexico.

I kept up with my responsibilities as a father of seven and husband. All with multiple sclerosis! Although I am weak physically, He has made me strong.

Nonetheless, the trials have not ended. In August 1998, I caught chicken pox along with all seven of my children. Chicken pox assaults the nervous system. For adults especially, it also assaults the immune system. I lost the use of my legs entirely for awhile when I had the high fevers, but I recovered after about two weeks. Ever since, it seems that my multiple sclerosis has gotten the upper hand, leaving my legs in a much weaker condition. I find myself needing to use my cane to keep steady on my feet. Walking is hard, and climbing stairs is difficult. Moving my body is an ever-changing challenge, and the future is uncertain. Yet God still enables me to do everything that is required of me: travel, lobby on Capitol Hill, testify, type, negotiate, manage, write, and be a father and husband. God's grace is sufficient.

The Battle with Ulcerative Colitis

Tracy has also had her own sufferings throughout the years. Back in 1989, she started bleeding through her intestines and was soon diagnosed with ulcerative colitis. Many of the drugs used to control the disease caused severe allergic reactions. The most powerful drug did nothing. For eight months Tracy steadily got worse. Each week she lost weight and blood. Her food passed though her ten times a day. She could not absorb many nutrients and soon weighed less than one hundred pounds. She looked like a prisoner of war. It was hard to watch my wife literally dying before my eyes.

I took care of then eighteen-month-old Bethany each night because my wife did not have the strength. The doctor thought it was likely that we would not be able to have more children. Tracy soon became dangerously anemic. The doctor even said she was too far past the stage to safely do surgery to remove much of her intestines.

The worst was yet to come.

Tracy caught the flu and was becoming dehydrated. I remember how little my faith was, and how I asked God out of my despair and helplessness, "Why God—why her and not me? Why did you let her get the flu when she is already so sick?" God showed me soon thereafter that He is in control. He taught me that He would do His good pleasure, and His timing would be perfect.

Soon, Tracy was taken to the emergency room where she was immediately placed on an IV and then given two pints of blood. The emergency room doctor ordered a test (something our other doctor never did) and discovered a strain of bacteria in her system that was complicating the ulcerative colitis. The combination was causing a dysentery effect that was killing her. As the doctors treated the bacteria and my wife was given blood, she began to get better.

God tested our faith and conformed us more to the image of His Son. He helped us loosen our grip on this world and look forward to heaven. God promises that He will not give us more than we can bear, and He never has!

Within a few months after Tracy started improving, I was hit head-on by a lady going too fast on a curve. The impact at sixty-five miles an hour totaled my car and caused me to smash the windshield with my head. For some reason God spared me from serious injury. However, the impact dislodged a kidney stone I did not know I had, and I was in excruciating pain off and on for the next few weeks.

I had to find a chiropractor for my neck, back, and shoulder injuries, so I stopped at the first sign I saw. Within six months of sharing the Lord with my chiropractor, Todd, he committed his life to the Lord, switched to a Bible-believing church, and led his family to the Lord.

I was in the car accident so that Todd would come to know the Lord. God was showing me to look for the opportunities He gives us in difficult times to glorify Him rather than feel sorry for ourselves or bemoan our bad circumstances.

Meanwhile, God blessed Tracy and she was able to stop medication within the year and control this incurable disease with nutrition. Although she still had periodic flare-ups, she treated them through her diet.

Twelve years later and after the birth of six more children, the ulcerative colitis became worse again. From September through October 2001, my wife lost more than thirty pounds. She experienced bad cramps, fevers, and weakness. She was passing food through her, and she bled from her intestines and colon twenty-five times a day and through the night. God's people prayed, and she was delivered, only to have the problems return a few weeks later. She has been on a roller coaster.

In November, as I write this chapter, I had to hospitalize Tracy for four days. She received two blood transfusions and forty-eight hours of IV fluids. She was allowed virtually no food during this time, and the doctors tried various medicines. I took some time off from work and ferried the children back and forth to the hospital. Juggling seven children, meeting work obligations, and trying to take care of my own declining physical condition was a struggle. Nonetheless, God continued to help us keep going. He also answered our prayer and moved in the heart of a godly home school graduate, Hallie Ray, to help us for the most intense two-week period. Our church also constantly helped us during this time with meals and help with our children.

God dramatically improved Tracy's condition, and, although not completely healed, she is doing much better. Life is harder for our family with both of us in poor health, but we have God's peace and still have joy.

Through it all, God keeps us focused on Him and doing His will. The home schooling of our seven children, although more difficult because of our health limitations, is thriving. We are so glad we kept home schooling through all our hard times.

The best and most lasting lessons for our children have come from participating in our struggles and learning to see God's hand in all that happens to us. To send them to school would be devastating to our family.

The Lessons of Suffering

Through all this, we have learned many important lessons.

First, we have learned that *nothing* can separate us from the love of God (Rom. 8), not even disease or tragedy. God's love abounds. He draws us closer to Him. He uses these hard times to conform us more and more to the image of His Son. He *must* prune us so we can bear fruit (John 15:2), and we were being pruned!

We learned to have joy in the midst of suffering: "Consider it all joy, my brethren, when you encounter various trials, knowing that the testing of your faith produces endurance. And let endurance have its perfect result, so that you may be perfect and complete, lacking in nothing" (James 1:2–4).

We must thank the Lord for these hard times too: "Exult in our tribulations, knowing that tribulation brings about perseverance; and perseverance, proven character; and proven character, hope; and hope does not disappoint, because the love of God has been poured out within our hearts through the Holy Spirit who was given to us" (Rom. 5:3–5).

Second, we know that "God causes all things [including suffering] to work together for good to those who love God, to those who are called according to His purpose" (Rom. 8:28). Through the eyes of suffering, we were blessed to see God's power and love so much more clearly. In addition, we saw lost souls saved, believers grow in the Lord, and the struggling conquer problems, all as a result of our suffering! The apostle Paul wrote, "But you know that it was because of a bodily illness that I preached the gospel to you the first time" (Gal. 4:13). Paul became ill and had to stop in Galatia. It probably was not on his agenda. However, he preached the gospel to the Galatians, many came to the knowledge of Christ, and a church was born. God works all things together for good.

Furthermore, God uses our suffering for good by equipping us to help others in distress. "Blessed be the God and Father of our Lord Jesus Christ, the Father of mercies and God of all comfort, who comforts us in all our afflictions so that we will be able to comfort those who are in any affliction with the comfort with which we ourselves are comforted by God. For just as the sufferings of Christ are ours in abundance, so also our comfort is abundant through Christ" (2 Cor. 1:3–5).

Third, we have found that God answers our prayers, but it is in His timing and in His way. For some of us, that timing will not be until we get to heaven. That is OK; God's will is better than our will. In the case of Lazarus, Jesus tarried for two days after hearing of Lazarus's sickness (John 11). He waited until Lazarus had died so that when He did come, He could raise Lazarus from the dead, giving God, the Creator, all the glory. The Gospel of John tells of a man who had been blind since birth. When the disciples asked why he was born blind, Christ answered, "It was neither that this man sinned, nor his parents; but it was so that the works of God might be displayed in him" (John 9:3). That man suffered all his life for the special moment when Christ would miraculously heal him. To glorify God is our sole purpose!

In other words, *God is sovereign; He is in control.* Before they were thrown into the fiery furnace, Shadrach, Meshach, and Abednego told the King: "[God] will deliver us us out of your hand, O king. *But even if He does not* . . . we are not going to serve your gods or worship the golden image that you have set up" (Dan. 3:17–18). Our attitude must be the same. This is the perfect balance: pray for healing but trust God and want His will to be done. As Jesus Himself said, "Not my will, but thine, be done" (Luke 22:42 KJV). Ultimately, we must bow to God's power and sovereignty.

Fourth, we've learned that God's grace is sufficient. No matter how bad the suffering seems, we can be sure that God will enable us to endure it. Although it may seem as if we can't go on, God will never give us more suffering than we can bear (1 Cor. 10:13). Certainly what Paul says is true: "'My grace is sufficient for you, for power is perfected in weakness'. Most gladly, therefore, I will rather boast about my weaknesses, so that the power of Christ may dwell in me. Therefore I am well content with weaknesses, with insults, with distresses, with persecutions, with difficulties, for Christ's sake; for when I am weak, then I am strong" (2 Cor. 12:9–10).

We were weak, yet God made us strong.

Fifth, we also know that we will receive the peace of God that passes all understanding. "Be anxious for nothing, but in everything by prayer and supplication with thanksgiving let your requests be made known to God. And the peace of God, which surpasses all comprehension, will guard your hearts and your minds in Christ Jesus" (Phil. 4:6–7).

God gave us peace in the midst of terrible suffering. This peace is supernatural; it is beyond our understanding. God will give it to us. It is a promise.

Sixth, we learned we must walk by faith and not by sight (2 Cor. 5:7). We walk so much closer to the Lord when we do not know what is ahead. Faith enables us to trust in the Lord our God and lean not on our own understanding.

Seventh, God taught us the necessity of rejoicing in Him always and being thankful for all things. In Philippians 4:4, we are commanded to "rejoice in the Lord always; again I will say, rejoice!" (also see Phil. 3:1 and 1 Thess. 5:16).

As my pastor, Jack Lash, pointed out, "If the joy of the Lord is not in you, how will nonbelievers ever yearn for what you have? How will they ever come to you and ask you to give an account for the hope that is in you?" (from 1 Pet. 3:15).

Joy is a fruit of the Spirit (Gal. 5:22–23), and only the Holy Spirit can give us this joy. In fact, it is called "the joy of the Holy Spirit" (1 Thess. 1:6). If we don't have His joy, we need to repent and ask for His forgiveness.

We learned that "the joy of the LORD is Your strength" (Neh. 8:10). He will give His people a supernatural joy that transcends all suffering and hardships, and it provides us with strength to go on. It is a joy in Him. If we have nothing else but Jesus, we still have joy. This helps us develop an attitude of thankfulness even in the middle of the roughest experiences. We truly have come to the point where we can do what once seemed impossible: *"In everything give thanks; for this is God's will for you in Christ Jesus"* (1 Thess. 5:18). We can thank God for the hard times because we know it is for our good—we have learned to complain less and look for the opportunity for our light to shine brighter.

Eighth, we learned that this life is very short and that we need to see it in light of eternity. What awaits us in heaven far surpasses anything here in this life on earth. Therefore, believing in Jesus as our Savior and seeking Him first in everything is all that really matters. Without Jesus, we have nothing.

The *last and most important lesson* we learned is that we must put our complete trust in the Lord Jesus Christ. Since He is the Creator of all things, He also controls all things and is completely sovereign. The Bible states in Matthew that He only needs to say the word and we are healed (10:1). God, in His sovereignty, may want us to remain handicapped or even die, but it is for His glory. And it is OK.

We can be assured of healing in heaven, where there will be no more tears or sorrow (Rev. 21:4). But we can be certain of our healing only if we know Jesus as our personal Savior. Without Jesus, we are bound for hell, where the suffering will never cease. "Therefore we do not lose heart, but though our outer man is decaying, yet our inner man is being renewed day by day. For momentary, light affliction is producing for us an eternal weight of glory far beyond all comparison, while we look not at the things which are seen, but at the things which are not seen; for the things which are seen are temporal, but the things which are not seen are eternal" (2 Cor. 4:16–18).

God's Continuing Care

Psalm 34:4 has been a tremendous comfort to us. "I sought the LORD and He answered me, / And delivered me from all my fears." Verse 8 goes on to say, "O taste and see that the LORD is good; / How blessed is the man who takes refuge in Him!" God has comforted us and strengthened us throughout this time.

Our troubles are not over. My multiple sclerosis is a daily struggle. The twins are a mighty responsibility along with our other children. God has even blessed us with a seventh child, John! Sleep is still hard to come by. However, God's strength is sufficient. He will see us through.

We wish many times that our health struggles would end, but He knows much better than we do. He assures us that "God causes *all things* to work together for good to those who love God, to those who are called according to His purpose" (Rom. 8:28). Even these health struggles are working together for good—not only for us but also for others.

We truly want God's will, not ours, to be done in our lives. We want more of Jesus and less of ourselves. We are willing to go through whatever it takes to let that happen. It is easy to say but sometimes hard to do, but God gives us His strength to keep our eyes fixed on Jesus.

God gives the most He can to us: Himself. Our God is with us. Emmanuel! His presence and comfort and strength keep us going. We can begin to understand and agree with Paul when he said, "But we have this treasure in jars of clay to show that this all-surpassing power is from God and not from us. We are hard pressed on every side, but not crushed; perplexed, but not in despair; persecuted, but not abandoned; struck down, but not destroyed. We always carry around in our body the death of Jesus, so that the *life of Jesus may also be revealed in our body*" (2 Cor. 4:7–10 NIV). We want the light of Jesus to shine through us. Therefore, we must die more and more to ourselves. God often uses hard times to help bring this to fruition.

I know many of you know this, and God has brought you through various hardships as well. God is still teaching us about the depth of His love, and we are still learning and, in some ways, relearning!

We have learned to thank God for letting us get up in the middle of the night in order to tend to Amy when she is sick. The frustrations melt away when we consider that we can help the twins now, when only a short time ago they were expected to die and we could do nothing to save them. We have learned to accept trials as our friends. God will give us hugs along the way and confirm His presence with us and His love for us through His church. Only in the body of Christ is there such deep love. God has given us help.

God loves us, and we thank Him for all that He has done. Praise God for Amy and Charity! We know that they will be used by God in a mighty way. We know that they already have been. We are so thankful to all those who diligently lifted up prayers on our behalf before the throne of God. The Lord used those prayers to bring us through and to continue sustaining us. We are humbled by the support we received from God's people. We are not worthy. We can only boast in His power, shown and done through us for His glory. We can say with Hannah: For these girls we prayed, and the Lord has given us our petition that we asked of Him. So we have also dedicated them to the Lord as long as they live (1 Sam. 1:26–28 paraphrased).

The mercies of God know no end!

(If you have further questions about what it means to walk by faith and how you can have a personal relationship with Jesus Christ, contact us: Chris and Tracy Klicka, 6779 Riley Road, Warrenton, Virginia 20187 or by E-mail klickaclan@erols.com.)

Evangelism and Home Schooling: How to Let Your Light Shine

He who wins souls is wise.
—Proverbs 11:30 NIV

What is our primary reason for choosing to home school our children? It's that we desire to train our children to love Jesus Christ with all their hearts, souls, and minds; to confess Him as Lord; and to do His will all their lives so that one day our children will be standing with us in heaven. We are not home schooling simply for home schooling's sake. Rather, we are home schooling to glorify and honor God by diligently training our children in His Word. In this way, home schooling teaches what really matters.

Evangelizing our children is our greatest priority. In preceding chapters I have spent a great deal of time on the fathers' responsibility to nurture their children's souls.

In the Scriptures God makes it clear that we cannot keep this good news simply to ourselves or to our families. He commands each of us in Matthew 28:19–20, "Go therefore and make disciples of all nations, baptizing them in the name of the Father and the Son and the Holy Spirit, teaching them to observe all that I command you; and lo, I am with you always, even to the end of the age." In order to be obedient to God, we must share the good news of the gospel of Jesus Christ with others. It is not an option.

CHAPTER TWELVE

I have realized that discussing home schooling with others outside our immediate family will almost always naturally lead to an opportunity to share the gospel. Strangers and friends alike will usually ask, "Why do you home school?" Of course, the reason we home school is inseparable from our faith in Jesus Christ and our desire to confess Him as Lord of our lives. We could ask for no better invitation to share the gospel.

Furthermore, by sharing the gospel in front of our children, we are demonstrating to them that our faith is real and that we sincerely believe what we are teaching them. Our actions prove that we truly believe that everyone is either going to go to heaven or hell. It is not just an intellectual doctrine. They see we really can't bear for people to go to hell, so we need to share with them the good news. This will deeply impact their spiritual growth.

Last, we must include our children in these times of witnessing so that they will learn early on how to share the gospel, overcome their fears, and appreciate the urgency and the utter importance of the task. I believe my children will never have to overcome the reluctance I once had to share the gospel because of my fears and lack of practice.

How God Impressed on Me the Need to Evangelize

I cannot hold it in. I have to tell others about Christ wherever I go. Sometimes I have a few minutes to share, sometimes a few hours, and sometimes more. It is especially nice when I am on an airplane and I have a captive audience sitting next to me for the next one or two hours! It is so much better to share the gospel, which has eternal consequences, than to talk about the weather or who won the latest basketball game! Unfortunately, I did not always have this fire in me.

Although I have been a Christian since I was a child, I was hesitant to share Christ. I could talk boldly about God's perspective on issues but not the heart issues. Then came the car accident in 1989, when I was almost killed. Then and there, I realized how fleeting life is and how crucial it was that we share the gospel . . . *now!*

During the next few years while I began regularly sharing the gospel, God confirmed the urgency of witnessing with the following events in my life: my legal assistant Kimberly Wray was killed instantly in a car accident; my twin daughters, Charity and Amy, almost died in Tracy's womb; and finally, I was stricken with multiple sclerosis. The Lord drilled the point home to me that life is too short and hell is too long. All we have in this life that will last after we die is our personal relationship with Jesus. As we hesitate, another soul will be lost. God calls us to participate in the spiritual battle that is taking place for men's souls and to share the gospel well.

In my personal devotions during one of my worst times of suffering, I came across a verse written by the apostle Paul: "But you know that it was because of a bodily illness that I preached the gospel to you the first time" (Gal. 4:13). And you know the rest of the story. God wants us to seek ways to glorify Him and tell others of Him, regardless of the hardship in which we find ourselves. My family and I find hundreds of opportunities to witness in the midst of the darkest times, and we see God save souls and change lives.

Follow Me, and I Will Make You Fishers of Men

One of my favorite authors is Charles Spurgeon, often called the prince of preachers. He was a man God used to bring thousands to Christ. He had an unquenchable desire to share Jesus with everyone. His book *The Soul Winner* (Grand Rapids, Mich.: Eerdmans Publishing, 1970) is a must read for every Christian serious about the Great Commission. In this book he gives many practical tips on evangelism. Some of his chapters include: "Qualifications for Soul-Winning," "Obstacles to Soul-Winning," "The Cost of Being a Soul-Winner," and "Instruction in Soul Winning."

Spurgeon focuses on Jesus' command, "Follow Me, and I will make you fishers of men" (Matt. 4:19). He explains, "If you yourselves are saved, the work is but half done until you are employed to bring others to Christ." Spurgeon comments, "Jesus' word is 'Follow Me,' not merely that you may be saved, nor even that you may be sanctified: but, 'Follow Me, and I will make you fishers of men'. Be following Christ with that intent and aim; and fear that you are not perfectly following Him unless in some degree He is making use of you to be fishers of men. The fact is, every one of us must take to the business of being a man catcher. If Christ has caught us, we must catch others" (*Soul Winner*, 275).

If you are wondering if you could ever have the boldness to share the gospel with someone, remember that He will make you, the fish, become the fisherman! It is not by your own power. Nor is it by your own power that you will save anyone, only God saves. Paul declares, "I planted, Apollos watered, but God was causing the growth. So then neither the one who plants nor the one who waters is anything, but God who causes the growth" (1 Cor. 3:6–7). Our concern is to obey. We cannot change hearts, but God has chosen to use our feet to bring the good news. God is sovereign. He is in control. Many times I have shared the gospel with individuals who have not responded, even though I thoroughly shared the gospel of Jesus Christ and they realized that they were sinners in need of a Savior. Yet they still rejected or postponed accepting Jesus as their Lord and Savior.

Just as the disciples asked Jesus, I am tempted to ask why the rich young ruler rejected him. This young man knew the Bible, obeyed all the commandments, was intelligent, and wanted to follow Jesus. Yet he still rejected Jesus. With frustration the disciples asked Jesus, "Then who can be saved?" Jesus' response is all that matters: "With people this is impossible, but with God all things are possible" (Matt. 19:25–26). God is reminding us again and again that He is in control. He saves souls, not us. We only need to be obedient and willing vessels to show His light to others.

You might say, *But I have no time.* The answer is simple. You must make time. We can never be too busy to share the good news.

You might also be wondering, *There are so many unsaved people out there. Where do we start? How can we possibly reach them?* Remember, our main concern is to witness to those who are within our reach. We each have a particular circle of friends, a unique set of relatives, and jobs that bring us into contact with many people. That is our mission field. You will find that it is much better to share the gospel than to talk about the weather and sports with strangers, relatives, or friends. We need to give them information that will determine where they will spend eternity. That is the most important gift we can give anyone.

God has given us a wonderful opportunity through home schooling to share the gospel without much effort. Therefore, let us prepare ourselves so that we, the home school families, can share the light of the gospel with others.

At this point, you might be saying, *Yes, I am convinced I need to evangelize, but how can I do it?* First, you must realize that you can do all things through Christ who strengthens you. This is a promise. Second, look at everyone you meet as a potential convert for Jesus Christ. You must come to grips with the fact that their souls will never die. You must have compassion on them, sincerely hoping and praying that no one will have to go to hell.

Where to Begin? Buy a Supply of Bibles and Tracts

Where do I begin? First, I recommend that you always have tracts and Bibles with you to give to people you meet. I joined the Gideons to have easy access to small personal New Testaments, which can easily fit into my pockets or briefcase. We carry gospel tracts in our van, truck, purse, and pockets. I also carry a *Bible Promise Book*, which summarizes the Scripture according to subject. I buy them by the case through my local Christian bookstore in order to get a substantial discount. Last, I use a written account of my own personal testimony about how God has worked through my multiple sclerosis, and how He saved our twins from certain death. Most of this testimony is recorded in chapter 11. Everybody has a story to share about God's deliverance. Take the time to type it up and carry it with you to distribute. Personal stories allow others to see your vulnerability, and this makes you more credible as you share the gospel.

Spurgeon in *The Soul Winner* emphasizes the importance of tracts: "When preaching and private talk are not available, you have a tract ready, and this is often an effectual method. Some tracts would not convert a beetle: there is not enough in them to interest a fly. Get good striking tracts, or none at all. But a telling, touching gospel tract may often be the seed of eternal life; therefore, do not go out without your tracts" (181).

Having one or more of these materials with you at all times will give you greater confidence. If you have only a minute to share with a stranger, give him a tract. If you have longer to share, give him a tract and a Bible. You can always hand him your personal testimony. I usually reserve the *Bible Promise Book*, which is about two hundred pages long, for individuals with whom I have had an opportunity to talk at length. You do not have to be concerned if you do not have enough time to finish a full gospel presentation; you can give the individual a tract or a Bible. These evangelistic materials will do it for you.

Second, realize that there are many opportunities to share the gospel. You can distribute tracts and Bibles anonymously in phone booths, bathrooms, public places, schools, and jails. You can witness to your relatives and family members. I believe that it is particularly effective to share the gospel and give tracts to people with whom you do business. An individual is more likely to listen to you and receive what you give him if you are also buying from his establishment, using the toll road, or paying for his service.

Third, remember that when you share God's Word, it never returns void:

> For as the rain comes down, and the snow from heaven,
> And do not return there,
> But water the earth,
> And make it bring forth and bud,
> That it may give seed to the sower
> And bread to the eater,
> So shall My word be that goes forth from My mouth;
> It shall not return to Me void,
> But it shall accomplish what I please,
> And it shall prosper in the thing for which I sent it.
> —Isaiah 55:10–11 NKJV

You cannot go wrong when you share the gospel with someone. Regardless of your ability, the seeds will be planted.

Home Schooling Opens Doors to Share the Gospel

Anytime you mention that you home school, this opens the door to talk about the Lord. You can talk with the electrician visiting your home or the plumber or the carpet cleaner. You can share with the person sitting next to you on an airplane, train, or other mode of public transportation. Bring up home schooling when you are in a barber or beauty shop, in the hospital, or sitting in a waiting room. Whether you are talking with a coworker, client, store clerk, or over the fence with your neighbors, just mention *home schooling*, and people will be curious. They will always have questions, and the question will finally come up, *Why do you home school?*

That question is your cue. At that point you will have the opportunity to share your religious convictions concerning home schooling. Tell them you believe your children must be taught the Word of God so they will understand the difference between right and wrong. Ask them where or if they go to church. Ask them if they are born-again Christians and if they know where they will go when they die. Explain to them how they can know for certain they will go to heaven. Some people will interact with you, while others will simply listen. Either way, the seeds are planted. You can end the conversation by giving them a tract or Bible and/or your personal written testimony.

Look for opportunities as a home school family to minister. Be sure to instill in your children, during family devotions and your one-on-one time, the shortness of life and the importance that they personally know Jesus Christ as their Savior; then explain to them how awful it would be for anyone to go to hell. They will begin to develop in their hearts a true and sincere desire for others to be saved.

Tips for Family Evangelism

Besides one-on-one personal evangelism to those within your reach, practice family evangelism. Home schooling gives us the flexibility to do more things as a family. Together we can do errands, go on field trips, take neighborhood walks, and meet visitors who come to the house. Here are some of the ways our family, through our home schooling, has been able to minister.

Neighbors

When our children are outside, they have opportunities to be witnesses for Christ by their good behavior. Our children often give tracts to neighbor children, or they do free chores for neighbors and then give them a *Bible Promise Book* or a Bible. Sometimes we make cookies and deliver them to our elderly neighbors. When we walk through the neighborhood, we always have a Bible or tract in the stroller. For the people we will see again, we build a friendship first and then give them the *Bible Promise Book* or Bible during another visit. We also invite our neighbors over for dinner or to go to church.

One family in the neighborhood seemed unlikely candidates, yet we shared the gospel and told them about our home school. The mother was disturbed about the negative impact that public school was having on her children, and she asked for more information on home schooling. I gave her the information and our personal tract. Later we invited them to church. One Sunday, they simply appeared at church. They have been growing in the Lord ever since and even started to home school! Nearly their whole family now professes Christ. It all started with curiosity about our home school!

Once, God sent a lost teenager to our house. She was living in sin and knew it. We shared the good news, gave her a Bible and tract, and took her home.

Another time, a young man named Mark stopped by our house to ask if we needed someone to trim our trees. I declined his service but started a conversation. He felt very guilty because he was living with his girlfriend. I told him about God's forgiveness and his need to repent. One of my daughters got a Bible from the house, and I showed him how to use it and gave it to him with a tract. You never know who might be open to the gospel or what seeds you are planting!

Rummage Sales

We generally hold an annual rummage sale. This is a wonderful opportunity to give tracts to everyone who comes. My children often give tracts to the men who are waiting in their cars while their wives shop. The men have nothing else to do, so they read the tract. I have talked to some people at our rummage sales for nearly an hour, sharing the gospel. The unsaved come to us because of our *good junk* and go away with the *good news!*

Restaurants

When we go to a restaurant, we take a stack of tracts with us. Sometimes the children will draw a special picture or a write a note for our waitress and will give her a tract. The children fan out in pairs to hand tracts to people at tables throughout the restaurant. They say, with big smiles on their faces, "This tells you how to get to heaven." Well-behaved children, especially small children, invariably draw a positive response from others in the restaurant. The testimony of our children literally draws others to come to us, and then we give them tracts too.

When we go to a drive-through restaurant, we always give the attendant a tract and say, "Here is some good news for you today!"

One night when my wife was very sick, Bethany, Megan, and I stopped to pick up an order at a Chinese restaurant and noticed two dogs looking at us out of a car. There was only one person eating inside the restaurant, and I commented that his dogs were well behaved. In no time, we found out that Bill was seeking God and knew he needed to repent. We shared the gospel with him and told him that many people will tell Jesus on the last day that they have done many things in His name. And Jesus will reply, "I never knew you; depart from Me, you who practice lawlessness!" (Matt. 7:23). We told him he needed to make a decision, and we invited him to church. We left him with a tract. God even had us meet Bill at a store a little later to exhort him again!

Barbers, Gas Station Attendants, Toll-Booth Operators, Bank and Store Clerks, Waitresses, Car Salesmen

Not every family is free to visit door-to-door on Thursday nights. But every family has to buy food, fuel, and necessities. You can turn nearly every errand into an opportunity to share the gospel. However, you need to be prepared, and you need to discipline your mind to see the opportunities you have to share the gospel.

For instance, when the bank teller gives my children lollipops, they give her a tract. Toll-booth operators and parking lot attendants have fairly monotonous jobs with a certain amount of down time. Giving them an interesting tract is almost always well received.

When we had to replace our ailing van, we decided to bite the bullet and invest in a new fifteen-seat passenger van. We found a great buy at a local dealer and began the long negotiating process. During our talks, we told the salesman, Russel, about our family, the twins, and our church. He told us about his background. During a break, I had one of the children get me a Bible out of the van, and I showed Russel how to use the Bible with a thorough gospel presentation. He listened intently and made a commitment to read the Book of John and start reading the Bible daily. I followed up with a couple of phone calls and a package with a copy of *New Beginning* by D. James Kennedy. Russel said he had committed his life to the Lord and was going to a Bible-believing church and worshiping with his family!

Barbers love to talk. I always bring up the fact that we home school, and I usually have children with me. Soon I ask the barber if he is a born-again Christian. At that point I have a lengthy opportunity to share the gospel, and I always leave our written personal testimony.

Store clerks have slow times along with periodic breaks. The children often walk up to the clerks taking a smoking break outside and give them tracts or Bibles. While we shop for groceries, I give each of my children a stack of tracts that they can pass out to shoppers in the store. Many times I converse with store clerks as I check out and introduce them to the gospel.

We need to look for every opportunity. Only God knows where it will lead. We only need to be faithful.

Vacations

Have you ever thought of turning your planned family vacation into a missionary trip? I do not mean going to Mexico. Instead, simply purchase a supply of tracts and Bibles and be prepared to pass them out.

Our family went to New York for a week and a half on a big field trip to see Niagara Falls, Six Flags, historic sites, and hotels. Everywhere we stopped, the children passed out tracts. At Six Flags alone, we passed out sixty tracts to people throughout the park. At one hotel, we shared the gospel at length with a handyman who knew he needed to change his ways. We challenged him to read the Bible we gave him and start attending church. Later that same day, a homeless man came up to ask for a couple of bucks. What an ideal opportunity to tell him about a life that would last forever and give him a Bible.

When I had to speak in Quebec, we decided to make it a family vacation. In advance, I bought a lot of French tracts to pass out. It was amazing to see the doors God opened for us. We shared Jesus at length with Roberto, the man who gave us a carriage ride in old Quebec City. We stopped to talk to a parking lot attendant at the beautiful waterfalls. God arranged that no one else came into the parking lot while we talked with Benois for about twenty minutes. He believed in a pantheistic God that was everywhere in nature, but he was still searching. We told him our personal testimony and gave him a Bible and a French tract. He was very excited and promised to read the Book of John.

We also met Chester at a fast food place while we waited for the car ferry. My daughter Megan gave him a French tract. The kids saw him again on the ferry as we crossed the St. Lawrence River. About two hours later, we stopped at a Chinese restaurant to eat. Suddenly a car pulled in, and the kids went wild. It was Chester! We asked him if he read the tract, and he said he did not read French very well. He accepted a tract in English, and I shared the gospel with him for the next thirty minutes. I explained that our meeting was no accident. He wanted to know the Lord, but was turned off by all the statues to Mary and the saints. As I told him that there is only "one mediator between God and men" (1 Tim. 2:5), he smiled and wanted to know more about Jesus. I gave him a pocket Gideon New Testament that he promised to read on the ship where he worked.

My wife booked us one night at a bed and breakfast in Ontario. We arrived at 10:00 P.M. in a seedy part of the downtown area and discovered that the place was run by and for homosexuals. We also discovered that one of the lovers had destroyed our reservation after a "domestic" dispute. My wife and I turned the situation into an opportunity to share the gospel to an untouched household. We left them with our personal testimony and a Bible. God had arranged it all and even had the homosexuals pay for us to stay elsewhere that night!

When I had an engagement to speak in Puerto Rico, my wife found a wonderful two-for-one cruise deal. To our surprise and dismay, we found ourselves on a party ship for five days. We just wanted to get off, but God opened our eyes to see the hurting people and the opportunity He had given us. We shared the gospel with many and led a Bible study in our tiny cabin that grew to seven people. We were able to lead two sailors, Danny and James, to Christ!

Bed and Breakfast Getaways

As supportive husbands, we need to take our wives on periodic overnight getaways to simply rest and relax. This simple demonstration of our love speaks volumes to them.

Yet even in this time of being close to our wives and making plans for our family, God puts people in our paths who need the Lord. As a result, Tracy and I receive great joy when we minister to our hosts and hostesses.

We have seen Unitarians begin to doubt, nonchurchgoers open up, and many hearts begin to melt as they hear the Word of God. On one occasion, we befriended and briefly shared the gospel with a young lady named Charity, who cooked at a bed and breakfast. I asked her if she wanted to talk more, and we decided to meet after dinner that night. She was eager to hear about the Lord. She had been separated from her husband for seven years, had one son, and no hope. The Word penetrated her heart, and she was saved within the week. She ended up coming to our church, and she soaked up the Word with fervor. She asked many questions, bought a nice Bible, and regularly visited our family. She even was convicted to restore her relationship with her husband!

We realize we just have to be willing vessels to share His gospel. God will do the rest. We also find ourselves uplifted and blessed as we witness together as a couple. It builds the bond between us and makes us closer soul mates.

Visitors and Repairmen

If your busy life is anything like ours, you do not have to leave your house to evangelize! Someone is always stopping by. So whenever someone visits our home, our children give him a tract, or cookies and a Bible, or something of that nature. We recently had a coal stove installed, and our children gave a *Bible Promise Book* to each of the men. When a man came to clean our carpets, the children made sure they gave him a tract and personal testimony. We shared the gospel for about two hours with a vacuum repair salesman. An electrician who came a few times had gone through a divorce and was searching for meaning in his life. He really wanted to commit himself to the Lord and left us promising to read the gospel materials we gave him.

When we built an addition on our house, we spent a lot of time talking with the workmen over a period of six months. We learned that each person had certain troubles of his own. One man returned to his trailer after work one day and found that his girlfriend had died. I had a long opportunity to share true hope with him. I also made certain I talked to the workmen about the Lord and gave each of them a copy of our personal testimony.

Many UPS men have received a Bible or tract at our house. Even our garbage man has not gone untouched by the gospel of Christ.

Telemarketers

Are you ever irritated by unwanted phone solicitation? Do you feel like simply hanging up? One time I was in the middle of a writing project at home and the phone rang. It was an AT&T salesman. I started talking to him about the latest deal and mentioned our phone needs and the size of our family. I talked to him for the next thirty minutes and found out he was searching for God but thought he had plenty of time. (He was only twenty-one years old.) I reminded him of the uncertainty of life and told him the story of my cousin who died suddenly in a car crash. He wanted to commit his life to the Lord but still wanted to read more, so I asked for his address. I sent him a package with a Bible, our family testimony, and *Beginning Again*. You never know when God is working on someone's heart.

Public Transportation

Riding in an airplane, train, taxi, or bus gives an ideal place to share the gospel. Why? Because you have a captive audience! Since I travel on airplanes frequently, I have had hundreds of opportunities to share the gospel.

Often the most unlikely candidates turn out to be the most open. For example, once I sat next to a feminist-looking woman. Esther was a divorced businesswoman who helped AIDS victims. I told her that Jesus wants us to help *the least of these*, and she asked me about who Jesus was. I explained the gospel and the grace of God. Tears welled up in her eyes, and she gripped my arm. She said, "It is as if scales came off my eyes and the fog cleared. I can finally understand!" I went through the tract "This Was Your Life" and gave her a Gideon Bible. She prayed the sinners' prayer. I sent her a package, and when I called her later, I found that she had been baptized and had joined a good church.

Taxi cab drivers also open up opportunities to share the gospel since they are stuck with you for awhile. Many are Muslims, and they always accept a Bible and take the challenge to read the Book of John when I tell them Jesus could not be just a great prophet because He said He was the Son of God. That means He is either a liar, or crazy, or the Son of God. Then I tell them of Christ's offer of forgiveness, and they are amazed because in their religion they must earn their salvation, and their god is not forgiving.

Tragedies, Car Accidents, and Funerals

I accidentally hit a car in front of me, causing minor damage. When I sent the other driver the check to cover the damage, I wrote him a letter telling him that "it was no accident" and that God had us meet for a reason. I shared the gospel and included a tract. Later my wife had an accident involving more damage, and we spent time sharing the gospel with the fireman and policeman, who subsequently reduced her ticket to nothing but court costs. We talked at length and gave a Bible to the tow truck driver and his fiancée. They were very interested and willing to read the Bible together while driving around in their truck.

Our neighbor David had three sons. His wife had died a year earlier, and our family befriended his family as I met with him a few times to share the gospel. Then one day at work I received a frantic call from my wife that his seven-year-old son had been struck by a car going forty miles an hour as he crossed the street in front of our house. David was crying as he held his bleeding son as they rushed him to the hospital. The doctors did not expect him to live. I left work and met Tracy at the hospital. For the next few days we cared for David's other two children and taught them of the Lord. Tracy and I took turns ministering to David in the hospital, helping him stop being angry with God. We prayed, our church prayed, and a miracle happened. The son lived and woke up from his coma on Easter Sunday! In this process, we led David to Christ and discipled him over the next few years. God uses tragedy to open hearts.

When Tracy's grandma died, she went to the funeral and spent time with relatives she had not seen in years. She was able to share the gospel with her estranged father and his wife. This opened a previously shut door and has made it possible for our family to minister the gospel to them since that time. I had a similar opportunity when my closest cousin died in a horrible car accident. I wrote a *public letter* to my cousin recounting our life together and sharing the gospel. I distributed it to my other seven cousins and two aunts and uncles at a time when they were most open.

When someone dies, it is a wonderful time to share the gospel because those who knew the deceased are suddenly thinking about death and where they are headed. We need to give needy people hope of eternal life with Jesus.

A Few Principles of Evangelism

Jesus, in the Great Commission, commanded all of us to share His gospel and to make disciples of all nations.

- *The unsaved need a preacher.* Paul said, "How will they believe in Him whom they have not heard? And how will they hear without a preacher? . . . 'HOW BEAUTIFUL ARE THE FEET OF THOSE WHO BRING GOOD NEWS OF GOOD THINGS!'" (Rom. 10:14–15). We cannot just keep the news to ourselves. We must not fear sharing the gospel. One of Satan's greatest deceptions is to make us fear sharing the best news we could possibly share with others. We often cannot bear the thought of penetrating another person's comfort zone or risking rejection. First Peter 3:14–15 encourages us, "'AND DO NOT FEAR THEIR INTIMIDATION, AND DO NOT BE TROUBLED,' but sanctify Christ as Lord in your hearts." Pray to God that He will send His Holy Spirit to help you overcome this fear. Remember, although you overcome the fear, it will never be easy to share the gospel. I have shared the gospel with hundreds of people one-on-one, and it still takes effort to break into other people's comfort zones.

- *Always be ready.* "Always being ready to make a defense to everyone who asks you to give an account for the hope that is in you, yet with gentleness and reverence" (1 Pet. 3:15). We need to be ready. One practical way for us to be ready is to always carry tracts and Bibles with us to share with those we meet. We also have to be prepared to explain the gospel to anyone so they, too, can hear and hopefully believe.

- *We are the light of the world.* Jesus made it clear that we cannot hide the light of the gospel under a bushel, but rather we need to put our light on a lamp stand so "it gives light to all who are in the house" (Matt. 5:15).

- *We cannot lose.* "But thanks be to God, who always leads us in triumph in Christ, and manifests through us the sweet aroma of the knowledge of Him in every place" (2 Cor. 2:14). God promises us that He will lead us in triumph in Christ every single time. But how can this be true, since not all are saved? The next verses state, "For we are a fragrance of Christ to God among those who are being saved and among those who are perishing; to the one an aroma from death to death, to the other an aroma from life to life. And who is adequate for these things?" (2 Cor. 2:15–16). When we share the gospel, it will either bring that person closer to Jesus and to a final commitment or push them further away and toward condemnation to eternal death. We need to stop making excuses that we are not adequate. In this passage, Paul admitted that none of us are adequate for these things alone. It is Christ who will strengthen us to be able to share the gospel.

- *Life is too short.* We need to come to the realization that life is too short and hell is too long for us to delay. Every moment we delay, more people die in sin. It is an intense spiritual battle that we cannot physically see, but it is raging all around us. God uses us to bring the message of salvation to lost souls. It is hard to accept the fact that some will die eternally. Some of them will be our friends. We need to truly desire in our hearts that no one should go to hell.

So how do you start sharing the gospel with a stranger? You can begin by talking briefly about some common ground. Once I was in a store and I heard a song being sung by Sonny Bono. I mentioned to the clerk how sad I was that he died so suddenly. She agreed, and we began talking about how easy it is to die. After a few minutes, I introduced the gospel to her and left her with a tract. I closed by simply saying, "You can know for certain where you will go when you die. Here is the way to heaven: Jesus Christ."

In another incident I was talking with a farmer named Rufus who was explaining how he loved walking through his fields and seeing the beauty of nature. He admitted that farmers, of all people, know there is a God. That gave me the opportunity to build on the understanding that he had in order to share the full gospel with him.

People often relate to suffering. Share your heart with them about someone you know who died recently or about a near-death experience that you had, such as a car accident. You might explain a personal struggle or hardship. If you are personal and vulnerable, people will open up.

I ask people if they are Christians, and then I quickly ask if they are born-again Christians. There are two questions that usually separate the true believers. I always ask them, *If you died today, are you certain you would go to heaven?* Most people are not. Then I ask them, *What would you say if God asked you why He should let you into heaven?* When answering this question, most people say that they have lived a good life.

Then I explain to them what *born again* means. I tell them the story of Nicodemus from John 3. I simply repeat the story with a lot of details so that they can relate to Nicodemus's situation. I tell them that they must be born of the Spirit. As Jesus said, this born-again experience involves the old man fading away and being replaced with the new man. It is an internal transformation. They can fool me, but they cannot fool God.

I then share John 3:16 with them and also explain Romans 6:23 KJV, "For the wages of sin is death; but the gift of God is eternal life through Jesus Christ our Lord." In sharing Romans 3:23, I emphasize that "all have sinned and fall short of the glory of God." Isaiah 64:6 NKJV, states that "all our righteousnesses [works] are like filthy rags." There is no way they can earn their way to heaven. I try to help them recognize their sin and need for a Savior.

The only way they can change and reach heaven is through Jesus. In John 14:6, "Jesus said to him, 'I am the way, and the truth, and the life; no one comes to the Father but through Me.'" As God says in Acts 4:12, "For there is no other name . . . by which we must be saved." Finally, I explain that they must truly repent of these sins (turn away) and confess them because 1 John 1:9 NKJV says, "He is faithful and just to forgive us our sins and to cleanse us from all unrighteousness." I quote Romans 10:9, "If you confess with your mouth Jesus as Lord, and believe in your heart that God raised Him from the dead, you will be saved."

There is a three-fold commitment. First, you must believe in your heart that Jesus is your Savior and that you need a Savior. He died and rose again for your sins. Second, He must become Lord of your life. You must read and obey His Word, the Bible. Third, there is urgency to make a decision, "Behold, now is . . . 'THE DAY OF SALVATION'" (2 Cor. 6:2) and "As it is appointed for men to die once, but after this the judgment" (Heb. 9:27 NKJV). There is no second chance.

It Is God Who Saves

Remember, the more you practice, the easier it gets. It does not get easier to break the ice or penetrate someone's comfort zone, but it does get easier to explain the gospel and to be able to respond to the various questions people ask. If you do not practice evangelism, it becomes more difficult. Commit yourself at least to give a tract to everyone you personally meet.

Don't get discouraged! God saves, not you. First Corinthians 3:6–7 KJV says, "I have planted, Apollos watered; but God gave the increase. So then neither is he that planteth any thing, neither he that watereth; but God that giveth the increase." We need only to obey. God will open blind eyes in His timing. I have had the opportunity to share with many people in an airplane. Most often I am convinced that people will not respond to the gospel; but amazingly, I find the good news of Jesus Christ brings tears to the eyes of the most unlikely candidates, and they willingly give their hearts to the Lord. Of course, many more people simply delay and say they will think about it. Some simply reject it outright. Just imagine if a third of the readers of this chapter started to incorporate this lifestyle evangelism into their daily routines. What a tremendous light home school families would be to those stumbling in the darkness!

May God guide you and richly bless you as you train your children and use your home schooling in this additional dimension for Jesus Christ. How beautiful are the feet of those who bring Good News!

Resources

American Tract Society
P.O. Box 462008
Garland, TX 75046
800/548-7228

Chick Publications
P.O. Box 662
Chino, CA 91708
909/987-0771
The tracts I find most effective are "This Was Your Life," "The Empty Tomb," and
"The Greatest Story Ever Told."

Living Water Publications
P.O. Box 1172
Bellflower, CA 90706
800/437-1893

The Gideons International
2900 Lebanon Road
Nashville, TN 37214
615/883-8533
This is an excellent source for Bibles and Bible distribution.

What to give new Christians right after they accept Christ:
Beginning Again
By D. James Kennedy
Coral Ridge Ministries
800/229-9673
Coral Ridge also has an effective evangelism program called "Evangelism
Explosion" and at least two excellent tracts.

The Home School Missionary Effort around the World: What You Can Do

Y ou could see it in their eyes. You could feel it throughout the room. The excitement and hope was welling up inside each member of the audience. They nodded knowingly as I reminded them of the inestimable value of their children and the dangers facing them in the present culture. Their faces showed mixed emotions of both fear and hope.

They drank up every word of each speaker that day as the reasons, rights, and practical steps of home schooling were presented. They were completely focused. This is what they were looking for as they sought a solution to their children's training and education.

The meeting ended, and they were enthusiastic. Many committed themselves to go against tradition and against the mainstream to home school. It was reminiscent of the home schooling movement in America in the mid-1980s, when parents were risking virtually everything to be different and answer God's call.

The place was Tokyo, Japan, in August 2000, and the parents had come from all over the country to be encouraged and instructed.

This was not a unique experience. I have seen this scene from Japan repeated in places where I spoke to thousands of parents in other countries near and far: South Africa, French-speaking Quebec, Mexico, Switzerland, and Germany. Parents everywhere are desperate for hope and

CHAPTER THIRTEEN

the opportunity to train their own children. The moral decay in the government schools is common to many countries. The parents are starving for more information.

It has become increasingly apparent to me as I have traveled that home schooling is no longer a United States phenomenon. Home schooling is gradually but steadily spreading across the world.

The Internet is playing a large role in bringing the world closer together. As parents in foreign countries find home school Web pages and learn about its invaluable benefits for their children, they want to home school too. However, they check their laws and find out it is not legal. In fact, it is very similar to the legal atmosphere in our country in the 1980s.

Reaching Out to Help the Least of These in Foreign Countries

These families in foreign countries hear the call of God to home school, but the legal barriers seem insurmountable. They do not know where to start, so they turn to that beacon of home school liberty: the United States. We are blessed to be living in the country with the most advanced home school freedoms in the world.

Inevitably, they contact me at the Home School Legal Defense Association in my role as Director of State and International Relations to find out what we did to win the right to home school.

When I started working for HSLDA in 1985, I would never have dreamed that we could help home schooling become legalized in other countries. We were just trying to survive in the United States. Yet God blessed us with many victories in the courts and legislatures to bring us to this day when it is clearly legal in all fifty states.

Although the home school movement in many countries is only a fledgling movement, it is beginning to take hold. But the first step in many western and Asian countries is to make it legal.

One of the goals of the Home School Legal Defense Association is to help the least of these in other countries by exporting the knowledge and lessons we have learned through our struggle as home schoolers to be free here in America. We also want to share the many benefits of home schooling, which involves distributing various studies demonstrating the academic success of home schoolers at the elementary, secondary, and college levels.

Most important of all is our desire to share the light of Jesus Christ through the vehicle of home schooling. Home schooling enables families to teach what really matters: knowing Jesus as their Savior and obeying Him as Lord. More and more families home schooling on the foundation of the Word of God will bring blessings to the nations around the world.

The HSLDA legal staff works regularly with home school leaders and home school associations in various countries. The assistance includes recommending legal and political strategies, sending home school studies and materials, corresponding and sometimes meeting with members of parliament and various government officials, organizing letter-writing campaigns to various foreign embassies, talking to the foreign press, visiting and speaking in the country, and helping establish national legal defense associations for home schoolers.

HSLDA has also provided seed money to start legal defense associations, purchase printing equipment, and buy other needed resources to home school leaders in various countries.

The Call to Be a Home School Missionary

My hope is that home schoolers throughout the U.S. will catch this vision of being home school missionaries, consider ways they can help, and pray for parents just like us who live in foreign lands looking for hope for their children.

To help you catch the vision, I will describe, in this chapter, the condition of education in various countries, the obstacles faced by parents trying to home school, and how American home schoolers have helped.

As you read these true accounts of the struggles home schoolers face in the several countries below, please keep in mind how the Lord might move you to help. I know how much of a blessing home schooling has been to our family, and I want other families around the world to be able to train their children in the Lord through home schooling.

Please keep in mind the following suggestions on how you can help these Christian families around the world as you read this chapter.

What Can You Do?

The world is a big place. The task of helping other countries legalize home schooling is daunting. The curriculum needs are great. We can't do everything, but we can do something. And what we can do, we ought to do to help the least of these who are desperate for our support.

Here are some suggestions on what you can do:

1. Adopt a country for your family. Learn all you can about the home school movement there by checking the HSLDA Web site at www.hslda.org. For each country, we summarize the laws, home school population, and the latest news. We also give a short history of the development of the home school movement in that country and a description of the Christian home school associations.

Use this ministry as an opportunity to instruct your children and do a unit study on the country. Have your children explore its history, culture, traditions, and geography. Consider developing pen pals by directly contacting the organizations listed on HSLDA's Web site.

2. Pray regularly for home schoolers around the world. There is power in prayer! We have seen the miracles God has done on behalf of home schoolers here in the United States. (See my book *Home Schooling: The Right Choice,* which recounts many of the times God delivered home schoolers from the authorities in the United States.)

If we do not pray for home schoolers, who will?

3. Join HSLDA to support our efforts to assist other countries in helping home schooling to become legalized. Without members, HSLDA could not assist home schoolers in other countries as we have to this point. This chapter tells many of the stories of how God used home school families who are members of HSLDA to turn the tide in countries like Ireland, South Africa, and Germany. You can join HSLDA by calling 540/338–5600 or visiting our Web site at www.hslda.org.

Not only will your membership support our foreign home school efforts, but it will also guarantee your family legal protection from the authorities if you ever are challenged. Membership in HSLDA is an investment in our work before the legislatures in all fifty states and the U.S. Congress to protect home school freedoms, parental rights, and religious liberties. We commission home school research, promote home schooling with the press, and help home schoolers get admitted to college. We handle hundreds of home school cases and more than six thousand legal conflicts faced by member families each year who are threatened by social workers, truant officers, prosecutors, and school officials.

4. *Respond to HSLDA alerts by writing or calling foreign embassies,* encouraging them to inform their governments that parents need to be allowed to home school. You can also share some of the benefits. These alerts have been very effective in influencing governments in most nations. It is amazing to contemplate that a letter from you on your home computer or a phone call can make a difference so far away!

5. *Donate money, used books, and home school products* to help the fledgling home school organizations succeed.

6. *Offer resources* to the foreign home school families to help them locate a curriculum.

7. *Convince your home school support group to do a fundraiser to help a particular country or foreign Christian home school association.* You can bring information to your local support group about the needs or troubles home schoolers are facing in a particular country. Then take up a collection or make a care package of curriculum materials to send the Christian home school association.

There are many other ideas, but these will give you a good beginning.

Let us take a moment and read the true stories of what God is doing on behalf of home schoolers in several countries. You will notice that each home school movement has its own unique trials and blessings. I will begin with the growth of the home school movements in Japan and Germany. The origins of the home school movements in these two countries, as you will see, are very different.

Home Schooling Grows in Japan and Germany

In Germany, the home school movement may be small, but the families are committed. Most of the home schoolers are Christians who believe that God has called them to home school. Much like the laws in the United States, the German compulsory attendance laws are enacted by each state. No laws specifically allow for home schooling, though each state allows school officials some discretionary authority to approve alternative education. While some families have obtained this approval, most families operate underground. Many families are taken to court.

In April 2000, I traveled to Germany, along with my wife and oldest daughter, to speak to American military home schoolers located there, as well as some of the German home school families. The German home school families that I observed were very excited about the conference and hung on every word spoken there. However, they were also worn out and somewhat discouraged because of the legal climate in Germany.

I met one particular father, Johann Harder, whose house had just been ransacked by the police. They broke in through the window, turned over furniture, emptied drawers, and dumped out the contents of the closets looking for their children. The police tried to find the Harder children so that they could force them to attend public school. A couple of the children escaped through an attic window and others remained hidden. The police caught and took one child to the public school that day. At the time, Mrs. Harder had a newborn infant, further escalating the trauma. Mr. Harder met with me and pleaded with me, asking if American home schoolers could do something to help him. He was facing court action that threatened to take away his children. I promised to see what I could do for him.

While I was in Germany, I met with half a dozen German lawyers to discuss strategy and to begin creating a network with many of the German home school families. My goal was to persuade them to establish a legal defense association for home schoolers so that home schoolers would not be picked off one by one in the courtroom. I was able to convince another organization, Christians for Truth, which has approximately one thousand members, to fully endorse a soon-to-be-established legal defense association. Rich and Ingrid Guenther, who helped follow up on all these contacts, have worked tirelessly for the German home school movement.

Upon returning to the States, we launched a nationwide alert on June 5, 2000, requesting American home schoolers to contact the German embassy to protest the criminal prosecution of the Harder family for their choice to home school. An embassy official confirmed that she received at least one thousand E-mails and between three and four hundred letters from concerned home schoolers. The official also said that the embassy informed the

German government about the outpouring of public opinion. In addition to the letter-writing campaign in the States, Terri Harding in Australia, Mike Richardson in Mexico, and home school leaders in other countries distributed our alert, generating calls to various German embassies throughout the world. Within three weeks, the scheduled court hearing for the custody of the Harder children was inexplicably canceled. A few days later, their attorney, Frau Eckermann, received a formal notice that the case had been dismissed and the charges dropped. The German home school leaders wrote: "We home schoolers here in Germany cannot offer thanks enough to HSLDA for your involvement and the involvement of thousands of home school families in response to your alert. Because of all of you, your prayers and actions, the Harders have been relieved of their heavy burden—the threat of their children being taken away from them. You being there for us, your counsel and actions throughout this whole ordeal, were so helpful, needed, and encouraging. You have given us real hope."

This was an amazing result and an answer to prayer. However, the work is not done: Other German home schoolers have pending cases in court.

Around the same time, four business associates of the Atmark Corporation from Japan visited me. Over the last couple of years, Japan has been plagued with tremendous dropout rates in their high schools and junior high schools: more than 300,000 children are dropping out of school each year. School bullying has also become a major problem. Japanese schools are experiencing moral decline that is similar to that in public schools in America and throughout Europe. The business community and the press also realize that the schools in Japan are suffering. Businesses no longer want factory workers. They want graduates who have ingenuity and individualism and can break out of the molds to create new ideas. As a result, the business community is seeking solutions that might give children who dropped out of school a good reason to return to their studies.

The four businessmen who visited my office were in the process of starting a business venture to provide a tutoring program to high schoolers in Japan. During their visit, they wanted to know everything I could share with them about the home school movement here in the States. I helped them expand their vision to provide a program not only for high schoolers but also for kindergarten to eighth grades. Because the Japanese government is most likely to listen to the business community, I encouraged them to work toward legalizing home schooling in Japan. Unlike Germany, the business community is driving the home school movement, and the Japanese press is enthralled. Shortly after my meeting with the businessmen from Atmark, the two largest TV broadcasting companies in Tokyo, Tokyo Broadcasting Service (TBS) and NHK-TV, came to my office to interview us about home schooling and our grassroots successes before the legislatures. Subsequently, two one-hour specials on home schooling aired in Japan.

I was invited by the Atmark Corporation to go to Japan to speak at the first meeting of a national home school conference. I had urged the businessmen to hold a conference and create a national home school association. The plan was to launch this organization, HOSA, at the time of the conference. I encouraged them to hold a press conference and to set up a meeting with the Ministry of Education.

As I made my travel plans for Japan, I learned that I could go through Frankfurt on the way to Japan. I asked the Atmark Corporation if they would pay for me to have an extended layover in Frankfurt so that I could help establish the national legal defense association for home schoolers in Germany. Atmark agreed to pay for the layover. During my layovers in Frankfurt, both on the way to and from Japan, we were able to establish a new national home school organization, *Schulunterricht zu Hause* (School Instruction at Home). Now German home schoolers' resources can be pooled together in one organization to help finance their cases and provide funds to negotiate with the German authorities for changes to the laws.

When my wife and I arrived in Japan, the Tokyo Broadcasting Service (TBS) was waiting at the gate and filmed us as we walked down the corridors to customs. After going through customs, the TBS reporters whisked my wife and me away in separate vehicles to take us to the hotel. During the trip to the hotel, a cameraman in the front seat filmed me while I was interviewed in the backseat.

Over the next several days, I had nonstop interviews with the Japanese press and spoke at a large press conference with all the major networks and newspapers in attendance. Some of the newspapers that carried excellent stories on home schooling were the *Daily Yomiuri*, the *Nikkei* (the *Wall Street Journal* of Japan), the *Tokyo Shimbun* (the largest paper in Tokyo), *Japan*

Today.com, and many others. The newly established home school association, HOSA, had been endorsed by the president of Microsoft of Japan and other major business leaders. The university community also endorsed HOSA. In fact, the president of HOSA, Shigeru Narita, is an education professor at Hyogo University. Akio Hata, a professor at the Saitama Institute of Technology, also serves on the board of HOSA. The vice-chairman of HOSA, Kozo Hino, is the president of Atmark. He and his advisor, Jun Adachi, were the main organizers of HOSA and were instrumental in involving the press. HOSA's magazine is of nearly the same quality as *Practical Home Schooling Magazine*, albeit shorter.

The business leaders arranged for me to meet with a high-level official in the Ministry of Education who, upon understanding the home school concept, highly endorsed the idea. Because Japan's compulsory attendance law is at the federal level, the Ministry of Education's decisions and opinions are very important to local school authorities. The official indicated that he was interested in possibly signing a letter publicly endorsing the home schooling concept.

TBS and NHK came to our offices in the United States for a second time to do additional programs. The last program aired by TBS resulted in well over three hundred phone calls to HOSA from interested persons. As a result, dozens of new home school families have joined the HOSA organization. My wife and I were utterly amazed at the professionalism of the HOSA organization and the 100 percent support of the Japanese media.

In the meantime, the Christian Home Educators Association of Japan (CHEA of Japan) has started with Hiro Inaba as president. I was able to network CHEA and HOSA and encourage them to work together as partners. CHEA of Japan mainly represents the small Christian community of parents interested in home schooling in Japan. They have both asked me back.

HOSA and the home schoolers of Japan are now looking for curricular materials to translate into Japanese and are also working with the Christian home schoolers to develop Japanese curricula. God brought many things together to help these Japanese and German home school organizations to be established. The new German organization, Schulunterricht zu Hause, can be contacted by E-mail at info@german-homeschool.de. The contact for

CHEA of Japan is Hiro Inaba, who can be E-mailed at HiroInaba@chea-japan.com. For more information on HOSA, visit their Web site at www.home school.ne.jp or contact Jun Adachi at adachi8@E-mail.msn.com.

Hungary Yearns for Home Schooling

As a former Soviet satellite, Hungary has now become a free country. Unfortunately, the most decadent aspects of Western culture are quickly filling the spiritual vacuum left behind. The school system is thoroughly secularized, and parents are looking for options. Dr. Gene Antonio, a home school father of seven and former missionary to Hungary, explained that "we are dealing with sharp, educated, English-speaking people who intend to home educate their children bilingually." He explained that the need and desire is there, but the families simply need to be reached, encouraged, and taught how to home school. Dr. Antonio said the greatest need is home school materials.

The main group establishing a national home school association with HSLDA's assistance is the Karoly Gaspar Institute of Theology and Missions headed by the Rev. Imre Scszokoe, who visited me in our offices along with Dr. Bob Rapp, a missionary to Hungary. Please pray for the home school movement in Hungary. Rev. Imre Scszokoe can be reached at kgtmi@matavnet.hu.

Mexico: Home Schooling
Is Discipling Families in the Lord

In 1999 in Mexico, more than six hundred Mexicans attended a home school conference in Saltillo, near Monterrey. Some families traveled as long as thirty hours to reach the conference! Nearly all the Mexican states were represented, as well as Costa Rica and Guatemala.

As I spoke, I saw how the Lord was working in a mighty way among the people at the conference. They were deeply sensitive to the convicting power of God's Word and eager to have His will done in their families. With many tears, the Spanish-speaking families expressed their profound gratitude for the conference (which was offered free of charge) and for the preaching and teaching on building godly families.

I discovered how the youth in Mexico and the Latin American countries are under the same secular assault as here in our country. I believe home schooling will continue to expand rapidly as more and more families find out about its benefits.

Without clear compulsory attendance laws, home schooling is flourishing legally. Quality education is hard to come by in Mexico, and many families are poor. Home schooling is providing an answer to this educational dilemma. It is enabling families to work together to make sure that each of their children receives a good and affordable education.

Mike Richardson, a missionary and home school father, had a vision three years ago to start an outreach ministry to encourage Latin American families to home school. His goal for this ministry is twofold: to serve as a conduit for the gospel and to restore families. He offers a free home school newsletter in Spanish that is sent to hundreds of families throughout Mexico and Latin America. He also organizes the annual home school conference outside Monterrey (Saltillo). HSLDA provided funds to purchase a professional printing machine to publish a Spanish home school newsletter that is now being distributed throughout Mexico and more than fifteen other nations.

To receive Mike Richardson's Spanish home schooling newsletter, *El Hogar Educador,* or to contribute to his ministry, E-mail him at vnm@characterlink.net or call 011.528.483.0377.

Brazil: *Fighting Home Schooling All the Way*

In 2000, the Home School Legal Defense Association received an urgent plea from a family in Brazil asking us to help them legalize home schooling there. The Carlos Vilhena family has been quietly home schooling since 1990. Carlos is a federal prosecutor who decided to boldly seek recognition for his home school. He said many people home school in Brazil, but they are underground because it is not officially recognized.

Carlos Vilhena explained, "The laws in Brazil are slightly less harsh than the ones in Germany considering school life. The peaceful nature of

Brazilians does not preclude the possibility of Brazilian [home school] pioneers suffering the same constraints as their German counterparts. With this in mind, we are asking for international help to bring acceptance of [home schooling] to Brazil and that it would serve as a model of peaceful change."

In Brazil the compulsory attendance law (ages seven to fourteen) is a federal law, and the federal Council of Education can issue a policy to allow or prohibit home schooling. Carlos submitted petition 9#23001000301/ 00–37 through his state government (Goias) requesting that the federal Council of Education recognize home schooling.

HSLDA alerted home school leaders around the U.S. to contact Brazil's Federal Council of Education and urge them to support home schooling. Unfortunately, although these efforts won over some of the council, the majority ruled that the Vilhena family could no longer home school—and then proceeded to prohibit home schooling for everyone in Brazil!

Since then, the Vilhenas' attorney, Dr. Aristides Junqueira, former Prosecutor General of Brazil, has filed a counter motion, petitioning the Superior Judicial Court to order the minister of education to reject the Federal Council of Education's opinion and instead to legally recognize home schooling.

This is a crucial juncture for home schooling in Brazil. The outcome of the Vilhenas' current crisis could set a permanent precedent—for better or for worse.

Irish Home Schoolers Avoid Restrictive Legislation

The home school movement of Ireland is small, but the right of parents to home school was about to be severely diminished late in 1999. The Irish Senate passed a dangerous bill that would have required home schoolers to register and be subject to periodic assessments at the whim of the school authorities. Worst of all, the bill would have required home schoolers to submit to home visits where the *education welfare officer* would observe instruction taking place, inspect the premises, and carry out an on-site assessment of the child's intellectual, emotional, and physical development.

The Irish home schoolers asked for our help. In response, HSLDA launched a nationwide alert and HSLDA members sent hundreds of letters and calls to the Irish embassy. I worked with home school attorney Elizabeth Bruton to help plan a strategy for organizing the home schoolers and lobbying the legislature. She corresponded with more than fifteen key members of the Lower House in an attempt to persuade them to derail the bill. The calls of HSLDA members in the United States to the Irish Embassy significantly contributed to the willingness of the Irish parliament members and minister of education to agree to a compromise. In the final passage of the bill this summer, mandatory home visits for all home schoolers were removed.

Home school leader Elizabeth Bruton wrote, "Thank you for the invaluable help given by HSLDA and your members in lobbying for changes to the proposed home school legislation. Home schooling in Ireland was facing a bleak future. Parents were to be confronted with mandatory home visits and wide ranging assessments of their children before being allowed to home school. As a result of the lobbying, the government has made significant concessions. Families who diligently educate their children at home can confidently proceed."

When home schoolers lobby, they make a difference—even across the ocean. We are thankful to God for blessing the prayers and efforts of home school families in the U.S. and Ireland.

Taiwan: Steady as She Goes

Home schooling has overcome a tremendous obstacle in the island country of Taiwan. Home schooling in Taiwan was officially legalized on June 24, 1999.

Until recently, elementary- and junior-high-school-aged (grades one through nine) children had to attend public school or private school—no exceptions. As a result, the great majority of home schooled children could only be preschoolers and kindergartners. Only a handful of them were school aged.

Some parents with school-aged children were able to reach an agreement with sympathetic local school officials to teach their children at home most of the time and take tests along with classmates. Some decided to withdraw their children from school completely, simply praying and hoping that school officials wouldn't bother to pursue them.

The Home Educators' Fellowship, a Christian organization, was founded in August 1998 to unite home educators, keep up with legal issues, and organize/share teaching resources, while adhering to biblical principles. Shou-kong and Chuo-chuin Fan are home schooling parents who founded the organization. It now has more than 120 member families nationwide (about 90 percent Christians, 15 percent pastors). Now that it's legal, the Fans are observing a big surge of families taking their children out of both elementary and junior high schools.

The government of Taiwan invited the Home Educators' Fellowship to help draft the new regulating policy. I had the privilege of providing counsel and helping model language that was used as the basis for proposals at the meetings with the government.

To support the home schoolers in Taiwan, contact the Home Educators' Fellowship at lfpower@ms26.hinet.net or skfan@tpts5.seed.net.tw.

Canada: Home Schooling Is Thriving

The vast country to our north, Canada, is experiencing a steady growth of parents who have chosen home schooling. Home schooling is presently legal in all provinces, but the requirements are varied.

In the early 1990s, the Home School Legal Defense Association of Canada was established. Michael Smith and I (of the Home School Legal Defense Association in the U.S.) are on the board, along with Canadian home school fathers Jack Baribeau and Dan Rhinehart. Mike and I have traveled to Canada many times to speak to home school conferences throughout most of the provinces.

Dallas Miller, senior counsel of HSLDA of Canada, is spearheading efforts in a number of trouble spots to protect the rights of home schoolers. For example, in Ontario and Quebec, school board officials are attempting to apply vague laws in an unfriendly manner against home schoolers. Problems also continue in the Maritime Provinces where school officials have discretionary approval over home schoolers.

In addition to dealing with school board officials, an increasing number of families in Canada are the recipients of unfriendly contacts from social workers. Home schoolers in every province are susceptible to investigations because of the methods of discipline or as a result of anonymous complaints. HSLDA of Canada has noted two cases in the law reports where home schooling families were prosecuted by social services and the courts found in favor of parental rights and family autonomy.

In May 1999, the newly established Association of Christian Home Educators of Quebec (ACHEQ) held their first Home School Conference and Curriculum Fair in Montreal. Dallas Miller and I addressed the audience on the rights and freedoms of home schoolers. The parents who founded the organization, Rod and Cheryl Stilwell, were the main organizers of the event. They were particularly pleased with the response from the French-speaking community. The Quebec home schoolers were clearly thirsty for information on home schooling and excited to have a province-wide Christian home school organization.

You can contact HSLDA of Canada at info@hsldacanada.org or visit the Web site at www.hsldacanada.org.

South Africa: The Battle Is Not Over

South Africa has come a long way in the last seven years. In 1993, home schooling was illegal in South Africa. When Andre and Bokkie Mientjies were sentenced to two years in jail for home schooling, South African home schooler Graham Shortridge, in desperation, contacted us for help. I launched a nationwide campaign for home schoolers to write to the South African embassy demanding the Mientjies release. The calls and pressure worked, and the Mientjies were soon released.

In 1995, the national government released a report indicating that home schooling would be legal only if the parents were licensed and approved at the discretion of the Department of Education. Over the next year and a half, I worked closely with Leendert van Oostrum of Pretoria, Graham Shortridge of Capetown, and various parliament members to spearhead three more nationwide alerts at key junctures of debate in the national parliament. Each alert helped turned the tide further in favor of the home schoolers. Finally, in December 1996, the education act passed, formally legalizing home schooling. But the battles continue as the government tries to impose burdensome, arbitrary requirements on home schoolers.

The South African leaders invited me and Tracy to speak in five cities in 1997: Pretoria, Durban, Capetown, Dundee, and Pietermartinzburg. The country is very diverse with eleven official languages. There are many black tribes, Afrikaners of European descent who arrived in the 1600s, English, Coloureds, and Indians. Yet parents from all these very different groups care about their children and are concerned about the secularization of their public schools. They have united to maintain the right to home school their children.

As we spoke and shared the American home schoolers' struggle to be free, the South African parents understood and took courage. When my wife spoke on how to home school and how to manage toddlers, the mothers gave her their undivided attention, thirsting for more. As I watched the crowd, I could see tears in the eyes of these loving parents.

We had Christian radio interviews wherever we went, and the interest in home schooling was high.

While I was there, I helped establish a legal defense fund and agreed to serve on the board. The Pestalozzi Trust, The Legal Defense Fund for Home Education, was formally organized with Leendert van Oostrum as president.

The Pestalozzi Trust is now growing in membership (this past year they went from one hundred to five hundred members). It counsels home schoolers throughout the country who have been contacted by the authorities. The board members and Leendert speak at conferences and network the home schoolers. Much tedious work is presently being done in province after province as they wrestle with very vague home school regulations.

Please pray for God's protection for the home schoolers during this volatile time. Also be ready to write or call the South African embassy if needed!

The Pestalozzi Trust uses the following E-mail address: defensor@lantic.net. Their Web site is http://pestalozzi.org.

Czech Republic: U.S. Home Schoolers Shut Down Parliament

I recently returned from a trip to the Czech Republic, where I met with Michal Semin, president of the Czech home school association. Nearly all the home schoolers in the country are part of his association. He described the uphill battle that home school parents faced to keep the freedom to teach their own children. He asked if we could send out an alert because he believed the international perspective would be well received. I also sent him two hundred copies of home school studies to give to parliament members.

Home education in the Czech Republic is only temporarily legal—pursuant to a governmental order that expires after a five-year experiment—and strictly limited to the first five years of elementary schooling, or for children from about six-to-ten-years old. Existing education law simply describes obligatory school attendance as the norm, with no mention of home education.

Under the five-year law, every home schooling family must enroll in one of three government-recognized schools, which minimally "supervise" the home education program. The schools issue a certificate of permission twice each year, and the children have to be tested. No federal agencies are involved in the process.

The Ministry of Education issued a new bill in November 2001, that continued to limit home schooling to the first five years and added a new set of restrictions. These require the home school parents to communicate with the local education agency that supervises area schools. This agency, then, would decide if there are serious enough reasons for the child to be home schooled. In the interview with agency officials, parents would have to specify their reasons for choosing home education and disclose other private information, such as their facilities and income.

We organized a massive blitz by members of the Home School Legal Defense Association to lobby on behalf of the home schoolers in the Czech Republic. In just twenty-four hours, over eight-hundred members E-mailed the two hundred members of the Czech Parliament, resulting in over 150,000 E-mails in support of the Czech home schooling movement. A local Prague newspaper reported that the parliament E-mail server was shut down by the volume of messages coming in on the home school issue!

So many E-mails came in on this issue that the Czech server stopped accepting out-of-country E-mail. The Czech home schoolers then asked us to do a "second wave" to make certain their government was aware that the home school legislation was attracting world-wide attention and to encourage them to recognize home school freedoms.

Thousands of E-mails to both the Czech Parliament and Embassy had a strong effect. We received a report from Michal Semin, the president of the Czech Republic National Home School Association, about the crisis in the Czech Parliament over their attempt to excessively regulate home schoolers.

Michal reported, "We are winning! The U.S. campaign has produced good fruit." He said there was "some angry noise among the parliamentarians because the E-mail letters had pulled down the whole server so not a single parliamentarian could use his personal E-mail account and Internet during the whole day." He then explained further, "On the other hand, they realize their work is being closely watched not only by Czech home schoolers, but around the world!" Michal believed the U.S. campaign was a complete success.

Michal personally spoke with many members of Parliament (MPs) and they all informed him that they were fascinated by the fact that the letters were not simply a copy of one original letter. They were impressed that each letter was different and personally written. The MPs said this is "the first time that any pressure group was so well organized in making itself heard."

The Parliament Committee on Education had a hearing on the home school legislation where many Czech parents came to represent the home schoolers. The Czech home schoolers were able to provide the members of Parliament with several documents about home schooling including two studies supplied by HSLDA. The central-right party succeeded, as a result, in postponing a decision on the home school legislation indefinitely. There was an effort by the Communist party to make home education illegal again, but there was little chance of this proposal succeeding. Michal Semin noted, "It is good to remind us how evil Communism is."

The Czech home schoolers also produced a ten-minute professional video clip on a computer CD for distribution along with the other materials to the parliamentarians.

The Czech home schoolers thanked all of the U.S. home schoolers for their assistance in preserving their freedom. Michal Semin ended with a note to me: "Please tell all your members how thankful we are for all their help and prayers!!! I wish I could thank each one personally, but then I would have to spend days and nights in front of a computer and would probably die from that!"

Conclusion: Many More Countries Need Our Help

In addition to these countries, we are also working with the authorities in Switzerland and Sweden. In fact, one of the largest TV stations in Sweden came to our office to interview us on home schooling. As a result, a nation-wide program on home schooling was aired, making many more people in Sweden aware.

We are also working with the Philippines, Belgium, Austria, Australia, South Korea, and Honduras. More nations are contacting us each month. The need is great, and the workers are few.

As I write the last few chapters in this book, I am visiting Germany and the Czech Republic to aid the home school movements again. I met for several hours with a producer, Peter Adler, of Channel 2. He is preparing to do a thirty-minute special on home schooling for 2.5 million viewers. This will help home schooling get off the ground in a big way and embarrass the aggressive school officials.

God is working throughout the world through home schooling. I am convinced that where home schooling goes, the gospel follows.

We need to support the fledgling home school organizations in these countries much as we support other missionaries of the gospel. I hope you will join us to help the least of these.

The Road to Heaven
Is a Narrow Way

T he road to heaven is a narrow way, but the doors to heaven's gates are open wide by the blood of Jesus Christ. We are home schooling, not for home schooling's sake, but for the glory and honor of God. Home schooling is not the end in itself: it is merely the means to the end. It also happens to be the best means for fulfilling God's commands on training our children.

But when all is said and done, the most important goal is for our families to all be standing together in heaven one day. The home school movement is causing a spiritual revival in our country, and it is beginning around the world.

But this revival will fail if home schoolers become complacent and fail to remember what is really the *heart of home schooling.* In this book, I have tried to focus on the most important areas.

We must each nurture our own souls and follow the Bible on how we must train our children in the Lord, shepherd their hearts, and consistently apply godly discipline. We must guard our hearts against the lusts of this world and the temptations of our culture. We must run the race, diligently loving our spouses, sharing the gospel with our neighbors and those within our reach, and equipping our young Christian soldiers in spiritual warfare.

Our home schools will fail and the home school movement will fail if our families break up and we abandon God and His laws.

We need to be certain we know Jesus Christ and have developed an ever-deepening relationship with Him. Therefore, you must ask yourself if you are truly saved and if you are continuing to thoroughly immerse your children

CHAPTER FOURTEEN

in the gospel and the whole counsel of God as found in the Scriptures. Are you so sold out for Him that you want to please Him in all things and particularly in these areas?

You might be wondering, *Why the urgency?* Because hell is too long, and life is too short. In addition, our children are never-dying souls entrusted to our care, and we do not know how long we will have them with us.

Hell Is Too Long

How long is hell? The Bible tells us there is no end. After you are there for ten years and think you cannot stand it anymore, you will be there one hundred years more. After you are there one hundred years longer and have suffered so terribly and think you cannot possibly exist any longer, you will be there a thousand more years—then a million more after that! And then on and on and on!

Life on earth is too short and hell is too long for you to delay another day. Today is the day of salvation (see 2 Cor. 6:2). You do not want God to say to you, "Depart from me, accursed ones, into the eternal fire which has been prepared for the devil and his angels" (Matt. 25:41).

All of us have sinned and fall short of the glory of God (see Rom. 3:23). This includes you and me. And "the wages of sin is death, but the free gift of God is eternal life in Christ Jesus our Lord" (Rom. 6:23). We are doomed. Our good works cannot save us because we continue to sin. Galatians 3:10 makes it clear that to earn our salvation, we must never sin again. So what can we do?

What Must I Do to Be Saved?

Accept Jesus Christ as your Savior! "For God so loved the world, that He gave His only begotten Son, that whoever believes in Him shall not perish, but have eternal life" (John 3:16). Jesus lived a sinless life and willingly paid the penalty for our sins.

You need to "confess with your mouth Jesus as Lord, and believe in your heart that God raised Him from the dead, [and] you will be saved" (Rom. 10:9). No matter what you have done, Christ will forgive you, as long as you sincerely repent from your sins: "If we confess our sins, He is faithful and righteous to forgive us our sins" (1 John 1:9). So you must *believe* in your *heart* that He died on the cross for *your* sins and then rose again. You must accept Him as Savior. He is the *only* way. Jesus said, "I am the way, and the truth, and the life; *no one* comes to the Father, but through Me" (John 14:6).

How Do We Live for God?

Once we truly believe, God sends the Holy Spirit to fill us and opens our eyes to understand His Word, the Bible. Next, we have to live our lives as followers of Jesus like we mean it! If we truly love God, we keep His commandments (see 1 John 5:2–3). We need to nurture a personal relationship with Jesus. That takes time. We must make time *every day* to read His words to us in the Bible. The Bible is how God speaks to us. It is His love letter to us. We must not only read the Bible but also apply the principles He gives us in the Bible. We must die to our own desires and live for Him. We need to go to a church that teaches the Bible to help us grow. The relationship we have with Jesus is the *only* thing we can take with us when we die! He has secured eternal life for us.

My hope is that everyone who reads this book, with the account of the miracle of the birth of Charity and Amy and how the power of God is working through my multiple sclerosis, will come to a saving knowledge of Jesus Christ.

Simply pray to God, confessing your sins and your need for a Savior. Accept in your heart that Jesus died and rose again from the dead, paying the penalty of death for you! Then ask God to forgive you and fill you with His Holy Spirit so you will be saved for all eternity. Repent and turn from your sins, making Jesus Lord of your life. Read the Bible daily and obey what it says. Let the Bible change your life so you become more like Jesus. The race will not always be easy, but the reward does not compare to anything on this earth: "Eye has not seen and ear has not heard, / And which have not entered the heart of man, / All that God has prepared for those who love Him" (1 Cor. 2:9).

We Cannot Keep the Heart of Home Schooling by Ourselves

The challenge is before us. We feel overwhelmed with the prospect of ever trying to fulfill all the aspects of nurturing our children, loving our wives, and being a witness as discussed in this book while still trying to teach our children academically, earn money, make meals, and fulfill our other responsibilities.

We feel it is impossible to do all this. I know I do. But I also know that we can do all things through Christ who strengthens us. Nothing is impossible with God. He promises He will not give us more than we can bear.

I believe if God gave us spouses and children, He will give us the grace to fulfill His commands. This is not saying it is easy, but the rewards are eternal. We only need to cry out to Him, and He will give us the power to do these things.

Always remember what is *the heart of home schooling*. It is teaching and living what really matters. We are not home schooling for home schooling's sake—but rather for the glory and honor of God.

May God bless you as you serve Him and love Him with your whole heart, whole soul, and whole mind!

A Quiz and
a Commitment
for Home School Fathers
and Husbands

1. Evaluation: Does my life reflect acts of a noninvolved home schooling dad/husband or a proactive one?

		Never Visible					Always Visible		Wife's Answer
a.	Do I assume the God-given role of spiritual leader of my home?	1	2	3	4	5	6	7	_____
b.	Do I lead in regular family devotions?	1	2	3	4	5	6	7	_____
c.	Do I assume the role of the legal and physical protector of our home school program and family?	1	2	3	4	5	6	7	_____
d.	Do I show interest to my children about their education?	1	2	3	4	5	6	7	_____
e.	Do I take primary responsibility for the discipline of my children?	1	2	3	4	5	6	7	_____
f.	Do I provide relief for my wife from the stress in her life?	1	2	3	4	5	6	7	_____

APPENDIX I

g. Do I demonstrate to my wife
my gratitude for the sacrifice
she is making for our family?   1   2   3   4   5   6   7   _____

h. Do I demonstrate unconditional
love to my wife?   1   2   3   4   5   6   7   _____

i. Do I demonstrate love and affection
to my children?   1   2   3   4   5   6   7   _____

j. Do I take time to shepherd the
hearts of my children?   1   2   3   4   5   6   7   _____

k. Do I lead my family in
evangelizing others?   1   2   3   4   5   6   7   _____

l. Do I ensure my children are taught
from a biblical worldview?   1   2   3   4   5   6   7   _____

2. In order to check your own objectivity and the accuracy of your observation, ask your wife to evaluate your answers.

3. For the wife: As your wife, the most important thing you can do for me as a home-schooling wife and mother is to

_____

_____

My Commitment:

I, _____, do prayerfully commit myself to make a conscious effort, by the grace of God, to improve each of the above areas related to my God-given role of leader of my family and to commit myself to pray for every member of my family regularly.

Signature_____Date_____

Personally Recommended Resources for Mothers and Wives

BY TRACY KLICKA

Bridges, Jerry. *Disciplines of Grace*. Colorado Springs, Colo.: Navigators Press, 1993.

Elliot, Elisabeth. *Keep a Quiet Heart*. Ann Arbor, Mich.: Servant Publications, 1995.

Fenelon, Francois. *Talking with God*. Orleans, Mass.: Paraclete Press, 1997.

God's Gift for Mothers (categorized Scripture for mothers). Waco, Tex.: Word Publishing, 1995.

Green, William Henry. *The Book of Job Unfolded*. Arlington Heights, Ill.: Christian Liberty Press, 1996.

Gwyn-Thomas, John. *Rejoice Always*. Carlisle, Pa.: Banner of Truth Trust, 1989.

Halliday, Steve and William Travis. *How Great Thou Art: A Daily Devotional*. Sisters, Oreg.: Multnomah Publishers, 1999. This book is a compilation of devotional thoughts based on scriptural passages from many godly authors including John Piper, Charles Spurgeon, John Bunyan, J. I. Packer, John Wesley, George Whitefield, Joni Eareckson Tada, D. L. Moody, Elisabeth Elliot, and many others. This book is a rich treasure showing us the glory of our God! This is one of Tracy's favorites.

APPENDIX II

Harvey, E. F. and L. Harvey. *Kneeling We Triumph, Book One and Two*. Shoals, Ind.: Old Paths Tract Society, 1982.

Miller, Rose Marie. *From Fear to Freedom*. Colorado Springs, Colo.: Harold Shaw Publishers, 1994.

Owen, John. *Sin and Temptation, The Challenge of Personal Godliness*. Minneapolis, Minn.: Bethany House Publishers, 1996.

Poems for Praise and Power. Crockett, Ky.: Rod and Staff Publishers, 1978.

Prentiss, Elizabeth. *Stepping Heavenward*. Amityville, N.Y.: Calvary Press, 1993.

Ryle, J.C. *A Call to Prayer*. Laurel, Miss.: Audubon Press, 1996.

Spurgeon, Charles. *Morning and Evening* and *Strong Faith*. New Kensington, Pa.: Whitaker House, 1995. Other devotional books by the same author are also available from Whitaker House. These are inexpensive trade paperbacks.

Watson, Thomas. *The Art of Divine Contentment*. Morgan, Pa.: Soli Deo Gloria Publications. Reprint of original 1653 work.

Resources for Fathers and Husbands

Training Children and Family Devotions

Meade, Starr. *Training Hearts Teaching Minds: Family Devotions Based on the Shorter Catechism.* Phillipsburg, N.J.: Presbyterian & Reformed Publishing Company, 2000. Excellent daily devotionals on biblical truths and doctrine for the whole family.

Brown, Joyce. *Courageous Christians: Devotional Stories for Family Reading.* Chicago, Ill.: Moody Press, 2000. Sixty true short stories of Christian heroes like Elisabeth Elliot, John Bunyan, Eric Liddell, and David Livingstone.

Sande, Corlette. *The Young Peacemaker: Teaching Students to Respond to Conflict God's Way.* Billings, Mont.: Peacemaker Ministries, 1997. 406/256-1583. Includes twelve student activity booklets with cartoons. It has helped our children to get along with each other much better.

Webster, Noah. *Advice to the Young and Moral Catechism.* Aledo, Tex.: Wallbuilders, 1999. Discusses authority, obedience, honor, service, respect, Bible as standard. I read and discussed this with my son, one on one.

Voice of the Martyrs and *LINK International*—two newsletters, for adults and children respectively. Bartlesville, Okla.: Voice of the Martyrs, 918/337-8015; http://www.persecution.com. This ministry, started in 1967, provides aid to persecuted Christians in fifty countries, prints gospel literature, and informs the world of these suffering brothers and sisters.

APPENDIX III

Each issue is filled with the accounts of Christians suffering for their faith in Jesus Christ. It is has had a profound influence on our children. We read them every week.

McPhearson, Joyce. *The River of Grace: The Story of John Calvin; The Ocean of Truth: The Story of Isaac Newton;* and *A Piece of the Mountain: The Story of Blaise Pascal.* Lebanon, Tenn.: Greenleaf Press, 1998. http://www.greenleafpress.com. These are factual biographies in conversational style. Reading these wonderful stories aloud will impact your children's lives.

Vos, Catherine. *The Child's Story Bible.* Grand Rapids, Mich.: Wm. Eerdman's Publishing, 1989. There are 202 stories accurately summarized from the Old and New Testaments. I have read the whole book aloud twice for family devotions. Good for discussion.

Grant, George. *Carry a Big Stick: The Uncommon Heroism of Theodore Roosevelt.* Nashville, Tenn.: Cumberland House Publishing, 1996. This is an inspiring story and part of the Leaders in Action Series promoting Christian character, diligence, and faithfulness. I recommend the whole series which includes the lives of Patrick Henry, Robert E. Lee, and others.

Henty, G. A. *The Lion of the North.* Mill Hall, Pa.: Preston/Speed Publications, originally published in 1885. Henty has written dozens of historical adventure novels for children and adults alike. Examples of his stories feature the lives of Robert E. Lee, the French Huguenots, Hannibal, William Wallace, Sir Francis Drake, Gustavos Adolphus, and many more. These stories are riveting, and your children will learn much about history, geography, and Christian character. These are the best to be found anywhere!

Especially for Training Girls

Andreola, Karen. *Beautiful Girlhood.* Eugene, Oreg.: Great Expectations Book Co., 1997. I have read and discussed this book twice with my two oldest girls, one on one. It enables me to discuss issues with my girls that I would not normally think of because I am a dad.

Alexander, J. H. *Ladies of the Reformation: Short Biographies of Distinguished Ladies of the 16th Century.* Choteau, Mont.: Old Paths Gospel Press,

2000. Originally published in England, these powerful, inspirational stories will provide your daughters with true godly heroines to imitate.

Fiddler, Carol. *A Girl of Beauty: Building Character in Young Girls.* Lincoln, Nebr.: Back to the Bible Publishing, 1999. http://www.backtothebible.org. This is excellent for your younger girls.

Sanseri, Wanda. *God's Priceless Woman.* Milwaukie, Oreg.: Back Home Industries, 1993. Chapters on Titus 2, Proverbs 31, and examples of Hannah, Mary, Miriam, Esther, Jochebed, Dorcas, Ruth, and others.

O'Conner, Lindsey. *Moms Who Changed the World.* Eugene, Oreg.: Harvest House Publishers, 1999. Biographies with principles about Susanna Wesley, Mary Beall Washington, Augustine's mother Monica, and others.

Marriage Books

Thomas, Gary. *Sacred Marriage: What if God Designed Marriage to Make Us Holy More Than to Make Us Happy?* Grand Rapids, Mich.: Zondervan Publishing, 2000. This perspective of marriage will revolutionize your relationship with your spouse and draw you closer to both God and your spouse.

Priolo, Lou. *The Complete Husband: A Practical Guide to Biblical Husbanding.* Amityville, N.Y.: Calvary Press Publishing, 1999. A must read for all husbands.

Devotional Books

Green, Keith. *If You Love the Lord: Uncompromising Devotions From the Heart of Keith Green.* Eugene, Oreg.: Harvest House Publishers, 2000. Awesome and moving devotions from a man who walked very closely with the Lord.

Tada, Joni Eareckson. *Holiness in Hidden Places.* Nashville, Tenn.: Thomas Nelson, 1999. Forty-seven moving stories and encounters from Joni that will stir your heart to be more holy.

Tada, Joni Eareckson. *When God Weeps: Why Our Sufferings Matter to the Almighty.* Grand Rapids, Mich.: Zondervan Publishing, 1997. This book is a must read for everyone! It is one of the best books I have ever read.

About the Author

Christopher J. Klicka is Senior Counsel of the Home School Legal Defense Association (HSLDA), a nonprofit legal organization dedicated to protecting the rights of parents to home school their children. Located just outside Washington, D.C., HSLDA has over 70,000 member families.

Chris is responsible for networking statewide home school organizations across the nation, directing HSLDA's legal and legislative strategies, and promoting home education on the international front. Chris also drafts federal legislation, lobbies on Capitol Hill, and provides expert testimony before the U.S. Congress.

Since 1985, Chris has successfully represented over 3,500 home school families in legal conflicts with public school officials, social workers, prosecutors, and police officers. He has handled hundreds of court cases and administrative appeals on behalf of home school families throughout the country, arguing before four state supreme courts and several state appellate courts. He has appeared before a dozen state legislatures and state boards of education to testify on behalf of home schoolers.

Chris has traveled throughout the world to speak and help home schoolers start legal defense and national home schooling organizations. He presently serves on the home school legal defense boards in South Africa, Germany, and Canada.

He has spoken at over 330 home school conferences throughout the country and has been interviewed by hundreds of newspapers, periodicals, and radio and TV programs, including *Newsweek, Washington Times, Chicago Tribune, Washington Post, USA Today, Family News In Focus,* Marlin Maddoux's *Point of View,* D. James Kennedy's *Truths That Transform,* Fox News, and CNN.

Heralded as "the standard-bearer of books on home schooling," Chris's newly revised book, *Home Schooling: The Right Choice,* has sold more than 45,000 copies. This easy-to-read, 480-page book gives a comprehensive view on home schooling, including statistical, historical, biblical, legal, and practical support. Chris also authored *The Right to Home School: A Guide to the Law on Parents' Rights in Education and Home Schooling in the United States: A Legal Analysis,* which takes a state-by-state look at the legal atmosphere of home schooling. He has published articles in the *Religion and Public Education* journal and the *Ohio Northern Law Review.*

Chris received his B.A. from Grove City College in Grove City, Pennsylvania, and his Juris Doctorate from O.W. Coburn School of Law, Tulsa, Oklahoma (renamed Regent University School of Law and relocated to Virginia Beach, Virginia).

Christopher and his wife, Tracy, home school their seven children (including a set of twins) in Warrenton, Virginia. He teaches writing, government, history, and Bible to his children. Chris makes loving his wife and training his children his most important priorities after loving God.